MW01178715

RAISE YOU TEN

RAISE YOU TEN

Essays & Encounters 1964–2004

Volume Two

Barry Callaghan

McArthur & Company

Toronto

Published in Canada in 2006 by
McArthur & Company
322 King St. West, Suite 402
Toronto, Ontario
M5V 1J2
www.mcarthur-co.com

Library and Archives Canada Cataloguing in Publication

Callaghan, Barry, 1937-
    Raise you ten : essays & encounters 1964-2004 / Barry Callaghan.

 ISBN 1-55278-566-1 (bound)

    I. Title.

PS8555.A49R343 2006   C814'.54   C2005-907828-6

The publisher would like to acknowledge the financial support of the
Government of Canada through the Book Publishing Industry Development
Program, The Canada Council for the Arts, and the Ontario Arts Council for
our publishing activities. We also acknowledge the Government of Ontario
through the Ontario Media Development Corporation Ontario Book
Initiative.

Every attempt has been made to secure permission for all material used,
and if there are errors or omissions, these are wholly unintentional and the
Publisher will be grateful to learn of them.

Design and Composition by Michael P.M. Callaghan
Cover Design by Tania Craan
Printed in Canada by Transcontinental

10 9 8 7 6 5 4 3 2 1

For

Ron Haggart
journalist

William Kennedy
who, as a reporter, never forgot
that journalism is storytelling,
and as a storyteller, never forgot
that he was a reporter

Special thanks to *Marilyn Di Florio*
for her longtime commitment and assistance

Words, after speech, reach
Into the silence. Only by the form, the pattern,
Can words or music reach
The stillness, as a Chinese jar still
Moves perpetually in its stillness…
Words strain,
Crack and sometimes break, under the burden,
Under the tension, slip, slide, perish,
Decay with imprecision, will not stay in place,
Will not stay still.

—T.S. Eliot, *Burnt Norton*

Contents

Year of the Horse ⌐ 1

Piano Play ⌐ 15

Irving Layton ⌐ 17

Dummling's Dream ⌐ 38

My Life in the Movies ⌐ 45

Berlin ⌐ 46

Sewing ⌐ 59

Churchill the Crisper ⌐ 60

Phoenix ⌐ 66

Sikorski, in a Pig's Ear ⌐ 68

All Found ⌐ 74

Flowers for the Forgotten ⌐ 75

I Love a Floating Apple ⌐ 92

Slaughterhouse-Five: Vonnegut ⌐ 93

Pencils and Pens: III – 1878 ⌐ 98

Woman in an Iron Glove ⌐ 100

A Stolen Kiss ⌐ 106

Archbishop Charbonneau ⌐ 107

What a Meece ⌐ 112

Fragile Moments ⌐ 133

The Public Ordeal of Bryce Mackasey ⌐ 135

Canadian Wry ⌐ 155

Of Winter and of Love ⌐ 164

A Motiveless Malignancy ⌐ 168

Suicide ⌐ 189

The Blues ⌐ 195

Muhammad Ali ⌐ 197

Crime and Redemption: Ramsey Clark ⌐ 212

LeRoi Jones: Death, He Grinning ⌐ 218

Mojo ❧ 231

Dean Acheson ❧ 249

Osip Mandelstam Moves His Lips ❧ 255

Nathanael West: *Miss Lonelyhearts* ❧ 256

Austin Clarke: Riding the Trane ❧ 263

On a Leap Year Night in Havana: A Man in a White Suit
   Who Said He Was Leon Rooke ❧ 270

John O'Hara ❧ 277

The Simian Irish ❧ 280

Cecil Beaton ❧ 288

Karsh and MacLennan: Power Lifting ❧ 290

About Face: John Reeves ❧ 298

A Performance of *The Exile* at Café Tristan Bernard ❧ 300

Salt and Toys ❧ 301

The G Spot ❧ 312

Edmund Wilson ❧ 323

Notes ❧ 367

YEAR OF THE HORSE

It all began in the South China Sea, in Macao, where I had gone to play the casinos, crowding into the gaming rooms with Chinese who stood sleepless for hours waiting for someone to surrender a chair at the 21 or roulette tables, and then they would hold onto that chair with a squatter's right for ten hours, a day, two, some men and women carrying plastic containers to piss in, all of them counting on stamina and hoping for a burst of luck from the steel ball clattering in the wheel, the hours slipping away, all sense of time and sense of self lost, playing fantan and roulette until – bored by the ache in my shoulders, bored by a profound sense of absence – I quit and went out to where only a few feet from the door, the ocean slapped against the breakwall, and there in the dim filtered light I walked along the ocean road, calmed by the curious milk-gel to the air before dawn, everything fresh, cleansed: but there were no birds flying or crying along the shore, and the few black birds that were clustered together on a slope of sand looked like coals abandoned by fire.

I took that as an omen and went to a temple and had tea with an old monk under a huge tree that was three trees twined together. He tossed the fortune sticks: . . . *dans l'Orient désert quel devint mon ennui . . .*[1] I went to Hong Kong on a jetfoil, passing between islands that are stone humps in the sea, arriving at the Peninsula Hotel, a palace of grace that caters to illusions, and I sat in the spacious lobby surrounded by the scurrilous and reputable, by film producers and perhaps a gunrunner, by exquisite

---

[1] . . . in the deserted East how divine my lassitude . . .

women and the odd counter-culture warphead. I strode between Silver Clouds, the white stone lions at the door, and little boys in white suits wearing white pillbox hats, and found my friend George Yemec – lean and aloof and greying at the temples – and he said, "Hello, can you get up at four in the morning? You should come with me and see the horses."

In the cold dark hours overcast with no stars in the sky I found myself hunched against the wind beside a racetrack and there were great amber floodlights high in the morning mist, suspended flowers, but I couldn't see anything, not around the turn in the rail, but I heard the muffled sound of hoofs and suddenly a huge horse broke into the half-light, lunging past.

"Aw, she's a might slow this morning," said the small Cork trainer, clocking the horse and staring into the gloom, waiting. Other horses, appearing out of the dark, disappeared.

After half an hour, I shuffled down the slope, shivering, to sit alone in a steel shed that cut the wind, but I was so cold I crouched down and thought, *Jesus, goddamned horses in the gloom. What am I doing?*

As the sun rose and the sky cleared, I went with Yemec to eat at a local market; sprawling stalls and narrow walkways covered with corrugated tin sheeting or corrugated coloured plastic, and the tables were piled high with fresh meats, fish, squid, eels, crabs, lobsters, melons, rice, fruits – and the gutters ran with water and blood. In the centre of this flesh and pulp, this hacking and chopping and slicing, women were sitting beside steaming chrome tanks sipping tea, eating delicacies. We sat down, warmed by steam from the tanks and tea, but in a near corner an old man was huddled beside a large wicker basket, lifting live quails out of the basket, and with his long thumbnail he slit the breast and belly, peeling the skin off each still live bird. The old man did this rapidly, stacking the pulsing purple bodies on a steel tray.

"Yemec," I said, "the omens are all wrong."

"Omens mean nothing," he said.

"You believe that?"

"Omens are for when you're confused."

A young girl came out and took the steel tray away. Another girl brought another tray and another basket of birds.

"I don't know what I'm doing here," I said. "I don't know anything about horses."

"I don't know anything about women."

"You mean I'll end up dreaming about horses?"

"I do all the time, wonderful dreams. I wish women were horses."

We were at Sha Tin racetrack north of the Kowloon foothills, an extraordinary racecourse on land reclaimed from the sea. We had our own air-conditioned box with a balcony, a small kitchen, a chef and serving boys. There were 35,000 people in the stands betting on geldings and a few odd mares (there are no pastures in Hong Kong, and therefore there is no breeding), and throughout the city another 500,000 people were crowded into off-track betting shops, wagering more than $15 million a day (the daily average at Woodbine in Toronto is $1.5 million). Pampered by escargots in pastry shells and soothed by white wine, I sensed something even more sensual than food in Yemec – a rush of energy, covert under his diffident graceful air, a channelling of all his attention while still making small talk.

I grew fascinated watching him read the *Form*, constructing out of circled fractions and underlined times a conviction about the upcoming race. Even when surrounded by backslappers he had a strange capacity for silence, sealing himself off so he could concentrate, and when we went down to the paddock to look at the horses, he disappeared, melted into anonymity, so that I was left looking around, wondering where he was – and then he appeared again out of the crowd, casually elegant in his Armani jacket, saying quietly, "I'd box the 2-4-7," striding off to the windows as if we were all grown men who knew exactly what to do. We began to win a lot of money, betting three-horse boxes, key-wheeling, back-wheeling, catching exactas. It was magical – and when the day was over, we had won several thousand dollars. It was like that for three days and I said, "Those exactas are terrific, the payoffs are so big."

"You should try the triactors back home."

"What's that?"

"It's the last race, and you pick the first three horses, in order. I once hit for $23,000 with a $2 bet."

On the last night, we celebrated at Gaddi's, the finest European restaurant east of Suez, eating quail breast, prawn dumplings in a champagne sauce, and pigeon with truffles. We drank Chassange Montrachet and a Chateau Pichon-Longueville, Comtesse de Lalande, sitting in the shadow of a Ch'ing Dynasty Commandel screen that depicted gay summer scenes with the emperor.

Back home, the weather was cold, the grey tail of winter, suspended time, the ice melting down to stubble on the ground. In the morning I considered what I was going to teach at the university that day . . . Camus' *The Plague,* Primo Levi's stories, Tom Kinsella's *Notes from the Land of the Dead* . . . and on some mornings I looked at the race results, fascinated by the triactor – $350 one day, $4,000 the next – and then one night I had a dream. There were three birds in white wicker cages, the cages like cubes or dice. The next night I had the same dream, except the birds suddenly became numbers: 2, 3, 9. In the morning I phoned Yemec and told him to book a table at Greenwood, the old track by the lake. It became a long meal. We lost race after race and I was almost tapped out, weary and saddened, but I held on until the ninth and last race and made the bet: it won – 2, 3, 9 – and paid $1,400. That was my first triactor.

Spring turned to summer. I sat at a window close to a ravine slope of ferns and tiger lilies and wrote poems about men I had met the year before – I had been in Moscow and Leningrad – who had stainless steel teeth, who smiled as ink fell on to a blotter and a name disappeared, and I had learned from a woman I'd met along the ice-locked canals that

we know what love is
when it's over,
the trail of two people
bending into the echo of their own laughter
across a lake fresh with snow.
'And this, this,' you cried, looking back
'is the whiteness of God's mind.
Without us he is nothing.'

At about ten o'clock, I drove to the university and talked for two hours to students seated on the lawn under a willow tree about Robert Lowell and Hart Crane and John Berryman, poets "freelancing out along the razor's edge," and then I had a light lunch at Cowan's Bottom Line in Yorkville, across the road from a firehall, the firemen regularly running their ladders into the air, practising, climbing high into nowhere. Toward two in the afternoon, I began to feel an almost sensual arousal and eased by the sun I drove to the Woodbine track by the airport for a late-afternoon outing, carrying with me a small notebook of poems I was translating from the Serbian poet, Miodrag Pavlović – a little work for between races.

There were several men I saw every day: my friend Yemec – entrepreneur, publisher and sometimes poet; the Bajan Shoebox Victor, in his blue suit and bow tie, a clipped moustache, and pockets stuffed with sweet pink candies and computer print-outs – soil conditions and speed ratings, quarter-fractions and breeding – all visioned in his mind along the arc of quantum mathematics; Patrick Donohoe, a gentle-spoken Wexford man, whose love was the horse, quoting not fractions but a whimsical line from Yeats or Service; Fat Saul Ellison, Yonge Street clothing salesman and raconteur; trainer Nelson the Bat; George Gardos, student, gambler, whose only disappointment in life came from not being born as Doctor J.; Statistician Steve, and sometimes Michael Magee, astute horseman, the most acerbic satirist in the country – he'd written a bestseller, *The Golden Age of BS* – an aficionado of military bands, brass bands, pipe bands and drum corps. Behind us all, the benign silent presence of the great old hockey player, King Clancy, on in his years, a man who seemed to know how to bide his time when there was so little time left to bide. It was always fine there in the afternoon, casual and yet intense – making a small bet or two, sitting in the open stands with seagulls far inland circling and swooping overhead looking for "crusts of bread and such" – until horses broke from the gate, striding beautifully, six or seven sprinters turning for home, to the wire . . . all of us together on our feet at the finish, yet each of us alone, the best at ease with aloneness, the worst filling every space with complaint, chatter, confusion. Myself, I was waiting, translating a line or two:

> *a curtain of smoke*
> *descends:*
> *an angel falling*

waiting for the last race, waiting until it was time to concentrate on the triactor, or as it is known, the Tri.

So: what had I learned since Sha Tin, what did I know as I waited for the Tri?

Though the track has been the last refuge of ontological man, I do not believe in systems. Distrust all men, whether in politics, poetry, or punting, who have a system.

Each race presents a new and special situation. The task is to see the situation clearly. Clarity is the aim, confusion the game.

Beware all men, whether in politics, poetry or punting, who say they are pros. It is the first excuse and their last resort.

I am not a professional. I am not even a handicapper. I have simply tried to understand what's at stake in one kind of wager, the triactor.

I am an amateur who knows what he knows. To actually know what you know is not so simple as it sounds.

It implies you know what you don't know.

The rest is intuition.

So: what do I know?

Among other things, the track – like the literary life – was a hive of opinions. Free advice, tips, tip sheets, doubts, touts, they were all about, beating like butterflies on my brain. The horses constituted enough confusion without all that clatter and clutter. So, the secret was to stand alone in the whirlpool, singing silently to myself. Silently. In that spirit – I never listened to losers. Losers cheered each other up by beating each other down. And if you lost, forget the loss immediately. Celebrate when you won and celebrate when you lost. Never let losing become a habit of mind. The more experience you had with losing, the more ways you'd find to lose.

There was one exception to this rule.

If I was lucky enough (for punting purposes) to have a friend who lost all the time, then I sought out his top choice and immediately stroked it out, even if it was the odds-on favourite. This required real strength, being the betrayal of a friend's best judgment, and such betrayal could only become, in the long run, a perverse bond.

I avoided the advice of players who never looked at the horses and only read the *Form*. They were like poets who never read poetry – or theologians who reduced God to checkpoints on a chalkboard (I once had a professor at the Pontifical Institute of Medieval Studies, a humourless man, who drew the operation of God's "intellect" as a series of little doors opening and closing, at the gate, so to speak).

So, I had to look at the horses as they saddled and paraded. But look for what?

The smell of liniment, iodine stains on the fetlocks, fatness, a horse "washing out" (over-sweating), a tail bolt-out from the backside (the horse was hurting), front bandages, etc.

Haw: once I'd seen what I thought I saw – then what?

Well, anything was possible, but unless a horse had a proven record of winning with front bandages, I never bet on it.

A horse dripping wet was usually washed out. But not always.

Fat was fat. But not always.

You had to use your own judgment. Anything was possible. Anything. I have never forgotten a schoolboy equation:

If $x = y = 1$
then $x^2 = y^2 = x2 - xy$
$(x-y)(x+y) = x(x-y)$
$x+y = x$
$x+y = 1$
$2 = 1$

And so I said to myself, *If only I knew someone in the back-stretch – the barn boys, the vet, the trainer.*

Well, in a way, I did. As soon as the odds for the triactor race went up on the tote board, I checked the "win pool" – the amount of money already wagered, the "barn money." I often found that long shots heavily bet by men who thought they knew something was a factor, perhaps for third place in the Tri.

Then there was that "gift" – the thing that fascinated me about Yemec at Sha Tin: the ability to simply "see" that a horse is ready. There was no way to explain this, but I had acquired it. The trap, however, was that you "tried" to see, and then you believed you saw what was in fact not there.

The same was true of hunches. You had to trust your hunches (intuitions) but not seek them. The sought intuition was a sign of confusion, a sign that you were afraid you were going to lose. The true hunch came to you clean, like grace. And like grace, it was preposterous.

So, what else did I pay attention to?

The *Racing Form*: but I never gave too much attention to speed ratings. Track conditions and situations were too variable. This was as bad as relying on statistics.

The opening mutual odds (or "morning line") of *each* horse in the program. This was the result, after all, of a considered judgment.

The horses carrying the five top jockeys: good jockeys tended to get good horses, or the sleeper that was ready. I'd won Tri after Tri because a top jockey had nosed out, for third place, an inferior rider on a superior horse.

The percentage jockeys: the leading riders were not always the top jockeys in terms of percentage finishes in the first three positions, and this was a crucial triactor consideration.

A marked low weight advantage.

The top trainers.

And the three-minute money move: the movement of the horses in relation to the morning line, from seventh position to fourth, for example, as a betting favourite. This calculation had to be done at the very last moment and factored into all the other information, judgments, intuitions, considerations.

All of this took place in some 25 minutes, and most of it in the seven minutes before post time. And even as I stood alone, I was confronted by all my confusions and calculations. Obviously concentration was the key: concentration while surrounded by shuffling, mumbling crowds, concentration while standing in line at the wickets, concentration while friends interrupted to say hello, ask advice, give advice . . . all of this as time, relentless time, clicked away. The secret was to lock your will, to focus on what you knew, seeking the conviction that had the most clarity. When the moment came – that still moment of lucidity – indecision ceased and I heard the sound of one hand clapping: a piercing, almost pure moment of perception. The immediate temptation was to suspect such clarity, to suspect myself. The solution, I thought, would not be so simple, so I was tempted to go with a last hunch or a word whispered in my ear. This was unavoidable, and then a certain panic set in, because even clarity of choice was not enough. I had to know how to bet my choice.

I had a simple procedure: if, in a field of 14, my top choices were 3, 5, 8, 11, 12, I would bet a five-horse box as a security (in a box, the three horses can finish in any order).

Then I constructed a series of bets that "pressed" those choices, so that when I got up to the window I had a card that looked like this:

3 5 8 11 12
5-horse $1 box, cost $60

5 8 11 12
4-horse $1 box, cost $24

8 11 12 6
4-horse box with long shot possible, $1 box, cost $24

8 11 12
3-horse $2 box, cost $12

11 12
12 11
2-horse bet on top, with the whole field for third, $1 cost $12 each; total $24

11 - 3 5 6 8 12
key wheel, in which the 11 must win and the others finish in any combinations, $1, cost $20

Total: $164

This was a minimum bet, and any individual move could be increased, but if – in the above series – the first three horses had finished 11, 12, 8, you would have had the Tri six times. If the payoff had been $1,000 for a $2 bet, you would have won $3,000.

This was not a system, this was a method that only an amateur could create, and only an amateur could afford. This was not the world of the pro. As Patrick Donohoe said, "Like the story of *The Song of Bernadette*, for those who believe, no explanation is necessary; for those who do not, no explanation is possible."

In August, as the summer Woodbine meeting shifted to Fort Erie, I went off with my lady Claire to Saratoga, the loveliest track in America, the Graveyard of Champions, a town of healing waters and a track with a long graveyard stretch run that sapped the spirit of frontrunners and broke the hearts of bettors who liked to put their money on favourites.

The rhythm of the town revolved around the track: the *Racing Form* arrived the night before the race, and gonifs, the addled rich, Bronx plungers and balletic puffs sat side by side on the balcony of the Rip Van Dam Hotel, hard at work over past performances in the half-light; there were afternoon cocktail and *petit-four* parties on the lawns of graceful mansions, the very rich nesting in town for the four-week meeting; lunch at Mrs. London's Bake Shop or Hattie's Chicken Shack was over by one o'clock, and the woman behind the desk at the Adelphi Hotel told the hour to customers in terms of how long 'til post time; after lunch, people hurried along the streets and through the park past the duck pond where orthodox Jews, who were in town only for the waters, took the sun, prayerful men wrapped in their black coats, like black birds: *"Prophet still, if bird or devil! / Whether Tempter sent, or whether tempest tossed thee here ashore, / . . . is there balm in Gilead? – tell me – tell me, I implore." Quoth the Raven, "Nevermore."* And the track – set among homes, so that the course seemed nestled in the neighbourhood – was groomed beautifully: a grassy saddling area under tall maple and plane trees with the horses within arm's length, a small jug-and-string band and step dancers and two fiddlers among the crowd, and restaurants that were open to the race course serving lobster, crab, and tender veal. It was a place of intimacy, grace, first-rate horses, first-rate jockeys, first-rate trainers, first-rate stewards.

For nine days, despite lovely sunlight and the close feel of the horses, I went into the graveyard. And when you are down in the hole "there's nothing to do but dig." I hardly held on through the daily card and nine times in succession my triactor picks placed 1, 2, 4. This was perverse and punishing. It kept me awake at night because it is hard to sleep when the devil has his porch light on. Too many good horses kept sneaking in from nowhere. I could not get a rhythm. Logic faltered, concentration slipped away. Losers began to talk to me under the maple trees. I began to smell loss between my own sheets, the loss of a sense of self: after all, betting was, among other things, a confirmation of the self. To fail was to fail yourself. Still, I tried to start each afternoon with a freshness: I looked for a sign, an opening, a move. To surrender was to suck wind: the tailing wind of the Holy Ghost.

On the day of the Travers, the big stakes race of the meet, I found myself in disarray, caught between anger and dismay. I'd fallen into the slough of the bettor's despond, second-guessing myself, making my choice and then betting against myself. So, I decided to just back off and wait, wait and see if that still moment of perception would show up. I would let the rhythm find me since I couldn't find it.

The Travers promised to be an extraordinary race, with the three winners of the Triple Crown – Conquistador Cielo, Gato del Sol and Aloma's Ruler – running against one another. Runaway Groom, a Canadian-bred grey, was also entered, a horse I'd bet on once at Woodbine, which had finished second in the Queen's Plate, and now I looked at it sentimentally but not seriously, until I saw that Jeffrey Fell was the jockey, an excellent rider who sits ramrod straight in the saddle, just the kind of rider to go into the Valley of the 600. The odds were 19 to 1 (Conquistador Cielo was 2 to 5) but then I thought, *Those are not long enough odds for an unknown horse: someone had to have put money on the grey.* For days I had been alone with the loneliness of the loser. Suddenly I felt a quickening and pressed close to the parade rail to look at the horses. I was astonished. Conquistador Cielo was wearing front bandages. I knew the horse had never worn bandages, and I thought, *No horse bandaged for the first time should be going off at 2 to 5.* I hurried to the windows, noting the odds had gone down another point, put $40 to win on Runaway Groom and, suddenly seized by conviction, by the belief that I was right, wheeled him for the late double (that is, bet him with every horse in the field in the next race). When, a few minutes later, the Groom turned into that graveyard stretch, coming from 20 lengths off the pace, surging, his long neck straining, the crowd roared in disbelief as the Groom ran down Conquistador Cielo and Aloma's Ruler and won at the wire. I felt as if I'd come back from the dead, blessed by my own best judgment, and that grey, running from nowhere, appearing as if he'd come out of the dark morning mist at Sha Tin, had suddenly put out the devil's porch light. Suspicion and second-guessing, gloom and disarray disappeared. Runaway Groom had come to me like a gift of grace, and when I left Saratoga ten days later, I had not only taken the healing waters but I had gotten both feet out of the grave. I had beaten the track. Down the killing stretch of the last days of the meet, clear judgment had clicked in, still moments had come to me; clarity of detail and gesture had fallen into place, leaving me with a rush, the gambler's sure sense of the harmony of all things.

As we left town on a bright morning, I saw two old men in their black coats, the coats billowing in the wind as they hurried away from me, birds of night, and somehow I knew that the strange fascination begun in the dark of that cold, steel shed at Sha Tin had reached a fruition. I had come back from the dead.

Having won the triactor 101 times by the evening of December 7, the end of the year's racing at Woodbine, Yemec called for a late-night supper at Cowan's Bottom Line. Jan, the chef, spent the day in the freezer carving a huge horse's head in ice. It sat in the centre of the table, surrounded by Claire, Yemec, Shoebox Victor, Yolande (the woman in the wickets who always got my late bets down, no matter the crowd), Gardos, Morley and me. We drank champagne. "Celebrate, Morley," I said, "We've got to celebrate more often."

"The horse is melting," he said wryly.

"Yeah, but he looks even more beautiful in his dying light."

Then I dedicated the book of Pavlović translations, *Singing at the Whirlpool,* to the boys of my summer:

> *for*
> *George Yemec,*
> *Patrick Donohoe, Michael Magee,*
> *Fred Dobbs,*
> *Shoebox Victor, Statistician Steve,*
> *Nelson the Bat,*
> *Gardos, Yolande,*
> *King Clancy,*
> *and*
> *the dream numbers*
> *2 3 9*

Toronto Life, 1983

PIANO PLAY

Al Rosenzweig was called Piano by his friends. He agreed to meet with me to eat a smoked meat sandwich at Switzer's Deli. Piano was a big man who appeared affable because he was slow moving and because of his ample pink cheeks and jowls. I knew he was a killer. The police knew he was a killer. They couldn't prove it but they knew that, after the Maggadino family from Buffalo had tried to kill Maxie Bluestein outside the Towne Tavern so that the mob could take over the gambling that was controlled in Toronto by the Jews, Al had driven to Niagara Falls and had strangled two of Maggadino's men with piano wire. But he was not known as Piano because of the wire. It was because he played the piano at a Bathurst Street high-rise social club for survivors of the holocaust every Thursday night, where he liked to sing Cole Porter songs: *Let's do it, Let's fall in love . . . .*

As I arrived at the table, Piano was singing to himself.

He looked up and said, "Take a pew with a Jew."

We ate our smoked meat sandwiches and then I said to him, "Piano, I know business is business but we both know Solly Climans. He's a good guy."

"So he's a good guy. I even knew his father, Fat. I booked his father's bets, too, but he owes money, too much money."

"I'm worried about him."

"Why worry? If he pays, he's good."

"He's beyond scared, Piano, he says he's gonna commit suicide."

"He ain't gonna commit suicide."

"I believe him."

15

"You believe him?"

"Yeah, I believe him."

"Jews don't kill themselves."

"Believe me, he's gonna kill himself."

Piano wiped his lips with his napkin. Drumming his fingers on the table, he began to hum, and then he said, reaching out to touch my hand, "Jews don't kill themselves. They sometimes kill each other, but believe you me they don't kill themselves."

He shrugged, as if I should have known we were helpless before a truth, a truth that allowed him his amiable consideration for me.

"Do yourself a favour," he said, "try a little dessert, a cheese-cake. It'll look good on you."

2004

IRVING LAYTON

I was sitting with Irving Layton in his apartment in Montreal. We were talking about fathers, about how his father had a black beard, and how his eyes were black, and how he had been harried by angels who had nibbled at his ears. "They talked to him, all the prophets talked to him, but he didn't talk much to me. But my mother, she did. My mother held me up by the heels. There I was, the first Jew since Moses to be born circumcised. To her, I was the Messiah. I could do no wrong. She gave me freedom. Of course, she was backward, ignorant, but a woman of power and feeling."

"Now I understand," I said.

"What?" he said.

"All that mad Montreal saint of the mountain stuff, all your arrogance and strutting, it's as simple as that. Your mother told you you were the Messiah."

Of course, it had not been as simple as that, and yet, on that evening, I saw how he had carried the peculiar vituperative fever of the prophet with him all his life; he'd always been on stage, the poet decrying other poets, calling them liars and trained seals; he'd always been the avenging angel, a little ridiculous, wrong-headed, striding out of his Judean hills; always in the stance of the lover, trusting no one, boxing half-baked intellectuals and poor-mouth professors of a Presbyterian bent about the ears, and yet . . . there he was on that evening in Montreal with his boy child standing beside him, holding the boy's little hands, then brushing back his hair, trying to urge a word out of him, saying, "I'm worried. He should be talking. I talk to him all the time and he says nothing."

We sat and stared at the boy who was about three years old, and the boy stood and smiled at us and then he left the room. "Since we are talking about prophets," I said, "I'll tell you who my favourite saint is, Simeon Stylites. An old Syrian in the days when the Church was in the desert, and he built himself a 60-foot stone pillar and he shinnied up the pillar and mounted it and lived and preached from that pillar for thirty years. He was a prophet to some, even a saint, but for me, he was the world's first flagpole sitter, sitting on top of the image of his own ego."

"The image of his sex."

"By the way," I said, "what does a man do with his shit for thirty years up on top of a pillar?"

"He sits in it. Any poet that's any good has to have sat in his own shit," Layton said.

The little boy had wandered back into the room and Irving took him in his arms and spoke softly to his silent face, almost singing to him, Irving, who'd always been so voluble and effusive, from the very beginning when he'd been a boy himself living with his family in a tenement room under a semi-brothel. Each night he'd been wakened by the screams and shouts of roistering drunks, wakened by brawling, and the crash of breaking beer bottles. His mother, Keine Lazarovitch, had begged her small son to get the broomstick and he'd stumbled through the dark and thumped its handle into the ceiling. The pole had always made a dull wooden sound in the darkness, but it was then that the miracle had taken place.

"The loud cursings and clatterings would stop suddenly, and silence like some mysterious night flower would blossom from the tip of my broomstick. It was uncanny, and in my child's imagination I saw myself as a boy Moses parting the filthy noise-filled blackness so that the long-suffering Israelites might pass safely into a region of peace and slumber . . . . Each time the mysterious flower of silence opened its invisible blossoms over my head I felt the same thrill of power, of exulting joy . . . I, I alone, had punched a rectangular space of quiet into the filthy drunken chaos and presented it to those older and stronger than myself."

Layton, in full stride in long pants, his arm thrust into the night, is still crying, "I, I alone . . . ."

> *I curse all the passionless worms*
> *that slide their fearful, grey forms*
> *over this astonishing earth; let them dissolve*
> *like rain into the sought-for mud;*
> *let their worm eyes explode from a sudden*
> *unlooked-for glimpse of God!*

Perhaps, with Irving as God's agent, there had been a moment of silence among the exultant, cruel whores of his house and the *sheeny* men of the neighbourhood and the English on the mountain who had seemed to have the mysterious power of huge mastiffs . . . a silence amidst all the noise and pain of the Jewish quarter, noise that had presented him with a huge possibility: the thrill of power, as if the opening up of silence could be like

> *A milk white kitten*
> *curled up*
>   *on the bough*
> *of an apple tree*
>
> *A gigantic blossom*
> *until*
>   *its green eyes*
> *blink*

Layton has said it: he has brazenly played the cock-of-the-walk but his world has never been narrowed to "only cock-and-cunt." Before copulation there was battle. "You broke someone's skull, anyway made a profound philosophical dent in it, or he broke yours. People were so mad they hated one another at first sight and sought their injury. They conceptualized and tortured; out of the same taproot grew their creativity and evil. They were neurotics – even the best of them – with an ineradicable penchant for cruelty . . . . As a boy I looked forward to the nightly battles with the youthful Jew-hating Christians who descended on the tiny Maccabean band waiting for them with stones, bottles and bricks or anything else . . . ."

Grey hair has not calmed the Maccabean.

Over the years, he has confused a lot of people by banging the drum for love, and all such delicacies thereof, while scourging – or sometimes just bullying – all prigs, mewlers, layabouts in academe, featherbedders in the dormitories of power, and self-anointed idealists, especially if such idealistic "world-savers" have had no guns or tanks:

> *Be none of these, my sons*
> *My sons, be none of these*
> *Be gunners in the Israeli Air Force . . .*

> *The up-to-date poet*
> *besides labouring at his craft*
> *should be a dead shot . . .*

The dead shot. That was bunk. That was the bluff side of a bravado that Israeli poets like Yehuda Amichai, who'd actually fought in wars, thought was childish. Mind you, it was easy to understand Irving's exultant joy in the victory of the Jews in June of 1967 – he'd no need to explain that joy, just as he has not needed to explain his contempt for liars and poor toadying poets. But, more and more the sounds he has made have been on the side of power, the men with the guns. Bang. Bang. You pick your side in the gutter-fight and bash it out; Jews against Italians, Italians against French, French against English. His output of vituperative rhetoric, if one could record it in linear feet, has been extraordinary. Of course, I always sensed benevolence beneath his belligerence, but there has been something altogether too contradictory in Irving: in the night, it seemed, he studied his Talmud – and in the light of day, since he couldn't shoot from the hip, he shot from the lip:

> *Idiot!*
> *The one human I'd trust*
> *is a deaf-mute paraplegic*
> *– behind bars*
>
> *In the absurd slaughterhouse*
> *that is history . . .*
> *make certain*
> *the cleaver is yours*
> *and the bared throat someone else's.*

That was not poetry. That was Irving on his loud-hailer, an angel dipping his wings into the political stink, an angel lacking any large sense of ethical affirmation, any sense of the wisdom of self-doubt.

And so, even during the 1970 War Measures Crisis, when the army was sent into our streets to apprehend an insurrection and all our civil rights were suspended, when the innocent were arrested in the night and the government lied because there was no insurrection – what a disappointment it was to read Irving when he wrote: "I sympathize with Pierre Trudeau having to struggle with a collection of boobs, windbags and second-raters inside and outside the House of Commons. They are not fit to tie the laces of his ski boots. However, he may take comfort in the thought that they speak for no one but themselves, for the overwhelming majority of Canadians are not interested in clever sophistries, debating points or the ready-made cynicisms of little men."

I remember the letters he wrote to me from Israel, defending the war in Vietnam, defending Johnson, sneering at the cynicisms of little men who questioned the morality of the war. With all the confidence in the world he dedicated a book to LBJ, as if he had never heard the groans of the napalmed, the mutilated, and then he told me – after the massacres at Shatila camp – that Ariel Sharon was "a great man, a great Jewish soldier." He insisted on it. I was flabbergasted because I knew that he cared deeply for the dispossessed, he felt in his bones for the mutilated – he wasn't stupid – and after all, I knew he had said, without equivocation, that no man can "remain decent and sensible / with absolute power in his hands."

So, what had gone wrong?

I can only think back to Simeon Stylites and Irving's remark, "Any poet that's any good has to have sat in his own shit." Irving has spent a lot of time sitting in his own shit.

Forget the politics for the moment. Irving, broompole in both fists, has been our self-appointed celebrant of life. He has been the *adelantado*, the front-runner of English poetry in our country. He has been good alcohol in our blood. He has gone among us "naked with mystery," condemning the joy-haters by telling them,

> *They dance best who dance with desire,*
> *Who lifting feet of fire from fire*
> *Weave before they lie down*
> *A red carpet for the sun.*

He has urged the injection of ecstasy into our slothful dry Methodist world. And early on, erection itself became his rare weapon, so mysterious in its power that even Circe – so he claimed – had to do a deal with him:

. . . your bewitched minions
Must scrape the oozy mud of the seafloor
For squids and periwinkles
To nourish me thereon
Should you want, O lovely and divine Circe,
Another erection.

Such a cock-and-cunt vignette, at the time – early in the Six-
ties – had a jolting effect, but now it has a comic charm, some-
thing of laughter and self-mockery, and a relish for the bed. He
has made it clear that bed has been good for his backbone. He
has recommended backbone. He has said foolish things but he
was no fool. He knew from the beginning that broompoles –
after that moment of silence – must turn to sweeping. He was
no man to sweep up. That was for critics. It was that miracle of
silence that he was after, because he believed in the miracle of
the imagination – he believed that through the power of the
word – the naming power, a word gift as primal as Adam's –
that he had the power to renew, the power even to redeem an un-
redeemable world. With the complete conviction of a poet born
circumcised he boasted that even the brightest apples on trees
– until he, the fabulist – named them, would remain only as a
rumour in our lives, twisting on a black bough:

In me, nature's divided things –
tree, mould on tree –
have their fruition:
I am their core . . .

He believed a poem could include and resolve – and there-
fore heal – all our contradictions – if only for a moment – just
"as a pool includes water and reflection" – achieving – if only
for a moment – a oneness between earth and time on the wing:
"*Sit here / beside me sweet,*" Irving the fabulist, sharing this gift
for oneness, said to his love as he gave God's lowliest of the

black angels – common houseflies – a moment of grace on gum paper:

> *They look peaceful*
> *as if they'd been*
> *suddenly overwhelmed*
> *by the sweetness of life . . .*
> *The pale yellow strip*
> *studded with their*
> *black stiffened bodies*
> *and swaying in the gentle*
> *morning breeze*
> *is not without a certain*
> *kind of beauty,*
> *like my mother's cursings*
> *preserved in amber*
> *or Baudelaire's*
> Flowers of Evil

"What pre-Belsen Jew did not promiscuously shack up with five or six gentile cultures?" Irving asked. As a post-Belsen Jew, he had shacked up with several gentile nymphs, with Circe and other fabled *shiksas*. He had refused to be *shtetl*-bound. It was as if Irving had stuck his nose over the wall of the Torah and had seen the Temple of Astarte, and he'd gone over that wall as fast as his feet would take him, banging down all the temple doors, pleading:

> *Lady, let me have your lips*
> *Lady, let my hands caress you*
> *Lady, let me embrace you*
> *O lady, lady, lady, lady*

He tossed aliases at the ladies – Ulysses, Apollo, Dionysus – or made them into old friends, or cousins – the world was his oyster – but then, in the middle of some feast or love tryst he would suddenly begin to cry for no reason, he would hear the whispers of bewigged temple women from back home – those segregated women, those feared women – they were hard on his heels, those devouring *mikvah* women. "Life itself is a cunt," he said, and if he was going to accept the admonition of the Torah – to "live in the blood" – to live in the unclean carnage of the world, in the filthy noise-filled drunken chaos of his own life – then he would have to remain erect, never let himself be limp, never be vulnerable, but always ready to impale life:

> *If I do not hold on*
> *to my maleness,*
> *my individuality . . .*
> *I shall return to the womb.*
> *I shall surely die.*

And so, it has been "Jig jig jig jig . . ." in an ecstasy of pride until, sinking down into the cunt he has had

> *to gasp for air*
> *as if he had fallen*
> *into an open latrine.*

It was as if each woman in his arms had not been wholly human, but had been some irresistible erotic life force, her cunt, seductive – a paradise in its sweetness – and yet unclean, waiting for

> *one of the male flies*
> *buzzing about her*
> *buttocks . . .*
> *to alight*

to inject
the sweet venom
of love
into the receptacle
prepared for it
to round out
the contour
of her belly
with another fly.

Flies breeding flies. Irving's misanthropy, his sense of life itself as a betrayal – his sense of Mother Nature herself as "demented," caressing her children before "choking them to death" – has always been centred brutally in paradise, the cunt:

your cold vagina
extruding
a solitary pink
worm

It was Keine Lazarovitch, his mother, who had first called him prophet:

When I saw my mother's head on the cold pillow,
Her white waterfalling hair in the cheeks' hollows,
I thought, quietly circling my grief, of how
She had loved God but cursed extravagantly his creatures.

For her final mouth was not water but a curse,
A small black hole, a black rent in the universe,
Which damned the green earth, stars and trees in its stillness
And the inescapable lousiness of growing old.

And I record she was comfortless, vituperative,
Ignorant, glad, and much else besides; I believe
She endlessly praised her black eyebrows, their thick weave,
Till plagiarizing Death leaned down and took them for his
                                                    mould.

And spoiled a dignity I shall not again find,
And the fury of her stubborn limited mind;
Now none will shake her amber beads and call God blind,
Or wear them upon a breast so radiantly.

O fierce she was, mean and unaccommodating;
But I think now of the toss of her gold earrings,
Their proud carnal assertion, and her youngest sings
While all the rivers of her red veins move into the sea.

In his mother, so it seemed to young Irving, was all cursing, all rending of the universe, all sacrilege and laughter, all proud carnality and fury and issue of evil, all the sadness of a hollow cheek, all suffocation, and finally, in her image, all the lousiness of growing old.

◖⊙◗

"An image was created of me," he said, "like I was some kind of unzipped lecher watching madly down college corridors to pounce on all the pert females that I could lay my wretched hands on. It came about, I would say, largely through the cooperation of a sex starved, anti-erotic, and puritanical society that wants to live vicariously on the sexual pleasures that it thought I had . . . . My point is that every society, every country, every people creates its own narcissistic heroes, the images that reflect their own longings, the images that pacify frustrated desires. If that hero happens to be the poet, he has his own image of himself and that image works like the way you start a poem. When you start a poem you are in full control. When you start an image you are in full control. The first few lines that you put down on the page – they are your own lines, and you're very vain and very proud of them, and you control them. But as the poem develops, something strange happens: democracy suddenly turns into a dictatorship, the democrat into a dictator. The poem begins to dictate to you: change that line, this line is no good, the poet finds that he is not the creator but the creature of the poem, and the poem is writing him and telling him what to do. So it is with the image the poet has of himself, this love-hate relationship between the creator and his image, it is his, this relationship, until the very end."

When Irving started to publish, when he started to create his image out of his poems, he lived in a country whose people bought more life insurance, per capita, than any other people on the face of this earth. He lived in a country of sober citizens who wore good sensible shoes and were busy investing in their own deaths. In such a time, in such a place, Irving appeared to have a fine bawdy recklessness. A needed recklessness. And he knew he was needed, he played to being needed, and so he loved to carp and complain and complain and carp in tedious preface after tedious preface to his books. Often he was just foolish, beating silly men silly. But he was, for all that, full of exuberance, not least for himself and for his work, his poems, which appeared aplenty. Robert Frost once quipped that it was easy for a fool to get into a poem; it took a poet to get out. Time after time, Irving didn't know how to get out. Blame it on his exuberance, a guilelessness: he wore poem after poem on his sleeve, each like a heart. In such a poem, "Plaza de Toros," he wrote:

> *I stand on a hill;*
> *my mind reels in terraces*

and I'm sucked into a whirlpool
of earth.
An evening wind rattles the almond trees.

In the hushed arena of the sky
the bloodied bull sinks down
with infinite majesty:
the stanchless blood fills the sea

Triumphant matador, night
flings his black cape across the sky.

Irving published tens and tens of such exercises. He showed no restraint. This was surprising, because he always insisted that he had a first-rate "shit detector" – that he could spot shit any-where.

Am I too harsh? Well, about "Plaza de Toros," his admirer, Charles Bukowski, wrote: "I'm afraid that this poem could have been written by any high-school girl with a bad case of acne who had missed the Senior Dance and was sorry for herself and creating a seemingly beautiful escapism."

Fair enough.

But at the same time, he wrote strong, sharply observed poems, like "The Bull Calf":

The thing could barely stand. Yet taken
from his mother and the barn smells
he still impressed with his pride,
with the promise of sovereignty in the way
his head moved to take us in.
The fierce sunlight tugging the maize from the ground
licked at his shapely flanks.
He was too young for all that pride.
I thought of the deposed Richard II.

"No money in bull calves," Freeman had said.
The visiting clergyman rubbed the nostrils
now snuffing pathetically at the windless day.
"A pity," he sighed.
My gaze slipped off his hat toward the empty sky
that circled over the black knot of men,
over us and the calf waiting for the first blow.

Struck,
the bull calf drew in his thin forelegs
as if gathering strength for a mad rush . . .
tottered . . . raised his darkening eyes to us,
and I saw we were at the far end
of his frightened look, growing smaller and smaller
till we were only the ponderous mallet
that flicked his bleeding ear
and pushed him over on his side, stiffly,
like a block of wood.

Below the hill's crest
the river snuffled on the improvised beach.
We dug a deep pit and threw the dead calf into it.
It made a wet sound, a sepulchral gurgle,
as the warm sides bulged and flattened.
Settled, the bull calf lay as if asleep,
one foreleg over the other,
bereft of pride and so beautiful now,
without movement, perfectly still in the cool pit.
I turned away and wept.

There are two problems:

Irving is well read. The line, "I thought of the deposed Richard II" is intrusive erudition to no point except Irving trying to be smarter than the poem.

And "I turned away and wept" is a ruinous last line.

Suddenly he has made his own weeping most important. I understand that his weeping, as in other poems – "A Tall Man Executes a Jig," "The Old Niçoise Whore," etc. – is important to him (in the old days, amongst the *shtetl* Jews in eastern Europe, when and if there was doubt between a man and woman, weeping was a way of showing one's love), but that last line spoke to Irving's great weakness: he couldn't stay out of the act. It is what Keats complained about in Wordsworth: "Are we to be bullied into a certain philosophy engendered in the whims of an egotist? Every man has his speculations, but every man does not brood and peacock over them . . . how beautiful are the retired flowers! How would they lose their beauty were they to throng into the highway crying out, 'admire me I am a violet! – dote upon me I am a primrose!'"

One night in Toronto, we argued this point. He was furious with me. We were in his house and after several scotches, he waved his arms, he stood up, he sat down, he yelled "*Goi*, you sophist, you *goi*, you sociologist, *goi*, you pipsqueak professor, *goi,* you fool, you non-poet, no greater fool among my friends, you . . . you *goi*." He sat down. He stared at me. I stared back at him.

SILENCE.

And then he began to laugh, almost weeping with laughter, and he threw open his arms and asked, "After the silence, what?"

"Weeping," I said, "and with any luck, laughter."

Concerning the increasingly inclement weather in his skull: he is still running to Israel, to Greece, to India, engaged in an act of life that is like a pinwheel in the night:

> *Spit great mouthfuls of water*
> *over the boats*
> *whining like tethered horses,*

and crack your long, green fingers
Neptune, on island walls . . .

But his seas are full of ghosts – the ghosts of the women he has impaled on a rumpled bed, the ghosts of Hitler's henchmen who still haunt him, the skeletons of grief-crazed Jewesses who still stalk him, but now – and this is a seismic shift – when he has been stung awake in the night, when he opens his eyes on the pillow, his first thought is not of corpulent worms amidst the carnage; he says his first thought is of someone he loves and while thinking of her he makes a silence of her name and he then dips his hands into that silence, to make a prayer, a poem – a poem of passion but no rancour, no remorse, no regret, even as he looks up to see the ghost of his phallus in a whitening sky.

He may have, in the past, declared himself a stiltwalker, fantastical and bawdy among those women who had ambassadorial eyes, he may have played the buffoon, he may have spoken of himself as a mad saint in an insane world, but – as the years have gone by – as he's stepped out of the skin of such stances – and as he has, in fact, belittled the idea, the image, of his being a lover on a pogo stick – it has become clear that at his best, in his best poetry, he has been more and more a probative sane man, acutely conscious of his manner, his music – often more Auden and Byron than bluster, more decorous than deranged – a poet for whom

Manner redeemeth everything:
> *redeemeth*
man, sets him among,
over, the other worms, puts
a crown on him, yes, the size of a
> *mountain lake,*

dazzling more dazzling!
      than a slice of sun

He is still, of course, self-absorbed, but now he seems to be certain only about death and the uncertainty of all other things, a man who has come down off his stilts to walk among us, to walk slowly, and "by walking to find out where he is going" and

By intensely hating, how to love.

By loving, whom and what to love.
By grieving, how to laugh from the belly.

And out of his increasing infirmity he has built a strength, and out of his untruth, truth. From hypocrisy, he has woven directness and

Almost now I know who I am.
Almost I have the boldness to be that man.

Another step
And I shall be where I started from.

❧

. . . for every man the shark smiles
              —Irish proverb

In some quiet bay
or deserted inlet
he is waiting for me

It is noon
there is a stillness on water and land
as if some primal god is about to speak;

in the sky
not a single bird is to be seen flying

I shall swim out towards him
bringing him my incurable moral ache
and my cancered liver,
memories of women laughter Greek islands
griefs and humiliations I could find no words for

I want him to be black, wholly black
I want him to be famished and solitary
I want him to be quietly ready for me
as if he were the angel of death

The last thing I want my alive eyes
to behold before I close them forever
are his ripsaw teeth.

He now has a patience and softness born out of sorrow – certainly a sorrow for himself, a greying man – "undone who am a clown" – swelling with images of white faraway bodies lost after the wind and wolves have had their fill, but also swollen with sorrow for his lady, hard done by, bruised and abandoned by other, perhaps younger lovers:

O rabbis and angels
and lovers marooned
forever in lost movies
when wind and wolves have had their fill
I shall unstitch the clawmarks
from my lady's lovely flesh
I shall sleep all night
beside her bruised and glistening body
on a lonely hill.

He still pumps out his poems, scourge of the scurrilous, but now they seem only a habit, a reflex. Dionysus is out there, still having his day, and Icarus is having his death, but what has been compelling is his increasing feeling of oneness, not with gods, but with aging men like himself, like the gardener who has made one large tranquillity of acceptance:

> *wanting no man's pity or compassion*
> *only*
> *the remaining strength*
> *in his seven good fingers*
> *disease*
> *hasn't twisted*
> *into black unfeeling claws*
> *and the bite of a solitary tooth*
> *standing firm*
> *in his jaw*
> *like a weather-beaten nail*
> *for his smile to hang on.*

I have seen such a smile hanging on Irving's face, the smile of a man who believes that there has been, in his life, no great defeat, and no great victory either; it has been and still is "a Greek tragedy without catharsis" in which the sniffing of human blood must go on, murderous pinheads must remain in political power, and "everyone must still live with some gas in his lungs." Life – no matter how protective he gets, how low he lies – can not be lived without its taunting, sorrowing moments as he grows more and more aware that he is being hunted down by his own years – betrayed by his own body, in exactly the same way that his sister was betrayed by hers – his sister who lost track of her mind out in that garden . . . . Somewhere, somehow, her mind had gotten away from her so that, one day when Irving went to see her, she was there but she wasn't there. She sat up in her bed, senile, silent, except for when she sang to him, sang to the singer, and she had sung to him with an exultance that could only be taken by him as an affirmation of life.

Of an afternoon in Café des Copains in Toronto – perhaps lacking pity – I asked Irving to read a particular poem to me, to read "Senile My Sister Sings." He was reluctant, modest before – and perhaps even a little afraid of – the power of feeling he knew the poem possessed. His voice cracked, his hands shook as he told me how his sister, like a white blossom, had blinked and had begun to sing the same snatch of song over and over for him, her lips trembling when she had tried for a high note, her white hair close-cropped like a prisoner's, her unobstructed tongue lolling while her dentures had grinned at him through a glass of water, and he had heard his sister – his own blood – his sibling image – singing like some kind of vocal chicken, her small raisin eyes darting about to pluck worms out of his clothes, his sister so frail and emaciated, her smile so dazzling that the roaches roaming the walls of their old kitchen, he said, had scurried behind the torn wallpaper to hide out till her incandescence had passed, and he read to me:

> Sing, my dear sister, sing
> though your trembling lips break my heart
> and I turn away from you to sob
> and let the tears course down my cheeks,
> my grief held back by pride and even a kind
> of exultance. You do not moan or whimper,
> you do not grovel before the Holy Butcher
> and beg Him to spare you days; or rock
> silently like the other white-haired biddies
> waiting to be plucked from their stoops. No,
> though His emissary ominously flaps his wings
> to enfold you in their darkness, you sing.
> Your high-pitched notes must rile him
> more than rage or defiance. You sing him
> no welcome, and if your voice trembles

it's not fear or resignation he hears
but the cracked voice of the élan vital
whose loudest chorister you are, abashing Death
and making him skulk in his own shadow.

As he ended the singing of his sister, as she sent Death skulk-
ing away into Death's own shadow, I wondered whether I had
been wrong about that last line of his "Bull Calf" poem because
for a moment I turned away from Irving, afraid I was going to
weep. When I turned back I saw no tears but only a wan smile
hanging on his face. I hoped that when his time came, if he was
anywhere near, I might be able to

Speak softly
 to this queer beast;
soothe him, soothe him

Saturday Night, 1972-1980

37

DUMMLING'S DREAM

There are many views of life – the view from the bridge, the bird's-eye view – but what is the view from the cradle, or from first light, when a child is hung by the heels in the air? Who knows? But there is a novel, *The Tin Drum* by Günter Grass, written in the wake of the last war, in which a child named Oscar has come out of the womb and what he sees is a light bulb. "Let there be light and there was light," and Oscar quickly saw that life was going to be a forest of light bulbs, the switch in the hands of daddy, mummy, schoolteachers, and cops. Little Oscar wanted to go right back to where he had come from but the umbilical cord had been cut. His father cried out, "He will take over the grocery store when he grows up. At last we know why we've been working our fingers to the bone." Words to make any man-child shudder: the future laid down like a law, a grocery store, with all that self-pitying justification that big people go in for . . . fathers sacrificing sons to their own failed dreams.

Big people! That is what a child says, and he knows who his friends are: Tom Thumb, pygmies, leprechauns, Lilliputians, midgets and Mickey Mouse. Not those big people. Little Oscar, clairaudiant in his swaddling clothes, a visionary, a poet, lay back and listened to a moth flutter and beat its head against the light bulb, a moth casting shadows much, much bigger than its wing-spread the closer it got to the light; but it was still only a moth and Oscar knew life could go on like that for sixty or seventy years, until that final short circuit would at last cut him off and send him back into the soothing darkness. That, thought Oscar, was no way to live or die; deluding yourself, believing you were the big moth on the block because you cast a big shadow. Besides, Oscar saw not only an overhead light bulb but a clock on the wall, and the clock was probably the most remarkable thing that grownups had ever produced, but being grownups, they no sooner had come up with an epoch-making invention than they became a slave to it. Clock-punchers and grocerymen, slaves, banging their heads against the 60-watt light bulb of life. Thanks but no thanks, Oscar thought, and – in an act of Nietzschean inversion – he decided to stop growing at three, to remain a small boy, a child; in a magnificent reversal of what life's ambitions are supposed to be all about, he refused to become one of the willful big people.

Oscar's vision of himself and his plight is mordant and comic, and though it is a view that lacks the sensual pleasure a child feels in just being alive, it is filled with the pure, instinctive comprehension, the total solemnity, gravity and earnestness of children who are, as Goethe pointed out, rigorous moralists who expect and demand perfection in all things and beings – and what they get is big people walloping or loving them, full tilt, and for no apparent rhyme or reason.

It is on this point that Oscar touches a special truth and tells us how children must see it. Decisions are made for them, imposed on them, arbitrary decisions and gestures, and arbitrariness is the key, accounting, I think, for the violence that inhabits a child's vision, the violence that sends him into a world of extremes, because children, when they play, are not playful. The child's passion for play is utterly serious – which is why it is so much fun, and so extreme. It is total belief, every day at every moment, in life or death, in cops and robbers, monsters or moonbeams. In his journals, William Kurelek, the prairie-born painter many parents love – they love those unblemished children of his with their pie-shaped guileless faces and stunned smiles – wrote of his memories of childhood:

> I vacillated between terror and timidity . . . I suffered
> hallucinations at night: the lynx-sized cat clawing at the

underside of the crib; the giant grey rubber hose in the shape of a rocking chair with a black sheet draped over one end, rocking back and forth on a bench under the window; the huge turkey vulture that tried to peck at my face and eyes, and since I kept tightly covered, it could only walk all over me, and I distinctly felt its feet as it stomped from one foot to the other. I let no air under my blanket, and terror left me drenched in sweat . . . . My parents laughed when I told them of these things.

As Kurelek later understood it, and talked explicitly about it, these were the images of his loneliness, bewilderment and terror as he cowered under the gaping smiles of parents who were either loving or admonishing him to death. He was an extreme case, of course, but what else does any child feel in his crib as the lights go on and he looks up, and is hauled out of the dark, blinking, confronted by big people, a man looming, a mother cooing and cuddling, and then suddenly they are growling and angry and dismissive. That's what parents do, that's how they are, though they are the last to admit it. They swarm with love, they swarm with rage, and surely none of it makes sense to a child. The smiling face, the mask for tomorrow's twisted face of rage – which is why, I suspect, all children's stories that children love are filled with violence, the unexplained and unexplainable deceit of wolves who suck about like friends only so they can eat you alive, or a huge rock falls, BAM, or deformed monsters close the door, SLAM, as the town's self-indulgent fathers, all of them double-dealers, double cross the Pied Piper. HAW. Every child learns who has to pay for the pipe as the piper tootles children toward the canal, toward a death by drowning, as the sins of the fathers are visited upon the sons . . . .

Slam Bam Haw. Violence. Glub. Three men in a tub. These are the rhymes of the dying. And as dying is serious to a child, it is also ridiculous. A child is told: "There once was a man who had three sons, the youngest of whom was named Dummling and on that account he was despised . . . ." Or this: "A child was born, who, although he was perfectly formed in all his limbs, actually was not bigger than one's thumb . . . and he remained exactly the height he was when first born . . . ." The child laughs, and sits forward on the edge of his chair as you tell him these stories of little people arbitrarily doomed. Or as he watches the Roadrunner run, BAM, a tree has boomeranged across the road from out of nowhere; leaving only the final big BLAM; earth, air, fire, water, sun and moon are all weapons on the side of some total, relentless, implacable power. And children howl with laughter, go into exultant glee. Tom Thumb and Dummling are doomed, SPLAT, across the face of the universe, and we hear a child's high-pitched laughter, and no blame.

As the ancients said: all art, whether epics, cartoons or fairy tales, gives us back the image of our mind. And what is fascinating about children is that, unlike adults, they not only laugh at the horrors, the arbitrary unfairness of it all, but they blame no one. In their minds, they take life whole, for what it is: they are the supreme realists. You can be sure that a child has ceased to be a child and has begun to become a big person when he not only begins to blame his parents for his plight but begins to enjoy irony and to take pleasure in ambiguity. You can be sure, as a matter of fact, that he has stopped believing in the stories he is hearing and the stories he is telling because he has begun to flesh them out with moments of morality and psychology . . . that is, he has begun to love Snoopy, the life of Woody Allen as played by a dog.

On this point, Søren Kierkegaard understood perfectly what kind of belief, what feel for the truth, is at the heart of storytelling for children. In his journal for 1837, he wrote:

> There are two recommended ways of telling children stories, but there are also a multitude of false paths in between.
> The first is the way unconsciously adopted by the nanny, and whoever can be included in that category. Here a

whole fantasy world dawns for the child, and the nannies are themselves deeply convinced that the stories are true ... which, however fantastic the content, can't help bestowing a beneficial calm on the child. Only when the child gets a hint of the fact that the person doesn't believe her own stories are there ill effects – not from the content but because of the narrator's insincerity – from the lack of confidence and suspicion that gradually envelops the child.

The second way is possible only for someone who with full transparency reproduces the life of childhood, knows what it demands, what is good for it, and from his higher standpoint offers the children a spiritual sustenance that is good for them – who knows how to be a child, whereas the nannies themselves are basically children.

The basic childhood state, that open embrace of nightmare laughter, of light and ghouls, fun and gnomes, is more than the nanny's unquestioning acceptance of arbitrary reality. Her child, her charge, is not only the future – that is obvious – but he has within him the dream of the future. He contains not only the continuity of the race, but all the possibilities of the race. So as he grows up, he must keep his head down, he must continue to dream as a child dreams, he must, as Virginia Woolf once put it, continue to go "Down, down, down, fall into that terrifying, wildly inconsequent, yet perfectly logical world where time races, then stands still; where space stretches, then contracts ... down the groves of pure nonsense we whirl, laughing—

They sought it with thimbles, they sought it with care;
They pursued it with forks and hope ...

And then we wake." We wake to reality, to adulthood, to the dying of the race, but – and this is the key – having been down among the children we can still try to do as a child does, we can try to create ourselves, or we can try to do as a Byzantine mystic once did: "Since we cannot change reality, let us change the eyes with which we see reality."

I spy with my little eye . . .

The child, when he sees the world for the first time, he creates it. All things – animals, trees, men, stones, forms, colours, voices, smells, light bulbs, and lightning flashes – all these things flow unexplained in a child's eyes and as a result he becomes one with the sky, with insects, sea, wind, wolves, grandmothers – one with whatever he sees or touches. But as things are magically re-kneaded in his realm, they come close to what big people call the abnormal. And big people, when they are faced with the abnormal in a child, the dreamer who sees the sky as a breast, the moon as a hole, the rain as God weeping, when they are faced with an Oscar and his drum, they turn to their psychologists and psychiatrists, those high priests of the statistical and the status quo.

"Drum the dream out of Dummling," they plead.

Everyone understands that the concentration camp crime beyond all understanding was the killing of children; when you kill men you kill the past, when you kill women you kill the present, but when you kill children you kill the future. To obliterate the future is unthinkable, suicidal, and we are repelled by the thought; we are struck dumb by such a dead end, and yet we determinedly assault and nearly always kill the child's dream of the future. We wipe out the possibilities of the dream in the name of grocers and true grit, all the job training programs, all the logarithms of fear, this is what we call school: a forest of light bulbs.

Sixty watts, 100 watts, fluorescent and neon, halogen – how do we step out of the constant glare, how do we keep a little of Oscar alive in a child, and how do we keep alive in ourselves that dream of an inner light – the illuminating idea, where everything is so strange that nothing is surprising. Nikos Kazantzakis, the novelist who learned from Zorba how to dance in the shoes of death, wrote as an old man about the child inside himself:

Whatever fell into my childhood mind was imprinted there with such depth and received by me with such avidity that even now in my old age I never grow tired of recalling and reliving it . . . . I remember frequently sitting on the doorstep of our home when the sun was blazing, the air on fire, the world fragrant with must. Shutting my eyes contentedly, I used to hold out my palms and wait. God always came. As long as I remained a child, He never deceived me. He always came, a child just like myself, and deposited His toys in my hands: sun, moon, wind. 'They're gifts,' He said, 'they're gifts. Play with them. I have lots more.' I would open my eyes. God would vanish, but His toys would remain in my hands. I possessed the Lord's omnipotence: I created the world as I wanted it. I was soft dough; so was the world.

1976

MY LIFE
IN THE MOVIES:
A LETTER FROM A
TENOR SAXOPHONIST

I have seen the room where I was born, I have seen it in several old black-and-white B-movies where there is a hotel room down in the east end of town by the old railroad station, and there is a single iron cot along the wall and the paper's peeling on the wall and there's an old leather suitcase on the floor that someone has made up into a child's bed, and outside, what you see through the window is a hotel sign that flashes on and off, which turns out later in the movie, after my mother, my real mother, a brunette with high cheekbones and marcelled hair, has gone downstairs to the bar, the sign turns out to be the sign for the Hotel Rex. The bartender, who happens to be a retired light-heavyweight boxer with a moon face and a bent nose, has always favoured my mother – that's what he says – he favours her for her beautiful skin. She smiles at him. "Peaches and cream," she says, touching his hand, and then touching her own cheek, "peaches and cream. That's how life should be." She smokes a Lucky Strike, tapping her ash into a heavy glass ashtray, and she blows a smoke ring, a pale blue ring that disintegrates in the light, and on her barstool she crosses her long legs and she says, looking me in the eye, "Don't you worry boy, when the world ends, the world's gonna end on B-flat."

2004

BERLIN

There used to be a wall in Berlin, and because of the wall, the left hand never knew what the right hand was doing. It was a time for the thought police. The left hand talked only to the left, the right to the right. People did nothing about the wall for forty years. Life was full of half-truths. But at last, nobody could stand it, people broke the wall down. It had been a strange wall, intended to keep people in, not keep people out. The bible said, Never let your left hand know what your right hand is doing. The bible was wrong. People don't want to know only half-truths. They want left-handed truth from the right people and right-handed truth from sinister people.

There is no Berlin. There are two sides of a wall called Berlin. The wall angles across streets, and through houses, it cordons off canals and rivers. On the western side the wall is covered with graffiti and white crosses for the dead; to the east the wall is penitentiary white. There are blue cobbled streets that dead-end into the wall and old rusty tram tracks, too. *Grepos* wearing jodhpurs and soup-bowl helmets stand in concrete flat-top machine-gun nests. There are street signs that point to where no one can go, the no man's land on the white side of the wall, a death zone of wire fences, dog runs, trip wires, tank traps (sawn-off steel girders painted white). The old dilapidated red-brick Church of Reconciliation is in the middle of no man's land, its doors nailed shut, rabbits feeding on the rough grass, the grass studded with fragmentation mines. There is no Berlin. There are two sides of a wall, one the double of the other, two sides of a mirror, and behind the mirror, the face of the other.

The graffiti side of the wall is a cluttered enclave of free citizen spenders trapped among collective citizen farmers in a police state. There is a fluorescent gimcrack energy in graffiti streets like the Kurfürstendamm – cut down colloquially to Ku-damm or even more colloquially to Qdamm – a tree-lined boulevard of terraces and sex shops, rock bars, street artists – where a child draws Mona Lisa's smile on the sidewalk – and motorcycle dudes and elderly couples walk elbow to elbow. So many old people! Sedate women dance together under bare light bulbs in tree-shaded beer gardens, table after table of old women who've left their childhood behind on the fire-stormed streets of the War and they are now hunched under little globes of golden light at Kranzler's double-decker café, smirking with a weary coyness behind a gloved hand, waiting for the table phone to ring, sometimes drinking a *Weisse mit Schuss* (a red syrup foamed with yeasty white beer), glancing up at a flirtatious boy who is flaunting his new silicone breasts as he passes out handbills, "See me *live* at Disco Joe's," he cries. On the corner, under the huge NeWs sign of thousands of pulsating light bulbs, pictures stipple the night sky, up-to-the-minute names broken by running time – always the up-to-the-second time (9:16) for people (9:17) with nowhere (9:18) to go – the young men, so few of them in comparison to women, young men who are all from somewhere else, tired but wide awake, and a woman says, laughing easily, "Moscow, the KGB, nonsense. The only thing I'm afraid of is another woman."

This street and those around the Qdamm – Joachimsthaler, Fasanen – are a hodgepodge of pre-cast concrete and chrome and steel, glass and aluminium, buildings bolted into place by a people who were eager to leave behind broken lives in a gutted city (in the north end, at Devil's Mountain – *Teufelsberg* – pre-War

Berlin is now in its grave: 18 million cubic metres of ornate stair-
cases, sewage piping, marble mantelpieces, tile ovens, toilet bowls,
roofing slate – cleared out of the rubble by crews of women
whose men had been killed – dumped, rotated and mashed;
Teufelsberg). Those stone-picker women who've now grown
old cradle their toy poodles and dachshunds as they stand on
small roughly hewn wooden platforms and look over the wall,
across no man's land to where

> *there are*
> *still songs to be sung on the other side*
> *of mankind.*[1]

and then they leash their little dogs and walk back into the no
man's land of widowhood, back to Kranzler's – passing by the
hideous shell of Memorial Church, No. 11 Ku-damm (1 to 10 is
a gap – "white" space – like the "white" of the Hitler years, "lost"
in the history books though his bunker is buried in no man's
land) and they sit down and talk with other people who have
nowhere to go, people who can have any titillation they want,
anything and everything that money provides: Von Karajan con-
ducting in the petal-shaped Philharmonic Hall, a bullet-proof
Audi 5000, *Specialité Sinistra: Strap-on-Dildos for Lesbians,* fish
tanks stocked with "whopper" piranha at a Burger King, a roul-
ette casino, Gatemouth Brown *preachifying* at Club Quasimodo,
the one-eyed head of Nefertiti at the Egyptian museum, child
hookers (girls and boys), transvestite fire eaters, and . . . speed –
crack – and smack . . . for sale at Bahnhof Zoo station (Joseph
Roth wrote in 1930, as if it were now: "Berlin is an unhappy city
in waiting . . . the wickedness, sheer cluelessness, and avarice of
its rulers, builders, and protectors as they draw up plans, mud-
dle them again, and confusedly put them into practice"), and
then, hungry, some walk over to the fresh-food floor at the

---

[1] The poems quoted throughout "Berlin" are by Paul Celan and Günter Grass,
translated by Michael Hamburger and Christopher Middleton.

department store KaDeWe – 10 lunch counters tended by cooks who, for a first afternoon course, prepare a fresh salmon crêpe with a glass of champagne and, after a half-hour stroll among ice-racks of seafood and stalls of sides of beef, sausages and roasted ducks, truffles, avocados, cheeses, cherries, almonds, puff pastries, cream pastries . . . there is a serving counter of broiled meats with red wine, followed at another counter by a superb plum sorbet to cleanse the palate and further down the line, langoustines with franconian white wine, completed by an apple and honey mousse . . . it is a salubrious afternoon lunch eaten among the well-heeled and self-absorbed who

> *live in an egg.*
> *We have covered the wall inside*
> *of the shell with dirty drawings*
> *and the Christian names of our enemies . . .*
> *We assume we're being hatched*

a hatching, a break-out into the streets where

> *senile chicks,*
> *polyglot embryos*
> *chatter all day*
> *and even discuss their dreams*

but then, at the end of the day, they stand in the shadow of the old Anhalter station, now only a dirty brick façade of ruined arches and empty rosette windows . . . stand in shadows as haunting as 1 to 10 Ku-damm, that hollow blackened tooth, the Kaiser Wilhelm Memorial Church, its doorway reeking of urine, an insistent ache, a

> *half death*
> *splayed beside us, true as an ashen*
> *image—*

Around the corner from the church, ashen-faced old folks are carrying string bags bulging with butter and spices as they shuffle into the Bahnhof Zoo station, all taking the Reichsbahn, the old rinky-dink railroad line that is still run by the East Germans, run by them – by treaty – on both sides of the wall. Dumpily dressed conductors loiter at the Coke and Sprite machines, the air is sour from backed-up drains. Down on a platform old people wait for the train to the other side of the wall. Zonked-out kids (who collect a government dole, a dole set up to pay young people to stay in Berlin) sit cross-legged on the concrete, transfixed by the air they are sitting in. ("Air, air, air," Dostoievsky said, "is what a man wants.") The old people have their space, too, taking the air as they travel "wooden class," in coaches that still have slat seats from the Forties.

Some are hobbled, going "over" for a day to try to find their childhood in the watery eyes of an infirm older sister or a cousin, the last one alive. At the checkpoint, you enter a grimy, greyly lit tunnel, you go up concrete stairs and stand alone in Passport Control, a constricted inspection closet, bent forward under overhead mirrors before a truculent customs official who is wearing a rumpled toneless brown suit. He checks your back in the mirrors and your passport under ultraviolet lights. There is a metallic tinge to the light in the mirrors, as if something in the lighting might be able to locate political infection . . . an individual weakness that would give you away . . . you wouldn't know what the infection is, you wouldn't want to know, you wouldn't want to be so paranoid that you believe your dreams, too, are being monitored by the *Stasi*, the secret police . . . . No, you want to look like no one, you want to be no one, to slip through . . . unnoticed. A buzzer goes off. A door opens. After paying the transit fee, DM25, and after a pat-down and search for books, newspapers, and money (any guileless traveller who has changed currency in the West is strip-searched: the discovery of substantial cash causes arrest and jail time), and you are given a fistful of featherweight grey coins and then bustled out into the almost empty windswept public squares on the white side of the wall – Marx-Engels-Platz, Strausberger Platz, Alexanderplatz . . . .

"Where are the crowds, where are the people . . . ?"

The old dressed stone walls of the rows of apartment houses are still, after all the intervening years, shrapnel-pocked from the War, the stucco seems stained by the perpetually worn-out faces of poster people (bleached and moldered, they are Brechtian figures mouthing joyless slogans), stone soldiers lie wide-eyed, stunned, their bodies broken in half in the long grass of abandoned churchyards while saints, still standing, are headless, with weeds growing out of their throats:

> *A strange lostness is palpably present.*
> *A privation.*
> *An absence of . . .*
> *Down to the last worn-out knot of breath.*

Along the river Spree, close by an old brewery building with a breached roof, at a small sidewalk café, the waitress complains about clients who have not only brought their dogs into the restaurant but their own homemade sandwiches. Clients who sit. And sit. Wearing shabby suits. Greasy lapels (suits that are shapeless, suits that have never fitted – always too big or too small as if belonging to another person, suits that seem to neuter everyone). The patron, in a frayed tuxedo, sits down beside a writer, a novelist, who has just got off a train from Prague:

Question: "How long have you been working on your novel?"

Answer: "Four years. I'll finish it this year. It fills sixteen empty notebooks."

Question: "What's the theme, what's it about?"

Answer: "The spoken word. Something is said; but a word, once spoken, vanishes."

Question: "How's it end?"

Answer: "I don't remember."

The novelist laughs. A high-pitched, mirthless laugh that has the weight of a fistful of coins.

Several customs officials, each carrying a cheap stiff brown leather briefcase, hurry across the street to the Opera Café (where Jules Laforgue had kept an apartment in the 1880s: and sitting at the café, he'd written the first influential essay on French Impressionist painting) while jackbooted troopers execute a *Gänseschritt* (goose step) on the Allee, legs rising, boots smashing back to the pavement of Unter den Linden:

> *Through a crack in the door we*
> *saw the world:*
> *a rooster with its head hacked off,*
> *running across the yard.*

The secret police, the *Staatssicherheitsdienst,* are felt like grease on the air, a clinging shadow in a blown-out lung (even the flat open spaces on the penitentiary-white side of the wall seem suspicious; there has to be a nook, there have to be crannies, envelopes in the air itself), and these police are known as the *Stasi* (stasis, in English, is a stoppage of the blood). Their forbidding central complex, "The House of One Thousand Eyes," is an entire city block on the Magdalenenstrasse. It has solid steel doors, a munitions bunker, a barracks, a hospital, two copper-lined rooms to prevent satellite surveillance, and 33,000 in-house employees who handle the files of one million full-time snitches, one million whispered betrayals week after week, miles upon miles of continuously rolling audio tape, an infestation of "bugs" as

> *we hang our sheets from the*
> *balcony,*
> *and we surrender*

to the 'Anti-Fascist Protection' Party and their cartographers who – after careful ideological consideration – have drawn up official maps of the country, leaving – in those maps – an area that is entirely "white space" – (the city had been worm-holed by "white spaces") – erased openings, a gap, a nothing where

> *the people of clouds . . .*
> *move about over orphaned grounds . . .*

and no ground is more of an orphanage site than the Pergamon. It is a dusty and ill-lit museum that houses stolen fragments of an ancient temple, all the fragments brought to Berlin decades before the First War, the sections of temple ruins uprooted from a rocky barren that had been situated close to Troy . . . a long, fractured altar of warriors wrestling in stone relief: Hecate, Artemis, Apollo, Zeus, Saturn . . . the immortal gods, who have been taken apart stone by stone, trussed and reconstructed – to stand close to a pirated Babylonian processional Allee (orange against Prussian blue) of glazed ceramic lions, the lions prowling under a row of tangerine sunflowers that open on to the temple stairs, and at the foot of the temple wall – amputated arms, a truncated leg, severed hands clasping each other, a reptile entwined around a headless hero, sheared rib cages, torsos, primal war:

> *And what if we're not being hatched?*
>
> *If this shell will never break?*
> *If our horizon is only that*
> *of our scribbles, and always will be?*
> *We hope that we're being hatched*

And as I stepped out into the Allee:
"Come out into the open," said the policeman.
"The open?"
"Come out. Out."
"I'm already out."

"Your papers please."

The broad Allee of spreading lime trees leads to the Branden-
burg Gate, a gate boarded up by wooden siding and concrete
slabs. Barricaded. It looms up over a road that could not be taken,
a road truncated by twelve Doric stone columns and four bronze
green horses that hauled the goddess' heavy wheeled quadriga
toward the Soviet's Red star in the East . . . but of course, before
the World Wars, she had wheeled around into the Prussian West,
and before that, she had charged into the East, always symbolic,
always on the expedient swivel of power in a no man's land:

> *Even if we only talk of hatching*
> *There remains the fear that someone*
> *outside our shell will feel hungry*
> *and crack us into the frying pan with a pinch of salt.*
> *What shall we do then, my brethren inside the egg?*

Getting out of Stasiland required a disheartening walk among
determined but mopey-eyed workers – a walk to the inside white
of the wall where I stood obediently for a pat-down search (the
only intimacy openly allowed!) by the surly pasty-faced guards
in the train station, and then I took the "wooden class" rickety
ride back through the wall to the gaudy nighttime Tiergarten –
necklaces of lights in the trees, craters of dark – the great zoo (at
night the howling wolves scat-sing in the city), past wide-open
fields of decades-old post-war rubble, halting close to an angel
goddess on a pillar whose gold wings seem heavy with what's
invisible. She is waving a gold laurel wreath at a winner of some-
thing long since gone down the road as she stands barefoot
between sawn-off captured cannon barrels – a glitzy woman hal-
looing conquering generals and politicians who are scattered
down the Allees and in the small squares, all leading to the nar-
row line of white wood memorial crosses that have been planted
over the dead "escapees" from the East – planted only a stone's
throw from the Reichstag, with its great glass dome "of the

future" that had long ago collapsed in the 1933 Nazi fire – and above the burial sites of the gun-downed escapees, there is the dedication carved on the Reichstag gable: TO THE GERMAN PEOPLE (though Metternich had said of the people: "No Bavarian desired to be an Austrian, no Austrian desired to be a Prussian, no Prussian a Bavarian, no Bavarian a Württemberger and no one in all the German marches desired to be a Prussian if he didn't already happen to be one").

An old Prussian is sitting on the Glienicker steel walkway over the river Spree (the bridge where several exchanges of prisoners and dissidents have taken place) and he is fishing with a long pole, watching the water with one eye, watching a guard in the East who has a gun slung over his shoulder with the other eye, knowing that any swimmer stroking toward the western shore will be shot out of the water by *Grepo* sharpshooters, and knowing, too, that the guard who is wearing steel-rimmed flight glasses on the Western graffiti side will not return fire because it is against the law; because – in mid-river – the swimmer is a no one from nowhere until he is fished out and claimed and buried under a small white cross:

> *Set free from the egg one day*
> *we shall draw a picture*
> *of whoever is hatching us.*

On the Ku-damm, a child has finished drawing Mona Lisa's smile on the sidewalk. Now he is drawing Hitler's moustache on her upper lip. Sitting in the morning sunlight with his left foot under Mona Lisa's chin, a man in his early forties says, "Of course, we learn the lessons of history. Ever since Hegel we have learned that history is a hatchery. Eggs get broken. Lots of ugly ducklings." He lights a cigarette, takes the hand of a blond woman, and says, "You see, you swallow and laugh at the same time. When I was a boy and the bombs came in our street, everyone ran out of the houses into the shelter, except for an old man who always smoked a pipe. He was a great pipe smoker and he refused to go, saying he would sit in his house and smoke his pipe, and when the bombs came and hit they hit only his house, a clean single hit like someone had pulled a tooth. Poof, gone, the old man dead and everyone else's house was okay. The lesson is," he says, taking a long drag on his cigarette, "smoking is bad for your health." He laughs loudly and then says, "Of course, this lesson is one thing, life is another."

He and the woman stand up. She is carrying two towels. "We're going out to one of the lakes," he says. "We have wonderful lakes and trees in the suburbs, lots of trees and grass. We will sunbathe. Germans love to undress and lie in the sun. You'll see whole hillsides of undressed people. Anyway," he says, "with secret police and spies everywhere, the only defence is to undress, so when you are able to see everything you see nothing."

Epilogue

You leave the enclave by car, driving out of West Berlin into Eastern Germany at Staaken, wanting to take the passage road to the West, to Hamburg. Lines of cars, red and white tubular barriers. Insolent guards lean into your face as it is framed in an open car window, the matching of the face to a passport photo, putting the passport into a leather pouch, the pouch disappearing into a slot: a long wordless wait, each traveller trying for casualness, an elbow out of the window, head in hand, trying to be unobtrusive, passive, yet keeping a quick eye for any tilt of the customs official's head, each traveller vulnerable without papers in a world where proper papers are necessary, are all. Then, a dismissive back-handed wave, a release – not into freedom but onto a narrow tree-lined highway through collective farmland, a tank in a gully, its cannon pointed back along the road, and machine-gun towers between the trees and then on a far hillside, a line of tanks on manoeuvre. Overcast. An air of mirthless vacancy:

Silence, cooked like gold,
In charred hands.

All movement is controlled, the strictly enforced speed limit on the highway abruptly changing: 100 klicks, 70, 40, 100, 40 . . . so that no one can stop and idle and snoop around and then make up lost time by speeding. The time the trip takes is known. There is a travelling standard, a common time, a uniform expectation, and any late car will be looked for. Five hours through grey stucco towns, fields half-tended, a moroseness in the passing faces, an unremitting wariness even at the one per-mitted stopping point, a shabby restaurant where the waitress, though she is probably an informant, depending on her whims, warns: "Keep your receipt with the time on it so they'll know you were actually here this long . . . ." Then, the last border cross-ing.

On time. "You know, already I can't remember the wall, where it goes, how it goes. I can't trace it in my mind's eye."

"Of course not," the driver says, "my father says it's a Schoen-berg song, nobody can remember such a song either . . . ."

"No?"

". . . twelve notes in no key, sharps and flats, so many that there's no key for the melody. Who can remember such a song?"

Sharpshooters with field glasses overhead, the customs guard, looking, probing . . . the photo, the face, the photo, the face, the time check

led through – by whom?
"Let pass" you say,
"let pass,"
  "let pass,"
the quiet scab works free

. . . the barrier is lifted to the road across another no man's land, a long expanse of lush green grass seeded with mines, flares, fragmentation bombs. Ahead, in the darkening sky of dusk, there is a lime-green streak, as if light is breaking, and a smear of red, as if at night the sun is going to hatch.

Leisure Ways, 1982

SEWING

After the shelling, under a cloudy sky and on the outskirts of the town, we drove past the caved-in roofs of farm houses, entering a road that was empty except for a cowering pariah dog and an old woman who was sitting on a red kitchen chair by the side of the road, sitting in a nest of black shawls in front of a burned-out shop. There were six or seven old foot-pedal sewing machines in front of the shop.

"Where is everybody?"

"Our sons, they are gone, they were the seamsters who worked those machines," the old woman said. "Soldiers coming through the valley wanted to know which of our seamsters was the poet, and, when the boys refused to speak up, a man in the militia sewed their mouths shut."

"Who did your sons say did that?"

"Their lips were sealed."

2001

CHURCHILL
THE CRISPER

Rolf Hochhuth is German. In his play, *The Soldiers*, Winston Churchill appears as the enthusiastic architect of firestorm bombing, the obliteration by fire of several German cities, most notoriously, Dresden. After London's Lord Chamberlain refused in 1968 to give *The Soldiers* a performance permit for the National Theatre on the grounds that it libelled Churchill, Kenneth Tynan leapt to the play's defence, saying *The Soldiers* belonged to "the ancient classical, integral theatre of high debate on great matters of public concern."[1]

The matter of public concern?

Was Churchill a blanket-bombing murderer in a Homburg hat, was he a war criminal?

Hochhuth announced that Theatre Toronto would mount the play in English. Critics came from across the continent and from overseas and by and large they echoed Tynan. The usually acerbic Nathan Cohen called *The Soldiers* "a gripping dramatic experience . . . very often it reaches sharp and disturbing depths." The

---

[1] In *The Soldiers*, Hochhuth has also suggested that Churchill – to appease his wartime ally, Stalin, whose plans for Poland were by then apparent – was complicit in the sabotage of a Liberator aircraft in which General Wladyslaw Sikorski, wartime premier of the London-based Polish government-in-exile, crashed to his death off Gibraltar in 1943. The allegation of sabotage appeared on the day following the crash in the Nazi newspaper, *Volkischer Beobachter*, under the headlines: "Sikorski murdered by London," which might lead one to believe the Nazis caused his death so that, by blaming Churchill, they could cause consternation among the allies.

gentle Herbert Whittaker said that Hochhuth had "undertaken a great and impossible task in *The Soldiers* – restoring the stage to greatness of purpose."

It was agreed: Hochhuth, having pilloried Pope Pius XII in his play, *The Deputy*, was the most provocative writer of his time.

The Soldiers, however, is an affront to stagecraft.

It is as clumsy in its dramatic construction as *The Deputy* was clumsy in its dramatic construction. The prologue and first act are mere scaffolding. The second and third acts are held together by a clever actor's rendering of the newsreel mannerisms of Churchill (the actor is John Colicos). Other players loiter about the stage for several hours, killing time, mulling over bits and tidbits of information, as if the increasing accumulation of information could advance an action, an action in which there is neither enlargement of character nor any rise in the emotions beyond a certain shrillness.

With no rise there can be no fall.

As a play, *The Soldiers*, like an old soldier, does not die, it fades away.

But, as with *The Deputy*, serious matters have been put in play.

Hochhuth – though he is German-born and was a patriotic youth during the Hitler years – insists that he not only despises Hitler but has only admiration for Churchill, not just as a statesman who was adept at backroom political expediency, but as a man of implacable right will (*right* used in the same absolute sense as a medievalist would when speaking of *right reason*), a man who had the *will* to firestorm German non-combatant citizens in their suburbs, in their homes, the *will* to burn them and so break their backbone. This, of course, is a portrait of Churchill as a mass murderer – a *good* mass murderer since he was instrumental in the defeat of that *evil* mass murderer, Hitler – but, a mass murderer nonetheless, and so firestorm bombing is up for debate as a matter of public concern, a debate as to whether the incendiary rendering of thousands of hapless citizens to grease could be justifiable, a rendering that took place because it was suddenly technologically possible.

Given this argument, the facts are, Churchill and his Chief Air Marshal, Arthur "Bomber" Harris, did order 1,000 planes to blanket bomb the city centre of Berlin; they did order a bombing of the residential areas of Hamburg that caused an incinerating storm of flame that not only moved at 150 miles per hour but generated temperatures of 1400 degrees Fahrenheit, killing 41,800 people; and then, Churchill did order Bomber Command to firestorm the transit city of Dresden, dropping 2,700 tons of bombs, half of them incendiary, killing between 40 to 60 thousand people, a substantial number of them refugees. Churchill and "Bomber" Harris did turn German streets – particularly in Dresden – into ovens in which women, children and refugees were baked alive, their bodies embedded in the molten streets, their bodies becoming feeding sacks for the fattening of slugs, maggots and rats. It was horrific but the admiring Hochhuth has Churchill say:

> *The man who wants to win must*
> *Be as wicked as he whom he must destroy.*[1]

This is a chilling line at a chilling moment in the play: it comes when Lord Cecil of Chelwood, Churchill's adviser, takes up red and white chalk and draws flight patterns on the floor to show how a firebomb raid could obliterate a city, could turn a city like Dresden into char and cinders. Since we are listening to two articulate and, so we want to believe, reasonably meditative men,

---

[1] It is true that on 8 July 1941, Churchill wrote: "There is one thing that will bring (Hitler) down, and that is an absolutely devastating *exterminating* [italics mine] attack by very heavy bombers from this country upon the Nazi homeland."

we anticipate a moment of probing uncertainty, a moment of anticipatory elation tinged by reluctance, a moment such as occurs even in the dank world of Macbeth:

> *. . . have we eaten on the insane root*
> *That takes the reason prisoner?*

However, as Hochhuth conjures them, Churchill and his Lord Chelwood are two uncomplicated and portentous windbags in pinstripe trousers. Talk, talk, talk, as the red and white patterns swirl into liftoff and motion. Bombers fill the air. More talk. The bombing happens, and after they receive reports of the horror – the reports of flesh turning to liquid – there is no alteration in Chelwood or Churchill. They remain men of stern motive, men of steel. No anger, no panic, no resentment, no remorse, no sense of revenge! Despite the largeness of his intent, Hochhuth has reduced Churchill (in his way) and Hitler (in his way) to a couple of crispers.

What we have, then, is Churchill as an erudite thug of hardy resolve, a thug who can be witty, petulant and quick with a verse, a thug who views war as a death struggle in which neither honour nor compassion carry weight when national interests are at stake. "This world," as Nietzsche said, and Hochhuth's Churchill agrees, "is the will to power – and nothing besides." As a man of such a world, Churchill is prepared – in order to defend and extend the national interests – to violate any and all conventions of war. This is Nietzsche – it is the *will* to *will* – sheer force that asserts itself as force: force that *wills* only its own *will* – force that is impersonal, incalculable, inescapable – force that is embodied in one man, the *übermensch*.

But, I have to ask, and any theatre-goer should ask: Is this in any commanding way true to the sometimes effulgent, sometimes incisive, sometimes acerbic, windily loquacious yet often times pithy, variously accommodating yet all too pigheaded Churchill that we have come to know through the chronicles of our time?

Or is this Hochhuth himself – unsympathetic in any convincing way to the victims of Dresden – is this Hochhuth indulging in an old Germanic dream, that Germanic preoccupation with the *übermensch,* the superman, the leader who is in possession of a moral force that "has nothing to do with whether a man is morally good or bad" – the old Rhineland dream of there being a man who is able to rise above both conventional wisdom and the prudence of active silence (Pius XII), a man who is able to act with a vengeance while believing vengeance is beneath him, a man not to be measured by common standards?

> *Greatness has its own dimension.*
> *How can you have the gall to condemn an action,*
> > *simply because*
> *You could not have performed it?*

Hochhuth celebrates Churchill as Nietzsche celebrated Napoleon – as an astonishing "synthesis of the *inhuman and superhuman"* – for just as Napoleon became, for Nietzsche, the "great artist of government," Churchill has become, for Hochhuth, the great artist of bombing. Hochhuth has restated, baldly and clumsily, not just the idea of the *übermensch,* but an even more ancient tale, the story of the great criminal who – in choosing to do what he does – is subject to neither God nor man, but is a pure power-lifter, a criminal beyond fact and physical necessity,[1] justified – as the victor is always justified – not in the eye

---

[1] There is, however, a dramatic and moral dilemma, a sin and a sorrow that is beyond resolution or redemption, lurking at the heart of *The Soldiers.* Hochhuth, by taking up the tired old tack of the *übermensch* and the great criminal, has missed it entirely. In deciding to bomb densely crowded cities from the air, in deciding to create a fire storm, Churchill made a choice, a choice that was made possible by the nature of the technology, but because of the nature of that technology he surrendered all choice to inadvertence. In exercising his decision to kill, he left himself with no control over who he was killing; this constitutes having the capacity for absolute power while at the same time lacking the capacity for any discretionary use of that power; this is the modern sin of inadvertence; inadvertent death through terror bombing; this, it seems to me, means living with a mushroom cloud in the heart.

of God but in his own eye, and therefore in the eye of History, because, after all, it is the victor – criminal or not – who writes history.

Criminal or not, that is certainly what Churchill did. He sat down – having been turfed out of postwar political office – and wrote his history of the War. With a sense of irony beyond Herr Hochhuth, the Nobel Prize Committee awarded Churchill one of their prizes, but not for history. They gave it to him for literature. Perhaps the Nobel Committee had taken Voltaire's witty aphorism to heart: history is an agreed upon fiction.

Maclean's, 1968-70

PHOENIX

Ivarr the Boneless,
bivouacked on the shore
of the White Sea,
pocketed a small stone
and warmed it in his hand
all the way home
to his garrison
south
of Lake Ladoga.

In a fit of anger
he had the stone sewn
into the mouth
of a spy,
the body beheaded,
burned,
and the face with its pursed mouth
fired
from a catapult
into the Dark Wood

where it was found
by a blond horseman,
his breast painted blue,
who hung the head
by the hair over his hearth,
and waited for it to speak.

The thread dried,
broke,
and the stone leapt out
into the fire pit.
He raked the coals
until the stone
cracked.
A black serpent
stood
in the flame—
flute,
flowering stem,
the hooded priest's
backbone,

coiling
into a bracelet of
ash,
a name in smoke,
Ivarr the Boneless,

and wearing a winged helmet
he rode south to the Black Sea
to redeem the world
by war if
needs be.

Hogg, the Seven Last Words, 2001

SIKORSKI,
IN A PIG'S EAR

Summer surprised us, coming over the Starnbergersee
With a shower of rain; we stopped in the colonnade,
And went on in the sunlight, into the Hofgarten,
And drank coffee, and talked for an hour.
Bin gar keine Russin, stamm' aus Litauen, echt deutsch.

—T.S. Eliot

General Wladyslaw Sikorski, Premier in exile of Poland during the Second World War, was also Chief of the Polish General Staff.

In 1920, after Soviet troops had occupied the eastern frontier lands of Poland and had then marched to the outskirts of Warsaw, they were met by General Sikorski's Fifth Army of light armour, foot soldiers and horse cavalry. Sikorski's troops conducted a counter-offensive that led to a Polish victory and a new Polish-Russian border, ratified by the 1921 Treaty of Riga. Poland renounced all claim to about 55 percent of her former land. This loss was treated as a victory and in 1922 Sikorski became Prime Minister. Four years later, after initiating considerable changes in domestic and foreign policy, he retired to private life.

The Riga border agreement remained in effect until 1939, when Poland was overrun by the Nazis. When Poland was partitioned by von Ribbentrop and Molotov on behalf of Hitler and Stalin, Sikorski escaped to Paris. There, he formed a Polish government-in-exile. After France fell, he, like Charles de Gaulle, removed to London.

In 1941, after Hitler double-dealt Stalin and invaded the Soviet Union, Stalin declared the Russo-German pact of 1939 null and void, met Sikorski in Moscow, agreed to the mobilization of a Polish army on Soviet soil, and agreed to the secure borders of a free Poland once the Germans were defeated.

By 1942, it was clear to Sikorski that Stalin was not going to honour their Moscow agreement. Stalin was bent on pushing westward into Poland. Sikorski knew this, Churchill knew this, yet Churchill solemnly promised Sikorski that "as long as victory has not been achieved, the problem of the future State boundaries in Europe will be in no way discussed." He then flew to Moscow to discuss the boundaries of Poland with Stalin.

Sitting down later with Roosevelt, Churchill told FDR that the Atlantic Charter should be interpreted to mean that the Soviet Union's postwar frontiers would include not only the three Baltic States – Estonia, Latvia, and Lithuania – but half of Poland. Churchill then told Stalin what he had told Roosevelt.[1] For reasons of military necessity and political expediency, Churchill had double-dealt General Sikorski and the Poles. But then, Roosevelt double-dealt Churchill by telling the Russians that he would not agree to any treaties until the war against Germany was won. Churchill, always worried about relations with the irascible Stalin, sent Anthony Eden to Washington. Eden double-dealt everybody by lying to Roosevelt, telling him that it was the Poles and not Stalin who intended to take over the Baltic states.

Relations between Churchill and Sikorski worsened in April of 1943. German forces inside Russia – striking toward Moscow – discovered strange mounds in the Katyn Forest, mounds seeded with young pines. These were mass burial mounds. Soviet divisions during the Soviet invasion of Poland in September,

---

[1] There are times when Churchill and Stalin seemed to be in collusion. Churchill, for example, had proposed to Stalin, in a note on the back of an envelope, that they strike a postwar deal: he would agree to the Soviet takeover of the Balkans if Stalin would agree to Britain controlling 90 percent of Greece.

1939, had taken 180,000 Polish prisoners, among them, 10,000 officers. The Polish officers had been brought back across the border and slaughtered by the Soviets and buried in the forest of Katyn.

General Sikorski insisted that the International Red Cross should carry out an investigation. The Germans encouraged such an investigation. Churchill, wary of upsetting or offending Stalin, cautioned Sikorski to consider the Allied relationship with the Kremlin, to consider the stringent political realities that called for silence. Sikorski refused to let the matter slide. Churchill assured Stalin, "We shall certainly oppose vigorously any investigation . . ." and Churchill, with Roosevelt, made it clear that he was prepared – if pushed too hard – to sacrifice the Polish government in London. Sikorski knuckled under. He abandoned Katyn Forest, and issued a lame warning: "There are limits to servility beyond which no Polish citizen will step."

Sikorski, aware that the Allied forces were about to invade Normandy, wanted to make sure that his Polish forces stationed in the Middle East would play some significant role in the landing. Before he flew to the Middle East to inspect his troops, he told Churchill that he "put an almost mystic trust in Great Britain and in your leadership."

Sikorski was nervous. Earlier, in Montreal, a British plane carrying Sikorski to Washington had been brought down by inexplicable engine failure and Sikorski, by sheer fluke, had escaped alive. Sabotage? The British said the plane had not been sabotaged. Roosevelt seemed to allow that the plane had been sabotaged.

Sikorski's plane for his Middle East mission, a British bomber, a Liberator, flown by a Czech pilot, after taking off from Gibraltar, flew for some 300 feet and then pitched straight into the sea. The General was killed. Everyone on board was killed except for the pilot who happened to be the only one on the plane wearing a Mae West life preserver. The English blamed the Germans. The Poles blamed the English or the Russians. The Germans blamed the English. Everyone suspected the pilot. He blamed no one and went to live in California.

No satisfactory explanation has ever been given for the plane's plunge into the sea.

When Sikorski's body was brought back to England, Churchill said, "Soldiers must die, but by their death they nourish the nation which gave them birth."

Mrs. Churchill sent Madame Sikorski an inscribed photograph of Winston and herself.

Sikorski's death did not nourish his nation.

On August 1 of 1944, as Soviet troops advanced on Warsaw, the inhabitants – encouraged by Moscow Radio – rose up against the occupying Germans. The uprising continued for two months but the Soviets stalled and did not relieve the city. They stalled as some 200,000 citizens – mostly young men and women fighting house-to-house and from out of the sewers – were killed by SS troops, and on October 2 General Tadeusz Bor-Komorowski, the Polish commander, was forced to surrender. The Germans obliterated the city – wreaking a final vengeance. At the same time, Churchill arrived in Moscow. On October 14, with Stanislaw Mikolajczyk, the new leader of the Polish government-in-exile at his side, he met with Averell Harriman for the Americans and Molotov and Stalin. Churchill's personal physician and confidant, Lord Moran, noted in his diary that he was suddenly able to grasp "Winston's attitude to the Poles at that time":

> Molotov invited Mikolajczyk to speak first. The Pole did nothing to placate the Russians . . . . The P.M. spoke next. He supported Stalin – 'The Curzon Line dividing Poland must be your eastern frontier.'
>
> Mikolajczyk: 'I cannot accept the Curzon Line. I have no authority to leave half my countrymen to their fate.'
>
> Molotov (abruptly interrupting): 'But all this was settled at Teheran.'

Mikolajczyk looked from Churchill to Harriman. They were silent. Harriman gazed at his feet, but the P.M. looked Mikolajczyk in the face.

'I confirm this,' he said quietly.

Mikolajczyk was shocked.

The revelation of what had happened at Teheran, in the absence of the Poles, only seemed to make the Prime Minister angry, as if he wanted to persuade himself that he was the aggrieved person and not Mikolajczyk. He demanded that Mikolajczyk should agree there and then to the Russian demands. The Pole would not give way.

P.M.: 'You can at least agree that the Curzon Line is the temporary frontier.'

At this, Stalin rose in his place. 'I want no argument. We will not change our frontiers from time to time. That's all.'

Churchill held out his hands, looked up to the ceiling in despair and wheezed . . . . Perhaps the P.M. was thinking of his own indignation when Chamberlain pressed Czecho-Slovakia to surrender a great part of her country in the interests of peace . . . .

Stalin sat down opposite Churchill and ate a pig's head.

With a knife, he cleaned out the head, putting it in his mouth with his knife . . . . (He then ate more of the pig's flesh), ate these with his fingers.

Churchill left Moscow knowing how hollow his assurances to the Poles had been: Poland, for whose freedom the world had gone to war, had not been represented at the Teheran conference or the Yalta conference, and in 1945, Churchill and Roosevelt had spoken on behalf of the Poles at Potsdam.

The Polish government-in-exile in London withered and, after the Germans surrendered unconditionally, the Poles, out of deference to Stalin, were not allowed to take part in formal victory celebrations in Berlin. The Soviet Union occupied the whole of Poland.

Twenty years after the plane crash, Madame Sikorski saw Churchill for the first time at the opening of the General Sikorski Historical Institute. She turned away to avoid meeting him.

The Telegram, 1968-78

ALL FOUND

With one eye
blue, the other brown,

the earth at sea,
the sea ran aground,

then the other way
around as the moon

came down to earth.
His blue eye turned

brown, the brown blue,
and the sea turned, too.

So grace abounds
in what was lost

and now is found
in the round.

Hogg, the Seven Last Words, 2001

FLOWERS FOR
THE FORGOTTEN

Tribes disappear, republics are forgotten. As borders shift, towns lose their names. Even the secret police get confused: "Where did that country go?" A man wearing steel-rimmed glasses and a double-breasted suit laughed. "I will tell you where that country went." His name was Vyacheslav Molotov. "Up in smoke." He didn't laugh very often, but it was 1939 and Joachim von Ribbentrop, a count from Prussia, had just agreed, over schnapps, that Latvia, Lithuania and Estonia were to become part of the Soviet Union. Maps were drawn and von Ribbentrop said to Molotov, "Nice suit," but what he really wanted to do was go to the Kremlin to meet Stalin, and – as it turned out – despite some disagreement with Molotov over, maybe, a fox fur hat – he did. He and Stalin shook hands and laughed and a fine-looking general standing behind them laughed, too. A little later, he disappeared, and then, after the general's son died in battle outside Riga, someone asked, "Where did that family go?"

Such is life: but where did Estonia, Latvia and Lithuania go?

Well, they still look out on the Baltic Sea, but they are sealed in Soviet amber. Through the centuries, their borders have been moved back-and-forth by overlords who spoke Polish, Swedish, German, and Russian, until the end of World War I, when czardom gave up the occupying ghost. That's when the territories became agricultural republics, exporting eggs, butter, grain, fowl, and intelligence. "Our life was written in the stars," one leading politician said, but he'd lost an eye in a hunting accident and he couldn't see that the republics were defenceless. The truth was, no one could really see what was coming, because along came *Kristallnacht* and then the sudden plundering of Poland by the Nazis, and that's when Molotov asked, as he signed a non-aggression pact with von Ribbentrop, "Is enough ever enough?"

"Too much is enough," von Ribbentrop said, and laughed.

Overnight, the people of the Baltic States became Soviet citizens. Many were sent to Soviet prisons. Schoolchildren and bus drivers learned to sing Soviet work songs and were given little hammer-and-sickle pins to wear on their lapels.

Except, it wasn't exactly thus: in June of 1940, the Soviets told the Balts that they needed military bases on the Baltic Sea. The Balts declined to cooperate. When two Russian footsoldiers disappeared (dead drunk), the Soviets said they feared for the safety of their troops and the Red Army rolled across the borders. The Soviet navy set up port in Riga and the Soviet secret police deported trainloads of political prisoners *(zeks)* to labour camps in the east, until 1941, when – after Stalin had ignored more than 80 warnings that the Germans were coming – von Ribbentrop announced that the German army had crossed into the Baltic countryside, naturally killing Soviet soldiers as they went and, of course, deporting prisoners to labour camps in the west, this time in Poland and Bavaria.

Stalin had something like a nervous breakdown and collapsed, finding it incomprehensible that Hitler had double-crossed him.

The German army marched on to Moscow.

However, all did not go well for the Germans. Their army, freezing to death in the winter of 1943, fled from the outskirts of Moscow with the Soviet army on its heels, and in 1944 and 1945 that pursuing army ravaged the already ravaged Baltic lands, and soon Soviet cattle cars were loaded up again with *zeks* who were sent to death camps in the far eastern arctic gulag. As the wind whistled through empty Estonian villages, Stalin, back on his feet, said: "Hitlers come, Hitlers go." His hangers-on laughed. In two or three years most of them disappeared, too. Then the war was over. The Nuremberg trials were held. Germany, to the west, was refurbished by the Marshall Plan. Germany, to the east, was collectivized. The world settled into a Cold War – into the acceptance of lost borders behind the Iron Curtain – lost peoples beyond the Berlin Wall – and one of those men standing behind Stalin was heard to say amiably, "There will be a Lithuania, but there will be no Lithuanians."

1985. There was a plan: a small cruise ship called the *Baltic Star*, with 400 Balts from around the world on board, was going to sail from Stockholm to the marine borders of Soviet Lithuania, Latvia and Estonia. Then, the ship was going to dock in Finland on the day Soviet dignitaries were to arrive to celebrate the tenth anniversary of the signing of the Helsinki Accords, those accords that had condemned the republics to inclusion in the amber of the Soviet Union. That was the plan. And after that, if the Finnish police would let them, the Balts were going to leave the ship and march to a central Helsinki park and denounce the Soviet Union.

"Do you think you can get away with this?" I asked a woman in charge.

"Why not?" she said. "After all, enough is enough."

"I know someone else who said that."

"Yeah?" she said. "Who?"

"Never mind," I said. "He's known for his cocktails."

The Soviets, of course, were not pleased. Their government – through its news agency, TASS – warned that such a cruise would find itself in the middle of naval manoeuvres. It was a threat. Moreover, there was no reason why the Finns – so nervous about their Soviet neighbours – would let the *Baltic Star* dock. As for the protest parade, the flags of the three republics had not been seen in Helsinki for 45 years – not since von Ribbentrop and Molotov had shaken hands over schnapps. The cruise, therefore, was going to be a political luxury – an affront to Soviet power – that only amateurs could afford. I packed for a flight to Copenhagen. I did not know why, since the *Baltic Star* was in Stockholm, the protest was starting in Copenhagen, but then very little made sense about this cruise, except the cause itself – to draw attention to three disappearing peoples.

☜

In Copenhagen, King Hussein of the Hashemites of Jordan – wearing a headwaiter's morning suit and looking a little pale – stood staring out the door of Madame Tussaud's Wax Museum, past a bronze statue of Hans Christian Andersen, to a crowd of Balts gathered in the Town Hall square. Some women wore peasant dresses with woollen leggings and others wore black-and-white striped prison jerseys. They were carrying a huge bulbous black plastic chain toward a speaker's platform where one of the founders of the Russian Freedom Movement, Vladimir Bukovsky, a grizzled dissident who had survived the brutality of twelve years in Soviet jails, rocked on the balls of his feet, waiting to speak. A young woman wearing a *Nyet Nyet Soviet* T-shirt leaned on Andersen's polished bronze knee, waiting to hear him. Her patterned skirt had a double row of ancient signs sewn along the hem: ᴧᴧᴧᴧ, the sign of Mara, Latvian goddess of water and earth, and sign of the fir tree, destiny's tree.

As the Town Hall bells tolled the hour, Bukovsky told the Balts that the ongoing threat to their homelands, to their countrymen, lay in the readiness of all governments in the West, but especially the Americans, to accept the expedient maintenance of the Soviet status quo – especially the Helsinki Accords. "What it means is the possible liquidation of the peoples."

A boy, beating the dead march on a big bass drum, led the Balts in a stroll past Hans Christian Andersen: lean old right-wing businessmen with pouchy eyes; a Lutheran clergyman who had confirmed his commitment to social justice by slitting his wrists during a march in Spain; a small unctuous man who seemed to be in the wrong parade because he carried a sign that said: "Free Ukraine," and 45 men and women (representing the 45 years since Molotov and von Ribbentrop had shaken hands) carrying the bulbous black chain; and behind the boy beating the drum, a silver-haired woman dressed in black – black veil, black sheath dress, long black gloves and black shoes – carrying a small black coffin. She was supposed to be Lady Death, but her dress was too chic, her pumps were an expensive patent leather, a gold charm bracelet dangled from her wrist, and behind her veil, Lady Death was chewing gum, smiling as she walked beside Bukovsky, who had led the hunger strike at Vladimir prison.

A woman wearing a blue cape said, "We are a ship of fools. Maybe you should forgive us before we begin."

"There are holy fools," I said. "The Russians know about holy fools."

Though the United States insists that it has not forgotten the republics, insists that it officially recognizes the republics, and though official legations continue to function in Washington, the U.S. government has never formally protested the 1944/45 Soviet reoccupation of Latvia, Estonia, and Lithuania, and does not intend to. Molotov, after the Soviets had collectivized farms and ruined the economy and murdered dissidents, said mordantly, "Some things never change." Because the Helsinki agreement had ratified the Yalta agreement and Yalta had ratified the "inviolability" of Soviet empire and the Soviet empire had ratified the "Russification" of all captured states and captive peoples, the Latvians, Estonians and the Lithuanians are part of a disappearing act that is underway all over the Soviet empire. The Czech novelist Milan Kundera has said:

If someone had told me as a boy, one day you will see your nation vanish from the world, I would have considered it nonsense, something I couldn't possibly imagine. A man knows he is mortal, but he takes it for granted that his nation possesses a kind of eternal life. But after the Russian invasion of 1968, every Czech was confronted with the thought that his nation could be quietly erased from Europe, just as over the past five decades forty million Ukrainians have been quietly vanishing from the world without the world paying any heed. Or Lithuanians. Do you know that in the seventeenth century Lithuania was a powerful European nation? Today the Russians keep Lithuanians on their reservation like a half-extinct tribe; they are sealed off from visitors to prevent knowledge about their existence from reaching the outside. I don't know what the future holds for my own nation. It is certain that the Russians will do everything they can to dissolve it gradually into their own civilization. Nobody knows whether they will succeed. But the *possibility* is here.

The *Baltic Star*, a small cruise ship, was docked in Stockholm. For three hours, Balts stood outside a wire-mesh fence watching Swedish police dogs sniff their luggage; there had been five bomb threats. A man with soft puffy hands and a sweet smile, one of the organizers, was excited. "KGB," he said. "They're across the road, they're talking Russian." There were three rumpled-looking men sitting on a curb under the statue of St. George slaying a dragon and they were speaking Russian. The organizer had a shoulder video camera and he was recording anyone who looked stern and brooding. He hurried close to a man wearing smoked glasses, who was himself taking photographs of people in the crowd. I began to watch who was watching whom: a stern old man with high Mongolian cheekbones who shied two steps away if anyone came close; a white-haired lady in a white trench coat who stood beside the wire-mesh fence with binoculars, peering at bags that were only ten feet away; and then, a circle gathered around Lady Death, who was wagging her finger at a little man in a baggy brown suit. He was buttoning his camera into its leather case.

"I know him," she cried. "He is embassy. He is KGB, he is taking our pictures."

The baggy man shrugged and someone said, "For sure he's Russian. No one else wears shoes like that." They were thick-soled with wedge toes.

The organizer spun through the crowd, flushed with excitement. "The local KGB director, he's back there. I know him. There was a photograph of him once in a magazine . . . ." Several photographers scrambled toward a middle-aged man seated on a metal suitcase. He glared. They took his picture. A squat man with a slight limp took a picture of them taking pictures. "Bomb," someone said. "We cannot afford to be careless." The woman with binoculars disappeared. The police and their dogs disappeared. We went single-file up the gangplank to our dimly lit rooms. The man with the Mongolian cheekbones said, "I don't know anything about KGB." He explained that he was always tense before he got on board a ship because he couldn't swim.

Sitting in the *Baltic Star*'s stateroom, Imants Lesinskis knew the KGB. Heavily set and in his late 50s, he had a grey moustache tinged yellow, the yellow of his nicotine-stained fingers. He spoke in a damp monotone. Behind tinted glasses, he had unflinching eyes, and he had that capacity, shared by criminals and the police, to convey intimate muted menace. His hand, as he drew a cigarette to his lips, shook . . . an alcoholic's shudder (one of his favourite drinks when he lived in Riga was a vile black bitter, Melnais Balsams – Black Balsam).

Born in Latvia, he had become – around 1968 – chairman of the Latvian Committee for Cultural Relations with Countrymen Abroad, a cover name for KGB agents who were in control of contact with Latvian exiles, largely those in the United States and Canada, exiles like those who were now on the *Baltic Star*.

In the 70s, however, Lesinskis had called his close friends in Riga together and he had said that he wouldn't see them again for 15 years, and then he had gone to Moscow; after studying diplomacy, he had appeared at the United Nations in 1976 and 1977. There, he had kept a low profile until one day in 1978 he had disappeared; he had defected. At least, that's what he said, and that's what the Soviets said. Since then, Lesinskis has passed like a shadow through the lives of Latvians in the diaspora.

"My targets when I was KGB," he said, "were businessmen, international businessmen with contacts, clergymen if they were influential, and writers . . . I had a list . . . there are always lists . . . at my disposal in Latvia."

"Did you do any work in Canada?" I asked, as he laid his umbrella on the table between us as a barrier and gripped the right arm of his chair so that his space was completely self-defined.

"I was there in 1967, met people, agents."

"I've always wondered," I said, "whether the KGB actually tries to keep ethnic groups in Canada alive as communities, like feeding ponds full of information about dissenters in the Soviet Union?"

"Yes, of course, but it is also the KGB's intentions to destroy these communities. It is contradictory. Soviet policy in general is full of contradictions."

"So this was natural for you to exploit?"

"Yes, family ties, private visitors."

"Have you actually secured information from such people?"

"My function was to . . . discover weaknesses." The overhead bare light bulb in the dimly lit room had created two white stars on his tinted glasses. When he lifted his head the stars fell. "Starting in 1967, every college graduate of Latvian origin graduating in the West was kept on file. Files and files. People were approached, involved in cultural exchanges. Spying, I would say, is the most boring business in the world." He laughed, a wet, clattering sound, but there was only unflinching cold appraisal in his eyes.

"Sometimes you work and work," he said, "producing disinformation." He smiled wryly, as he gave me information about disinformation. "For years you send articles, doctored photocopies of files, and then suddenly there's an explosion. Your disinformation is in the headlines. We produced such materials about apparent Latvian war criminals . . . some half-truths sent in English translation to the U.S. and Canada and Israel. Nobody was interested. I thought it was dead." He paused, as if reflecting, but he didn't look up or away or to the side; he kept absolutely still, unmoving except for the hand that held his cigarette, the hand that shook a little.

"Then around 1977," he said, "a certain Howard Blum published a book with one of the big publishing houses and there was all our material. Congress created a special unit of investigation. You see, Jewish people are not different from others. They believe what they want to believe."

"But there were collaborators with the Nazis."

"I do not want to say there are not Latvian war criminals. There are, but they are not so many. Most of the criminals have died. But the Russians are not interested in establishing the truth. If a Latvian is active in the West," he said, taking a drag on his cigarette, "if he is active in a way that displeases the KGB, he is easy to slander."

Everything about Lesinskis was contradictory: he was a solid presence, yet I felt only the absence of who he was; he was full of menace and yet he seemed alone and even vulnerable; he talked freely about sinister situations – seeming to implicate himself – and yet he never was specific – seeming to extricate himself; he was plodding in tone and yet was agile and never careless with words; he reeked of guilt and yet, as a defector, offered himself as a cleansed soul.

Such a man has to be wary.

I asked him if the Soviets intended to liquidate the Latvian people. He suddenly went silent and pale. I asked the question again but he did not answer. He sat absolutely still, his eyes fixed on a face in the crowd. He was asked the question a third time. "Yes," he said in a hushed voice, and stood up and said, "My life is in danger, I must leave." He hurried from the ship's stateroom. No one followed him. "How strange," a woman said, "for him to just disappear like that." [1]

Each afternoon at sea, there was a service on the upper deck as the ship skirted the 12-mile marine borders of the republics. On the second day, after the passengers had gotten their sea legs by singing and drinking into the night, the Latvians gathered on deck on a damp afternoon. The wind was brisk from the east. They all stared, with the wind in their faces, at the homeland – but there was nothing to be seen, only the grey sheen of seawater on a dank day. Still, they knew Latvia was out there, they'd been seeing it in their mind's eye for years. So, three girls in embroidered dresses sang a mournful song in a minor key and trochaic measure, a recitative of longing and privation, accompanied by a

---

[1] In 1960, while ostensibly covering the Olympic Games in Rome for the Soviet newsletter, *Homeland Voice*, Imants Lesinkis had actually been working as a KGB agent, making contact with Australian athletes of Latvian descent. During the games, he requested political asylum at the U.S. Embassy in Rome. Their agents convinced him that he could do more harm to the Soviets by spying for the CIA. He apparently worked as a double agent until September of 1978 when, as a Soviet translator stationed in New York, he defected. He, his wife and daughter became, officially, West German immigrants: Peter and Linda Dorn, and Evelyn. Once he reappeared and began to circulate in the Baltic communities, some suspected he was acting as a "triple" agent – still working for the Soviets. He died shortly after taking the voyage on the *Baltic Star*, suddenly and mysteriously in a Virginia shopping mall. Rumour has it that it was not a heart attack but an assassination, but the cause of death is still unclear. He was buried as the fictitious German, with only his direct family and two or three emigré Latvians present.

girl playing an ancient *kokle*, a zither-like instrument that rested on her knees. As the crowd sang, there was no wailing but only wistfulness and tears, and a glimpse of a phantom grey streak of land. Some stood waiting for a shock of recognition. It did not come. Then the woman who always wore a blue cape, wearing it this day over a costume that had a fringe of tinkling brass squares, read from an epistle:

"We are running water . . . . Water is strong. It can create floods. With time, water wears down the hardest stone. Our water wheel is driven by drops drawn from all over the world, and this afternoon we are a single current, different as raindrops, dew, melting ice . . . trying to create storm clouds so everyone shall hear thunder speaking of Latvia."

Many were weeping.

Led by the clergyman who had slit his wrists in Spain, they went to the railings to cast flowers into the sea, flowers for the dead and imprisoned, flowers that lay in the ship's wake like red stars and then the flowers disappeared, the prayerful hoping they would wash up and be understood by someone on the shore picking a flower from the sea, a star . . . .

It is easy to disappear into the night in a Soviet republic: you can disappear *for* singing the national anthems, *for* having forbidden books, *for* showing the national flag, *for* teaching religion to children, *for* doing any statistical survey, *for* talking to Westerners, *for* putting flowers at the feet of the monument of Mother Latvia who holds three stars in her hand . . . .

Over the decades, the Latvians have been decimated by war and deportation, and now – with one of the lowest birth rates in the world – they are dwindling. Depression, despair and drunkenness have drained the people. Their young men are now dying in the Soviet army in Afghanistan, and when they come home in sealed coffins they are buried far apart from anyone else in the boneyards; it is against the law to mark their graves, against the law for anyone other than the family to gather at their graves.

"This is the triumph of reason," Stalin had said of their agreements and Roosevelt had beamed.

And so, the clergyman, a lean man whose casual air belied an inner tautness, spoke to me about the diaspora of these people.

"The one thing we Latvians do exclusively in Latvian," he said, "is worship and I'm convinced that the language a person uses in talking with God retains an importance that no other language has."

"But if you're worshipping in a language that you don't use with those you love," I said, "the language you use between the sheets – isn't it possible that your young people, cultivating the language of the lost homeland, will lose touch with themselves, lose touch even with their God?"

"There is that," he said.

"And isn't there a real possibility that the homeland, the republics, will end up as a state of mind?"

"Sure. We are already disappearing into a state of mind."

"Is this trip a last gasp?"

"Well, here's where theology plays a large role, the Old Testament theology of the remnant. There is a remnant, and who knows how long it will take, but they are the ones who eventually will go back home."

"But you remain, you live in the diaspora."

"Yes, and if they ever return home, they will return to something that has never been before."

"To never-never land."

"That's not quite the way I'd put it."

It was dusk, the sea wind blew cold across the blackish water, the coast a grey smudge on the water line. "That's Estonia," the captain said, a man with a florid face, always smiling, but with hard, shrewd eyes. We were on the bridge watching the radar screen, the line sweeping over blips that flared a luminous green for a moment. "This is serious," the captain said and laughed, as he always did when there was a problem. We were just outside the 12-mile Soviet limit, off the island of Hiiumaa, entering waters in which thousands of Balts had drowned during the War, fleeing to Sweden in small boats in winter storms. "It is a Soviet gunboat," the first mate said. "See, there it is," and he pointed to a ship some three kilometres away, a wedge on the water line leaving a white wake as it sped parallel to our course and then curved sharply toward us.

"This is serious."

"What are the other ships?" I asked, looking at four or five blips on the screen.

"One is a fishing trawler, just ahead," the first mate said. He handed me his field glasses. "See, dead-ahead."

There was a red and white squat trawler moving across our course on the starboard side.

"It is Russian, too," the captain said.

"They are speaking about us in Russian," the first mate said and turned up the radio. "They are checking our position. They are setting a collision course."

The gunboat was cutting the water at high speed. Behind it, a gathering grey haze, streaks of rose in the grey. A tender colour. The trawler, now lying in the *Baltic Star*'s path, had come to a drifting halt, its engines turned off.

"Is this really serious?" someone asked.

"Who knows?" the captain said.

"Serious for sure," the first mate said. The gunboat was only two or three minutes away. The captain changed course, away from the maritime border, to avoid the trawler. It was not flying a flag; there was no one on its bridge.

The gunboat changed course and swerved toward the channel between Hiiumaa Island and the shore. In a few minutes it was gone, a shadow leaving a white crease in the water, and then the unmarked trawler was left behind, seemingly dead in the water.

"That was close."

"Close to what?" I asked.

"A gunboat is no laughing matter."

"A little laughter doesn't hurt," I said.

It was Sunday, a few hours before dawn when the captain received radio confirmation that the Finns would allow the *Baltic Star* to dock in Helsinki, across the port from the main piers and terminals, in Hietalahti, a canal cul-de-sac used for repairing and refitting tankers. He docked and, as the mist lifted, a police inspector came aboard. He took off his cap. He put on his cap. He held his cap, silver-haired with a softness of tone, full of assurances for the captain (who'd put on his cap), and he said that even though there was "an order in law" that allowed the police to call a halt to any disorderly activity, the protesters could not only conduct an orderly parade to a central park, but the order had been given that they could use hand-held loudspeakers. "You have been docked on this side of the harbour for your safety," he added.

Singing *Finlandia*, the Balts unfurled their three flags, flags that had not been seen by Finns since the War, and then the 45 "prisoners" carrying the big bulbous black chain lined up behind Vladimir Bukovsky and the requiem drummer boy. Lady Death, in a red and white peasant dress (colours of the Resurrection), still carried the small coffin, but her purse and her bangles were in the coffin. "When we started the human rights movement in the Soviet Union," Bukovsky said in a wry, placid tone, "everybody – including our parents – told us it was impossible and crazy. Now it exists. Unless you question the impossible you don't achieve anything. I had a Polish friend," he said, laughing, "who asked me how many dissidents there were in the Soviet Union in 1977 and I said there were enough for the moment, and he said: 'Well, unfortunately, in Poland there are so few because the Poles are such conformists, they're so afraid of everything, living their small lives, not wanting to question anything.' But within three years from that conversation, ten million Poles united in Solidarity."

Bukovsky led the protesters through the dockyard steel gates, the protesters carrying crude placards – the names and faces of men in Soviet prisons on the placards – and banners proclaiming the free republics. The requiem bass drum boomed and echoed in the empty road along the canal as two policemen led the marchers past waterfront warehouses that had been blistered by polar cap winds. Stragglers began to sing as they were led into a broad street of dour four-and-five-storey apartment houses. They began to chant *"Nyet Nyet Soviet,"* clapping hands like schoolchildren. At a café on the corner, a beefy man wearing a broad white apron watched in silence, impassive, and then he began to applaud, alone on the sidewalk, and someone else came out of the café and began to applaud, too. "Freedom – Now. *Nyet Nyet Soviet, Nyet Nyet Soviet.*" Cowled women were leaning on windowsills and coming out of the houses, women who'd survived through the years by keeping a closed mouth, grim women in black shawls and black dresses. *"Da da Latvia."* There were old men in some of the open ground-floor windows, standing between shutters, holding their heads between their hands, as if in pain at this apparition, and a crook-backed man who had white moustaches said, *"Kauan Eläköön Vapaa Suomi"* and then, "Thank you, thank you for coming." The town's chief inspector of police, wearing a double-breasted suit, pushed through the crowd to stand beside Bukovsky and the bass drum.

Soon, there were a thousand Finns in Vanhan Kirkon Parks, standing at the memorial to the volunteer Finnish war dead who had fought for free Estonia during World War II. The boy beat the drum, *boom boom boom,* a high-cheekboned old man stepped forward, wearing a worn soldier's uniform, a long black coat, and ribbons three rows deep. He could have been from any war, any army. Maybe he was. As a church bell tolled the 11 o'clock hour, a wreath was laid for the Estonians. Bukovsky, flowers strewn at his feet, said, "My friends, real peace cannot be bought at the price of freedom . . . peace and human rights are indivisible. At this time, when the leaders of countries are coming together to celebrate the Helsinki Accords, we have to speak on behalf of those who have no right to speak in their own country. We ask those leaders to tell the Soviet leaders to recognize their obligations, or to abrogate the treaty, which has become an empty word. Peace in Europe is impossible until the nations of Latvia, Lithuania and Estonia are no longer oppressed. A shameful deal with Hitler must be repealed. To those thousands and thousands who are in the Soviet prisons," and he intoned a litany of names, names that were on the placards, "we say we are with you. I believe our mission is not in vain. We've done what we had to do, and I'm sure that it wouldn't be forgotten."

More wreaths of flowers were piled and stacked against each other at the foot of the monument. Then there was silence. The Finns sang their national anthem and the Estonians sang theirs, too. The grand moment had slumped to a halt. It was over. Shuffling, uncertain, and then breaking apart, the protesters seemed to leak away, to disappear. The sky suddenly seemed very low and grey. Placards and flags were put down beside a taxi stand, presumably for pick-up. "There's nothing more to be done," a Latvian man who was a lab technician from Boston told a young woman. She said, "This will be the biggest moment of my life."

"What'll you do with it?" I asked.

"Tell my children," she said, "we were here."

Lady Death wanted to know, "Where," lifting her veil, still chewing gum, "where did everyone go?"

"I wonder where Bukovsky's gone," I asked.

The park was empty. A segment of the black bulbous chain had broken off. It was lying on the grass. Stooped and shawled women disappeared into their dark doorways, broken bouquets lay by the cobbled curb. "It was enough," the woman wearing the blue cape said.

"We were lucky the whole way," the technician said to her. "I don't know why the police were so good to us."

"You never know why the police do what they do," she said, looking radiantly happy.

"We feel terrific, right?" he said, seeming reluctant to leave, reluctant to go back to the ship, as he turned a single torn red flower in his hand. "But what does this do to change the lives of the people in the homelands? Nothing!"

"It's not true," an old man with pouches under his eyes said, joining him. "They know what we did."

"What did we do?"

"What we wanted to do. It's not so easy."

"So what do we do next?" the technician asked.

"I don't know." The old man wiped his glasses.

The technician handed me his torn flower. "It's all yours," he said. He headed back to the *Baltic Star,*[1] heading home to his diaspora.

"Don't feel bad, even the police get confused" the old man called after him.

Toronto Life, 1985

---

[1] In 1989, Berliners took down their wall. The Soviet Union soon collapsed from within. The forgotten republics were found, still facing the Baltic Sea. They declared their borders and their independence in 1991. Some exiles came back from the diaspora to their homelands. One or two slit their wrists. Others prospered. Such is life.

I LOVE A FLOATING APPLE

I love a floating apple in the night.
Treeless, twigless,
I love the floating apple tree in the night,
rootless, weighing down branches in the night.

And the whole earth, afloat in the night
neither borne nor braced by anyone
I love darkness – that doesn't disappear
as I wake again

But keeps a distance, unseen
and then, as the sun sets, draws near.
I see someone approaching:
emerging from the dark, merging into the dark again.

Translated from the Latvian
of Imants Ziedonis, 1987

SLAUGHTERHOUSE-FIVE: VONNEGUT

The frost makes a flower,
The dew makes a star,
The dead bell,
The dead bell.
Somebody's done for.
                                        —Sylvia Plath

If you had taken refuge and shelter underground on the night
Dresden was firestormed and if you had heard overhead the
foot-stomp of giants all night through the storm, would you have
wept in the morning when you came up for air, and found that
there was nothing there but charred flesh and cinders, skulls
tanned to the colour of old ivory and knuckle bones sheathed
in melted glass, would you have wept as you crawled over rise
after rise on the new face of the moon realizing suddenly that
there, in fact, were supposed to be no men on the moon, none,
but there you were, a man, an actual man, and you were some-
how alive amidst some 60,000 who were dead, cooked, and there
was no water on the moon, only ash, and craters full of ash?

Kurt Vonnegut has taken twenty years to write this book, to
find the tone for this dance of the Dresden bones.

He knew that there had been, in history, many wheels of fire
within wheels of fire, and that even the Lord Himself, through his
angels, had rained obliterating fire and brimstone down on

Sodom and Gomorrah, and thinking back to that particular moonscape by the Dead Sea Vonnegut wrote: "Lot's wife, of course, was told not to look back where all those people and their homes had been. But she did look back, and I love her for that because it was so human. So she was turned to a pillar of salt. So it goes."[1]

Salt.

Vonnegut says his book was written by a pillar of salt, Billy Pilgrim, an optometrist – what else? – from Illium, New York, who survived Dresden but came unstuck in his head on the morning after the firestorm while sitting perched on the back of a coffin cart as it rolled out of the ruined city. And for two decades Pilgrim has crawled across the moonscape of his mind – listening to a little light opera on the edge of the abyss – trying to persuade himself, though he was once a member of a firing squad, that he had done no harm, complicit, yes, but he had done no real harm and he has even tried to step out of himself by stepping out of time – transplanting himself back to the workshops of Nazareth where he found out that the gods, too, are stained, that they too are complicit, even in their own deaths: "Jesus was learning the carpentry trade from his father. Two Roman soldiers came into the shop with a mechanical drawing on papyrus of a device they wanted built by sunrise the next morning. It was a cross to be used in the execution of a rabble-rouser. Jesus and his father built it. They were glad to have the work. And the rabble-rouser was executed on it. So it goes."

Salt.

Billy – he's so American: he's an optometrist of guileless goodwill who knows only what he sees and he sees only what's in front of his nose, and for him, what's in front of his nose is the whole world – so he does the only thing he can think to do: he turns the memory of his moment in history into a movie

---

[1] In *Doctor Zhivago*, Pasternak says that Lot's wife, as she turned to look back at the firestorm, was made into salt as punishment for (the sin?) of compassion.

and he throws the action into reverse, playing history backwards: American planes, full of holes and wounded men and corpses, take off from an airfield in England. Over France, a few German fighter planes fly at them backwards, suck bullets and shell fragments from some of the planes and crewmen. They do the same for wrecked American bombers on the ground, and those planes fly up backwards to join the formation.

> The formation flew backwards over a German city that was in flames. The bombers opened their bomb-bay doors, exerted a miraculous magnetism which shrunk the fires, gathered them into cylindrical steel containers, and lifted the containers into the bellies of the planes. The containers were stored neatly in racks. The Germans below had miraculous devices of their own, which were long steel tubes. They used them to suck more fragments from the crewmen and planes. But there were still a few wounded Americans, though, and some of the bombers were in bad repair. Over France, though, German fighters came up again, made everything and everybody as good as new.

When the bombers get back to their base, the steel cylinders are taken from the racks and shipped back to the United States of America, where factories are operating night and day, dismantling the cylinders, separating the dangerous contents into minerals. Touchingly, it is mainly women who do this work. The minerals are then shipped to specialists in remote areas. It is their business to put them into the ground, to hide them cleverly, so that they will never hurt anybody ever again.

It's a childish dream: "Daddy, make it all go away." As childish and as old as a *Saturday Evening Post* dream of a naked sunlit boy making pee-pee into a river in a land of no hurt, no sin.

But Billy, the veteran of foreign wars, has become so heavy in his heart with what he knows about war and he is so sorrowfully out of whack with his time, that even fantasy doesn't help.

He's been bent. All is aslant. He has long since been the enemy of his own best intentions:

"Billy didn't want to marry ugly Valencia. She was one of the symptoms of his disease (listlessness). He knew he was going crazy when he heard himself proposing marriage to her, when he begged her to take the diamond ring and be his wife for life."

The diamond was loot from the rubble of Dresden.

On his wedding night, his wife of course said she wanted to know all about the war. He wasn't talking. No. Mum was the word. On his wedding night he kept her busy "in a tiny cavity in her great body (where) she was assembling the materials for a Green Beret."

Mum!

Mother earth, Mother death!

A Green Beret!

Vietnam! History on its forward reel. More pilgrim soldiers. More salt.

Billy can't win; he is in lock-step with other broken men, other mind-bent cripples, he is a pilgrim – at home among the homeless of the heart: "On the eighth day, the forty-year-old hobo said to Billy, 'This ain't bad. I can be comfortable any-where' . . . . On the ninth day, the hobo died. So it goes. His last words were, 'You think this is bad? This ain't bad.'"

There's been worse. *This* is so. There's always been worse, there will be worse.

So how do we hear this tale of worse?

And worse?

It's all in an oboe tone.

The Vonnegut effect is one of tone.

Tone is Vonnegut's tactic.

The tone – "a sympathy of woe" – is one of consolation, one of remorse modulated by whimsicality. Sometimes the whim-sicality is laid on with a trowel: as if Job were being played by W.C. Fields, a wry charm amidst the knuckle bones and ashes, a forlorn smirk at the lip of the oven. Vonnegut throws this consoling voice back to frail children, he throws it ahead to huddled grunts in the rice paddies, all of them engaged in the greening of death. It's a tone as old as the Anglo-Saxon:

> *Many have heard of the rape of Hild,*
> *Of her father's affection   and infinite love,*
> *Whose nights were sleepless with sorrow and grief.*
> *That evil ended. So also may this.*

And older.

Amidst all this sorrow and grief, this salt in the air, it is hard to be a man. It is, in fact, harder to be a man than to be a god. If you are a god you drink blood: there's lots of it around. If you are a man, you thirst for your own humanity, for the compassion that makes you human – especially when you wake up one morning and you wander out of your underground shelter onto streets that are shadows of themselves, you wander amidst cinders and globules of glass, on the moonscape of your own mind. There is no traffic, nothing, only blue skies – and you want to go to heaven singing *Blue skies, nothing but blue skies* as you sit on the back of an abandoned wagon that is drawn by two horses. The wagon is green and it is coffin-shaped.

Birds are talking.

One bird says, "*Poo-tee-weet?*"

1969-1981

PENCILS AND PENS: III — 1878

A gentrified sitting room,
Pompadour easy chairs,
And, on pedestals, here and there,
A bronze in the half-gloom.

A basket of white Sweet William
Falls by the music stand to the floor.
An Érard* open from the night before.
A guitar, a violin.

A window. Red drapery.
And on the horsehair settee,
A child asleep. Serenity.
Morning, it's ten, it's early.

*Érard, Sebastien: a French manufacturer of musical instruments, born in Strasbourg – 1752-1831

Translated from the Québécois French
of Eudore Évanturel

Eudore Évanturel was born in 1852 and he studied at the Petit Séminaire in Québec. When his first book of poems was published in 1878, it caused a scandal among established critics and he was attacked by the ultramontane novelist, Jules-Paul Tardinel. The edition was reissued in a modified form, to the chagrin of the poet. He *exiled himself to Boston in 1879, where – as an archivist – he became Francis Parkman's secretary. In his poems – that fall in tone and style somewhere between Musset and Verlaine – he touched on a note that has prevailed through the poetry of Quebec: a silence and stillness in the closed room of the heart. He died in Boston in 1919, his work almost totally neglected, and it still is.*

1984

WOMAN IN AN
IRON GLOVE

The time is Québec, just before the Quiet Revolution, a time of monstrous husbands, monstrous priests, capricious nuns, and God, His eye on the convent school wall, is a spy, a bald-faced Snoop. Young schoolgirls, escaping these nuns, after a winter semester, went back to their small towns and villages with dreams diminished, hoping only for marriage to a pale recalcitrant shop owner or *petit avocat* – a man who would not break their backs in bed or over the washboard.

Rage, rage at dying into such a life!

Whether it is Anne Hébert or Marie-Claire Blais or Claire Martin, the same cowed little girl emerges out of the shadows of the Québec family – innocent and intelligent, set upon by over-scrupulous, vicious parents and priests reeking of repressed sex ... a little girl set upon by phantoms who live in her mind, phantoms who haunt her to death. Anne Hébert's novel, *Le Torrent*, opens with an epigraph for all these tales: "I was a child dispossessed of this world."

As the Québécois philosopher Jean Le Moyne has put it: "Three centuries full of triumph for the family, full of the sacramental blessings of marriage. Three centuries spent in faith and piety, sheltered from revolutions, skepticism, perversions, sheltered from everything, to end in this unhealthy havoc! ... the over-scrupulous race we have become, an intimidated race, haunted by the flesh as if we had never known it ...."

The French-Canadian mother, Le Moyne says, the Madonna of folklore, that fat Mama on her *lino* (linoleum) surrounded by clinging children, has played an insidious role. Fecund. Sexless. Wrecked by childbearing. Virginal. It is, he says, this woman of contradictions, this object of "admiration, distant love, fear, subjection and scorn," who has humiliated the men of the province until they have become brutes – men who, in their own pallid belittling dreams, have turned to two ineffectual icons of the Faith for solace – Joseph (a cuckold to the Mother of God) and John, the Baptist (who lost his head to a seductress). Le Moyne says this monstrous Mama with her daughters in tow – though they have taken up the liberating pen – share her unhealthy strength, her vehemence, her fear of love and her pitiless triumph.

What is one to say?

The novelist, Claire Martin, as if to answer this question, has written her memoirs, *Dans une gant de fer* and *La joue droite.* They have been translated into English in one volume, *In an Iron Glove.* There are many monsters in her story – sisters, spinsters, stepmothers, mother superiors, and mothers – but most monstrous of all is Claire Martin's father. She loathes him, she cannot call his name. He is known only as *him.*

Him was prosperous. He had land and a large house far out in the suburbs of Québec City. A civil engineer, he was six feet tall and weighed 230 pounds. He beat his wife and children, stomping on their ankles, splitting their lips. "It began with open-handed blows which immediately became very heavy, then, getting into the swing of it, blows with the closed fist, and if he got really swinging he would finish off with kicks .... Year in, year out, he never put aside his anger. Never. It was the only thing he really liked, anger. He enjoyed our cringing silence. He wanted us chronically terrified."

When he found two of his daughters together under the bed-covers he exploded: "What's all this about? Why do you want to sleep in the same bed? Haven't you got any decent instincts?"

He told his daughters that their mother was too evil for salvation and broke her nose, blackened her face, watched her die, took another wife, and lashed out at his girls with renewed vigour. He worked one daughter so hard that her hands were "cracked, bleeding, swollen, and of a rich lobster-red – it seemed as if some forerunners of the Nazis had been at work there with pincers and cigarette butts." His contempt for the flesh of women, especially his women, was common to the back country Jansenist parishes: – women were predisposed by the Stain of Sin to become slatterns and sluts, and any woman who had been "had" – even in the holy marriage bed – was not only diminished, she was abhorrent. Temptation itself was believed to be a sin and such "slatterns" were a source of temptation, a source of evil, and so all men, especially uxorious men – while seeking paradise – were the helpless victims of their women.[1] It was easy, therefore, for a man "when bile entered the pious heart" to justify his brutality – to justify a blood-letting – the beating was done in the name of his faith. He battled to save himself, as an exemplary man, from perdition – to save himself not just by setting his women apart, not just by healing himself in the splash of their blood,[2] but by "forgetting everything except the paradise of himself," by getting rid of his mother by becoming his mother.

---

[1] Connor Cruise O'Brien, in his *Maria Cross,* interpreting Leon Bloy, has described the horror of sex that is at the heart of Jansenism this way: "Man remains nailed to his mother. When he seeks to break loose, to find 'paradise' in loving another woman, he becomes aware of his crucifixion. Crucifixion, in which the cross (the woman) suffers equally with the sacrifice (the man), is punished for being the cross, is the only form of love. This balance of pain and punishment subsists until death. It can...reach the point of ecstasy where man the crucified identifies himself with his female Cross. Death then is the triumphant and paradisiac hour when the dying hero gives birth to himself."

[2] Through the 13th and 14th centuries, the sacrifice of life, the blood-letting brutality of knights on the battlefields of France and Italy, gave rise to a belief that the "sublime" sacrifice – the laceration of the body of Christ – demanded even more sacrifice, more bleeding flesh, and so, it was said, to

The Eye, the all-seeing eye of God on the walls of the convent schools, was always on the lookout, peering into the lives of girls and women. And so sin loomed large in the imaginations of the little nuns who had been "born into a society where women either married or simply didn't exist . . ." nuns who were encouraged by sin-snooping parish priests to hound, torment, and snitch on their little girls, nuns who were bogged down in the dreariest classroom stupidity, who ruled their sinful world by punching and slapping. In their wimple-encased minds even the discussion of childbirth was forbidden, for birth implied a direct canal to hell. The carnal blood canal. Disobedient girls were ordered to undress, to strip down and then, in order to draw the cleansing blood, the sister armed "with a stiff brush, scrubbed their faces with laundry soap" till their faces were raw, till they peeled and oozed blood. "I knew all about blows delivered in anger. But I had not yet heard of such meticulous and patient tortures."

In this unrelentingly dour world, kindness did not exist. There was little or nothing to choose between the wintertime cloisters and the family home at summer, for when the Martin children – Claire and her sisters – returned to the family house for the summer they found that their father was unchanged; so miserly, ruthless, awash in self-pity, full of nutty ideas, and so completely self-absorbed that he still believed his children loved him unreservedly.

---

affirm and to ritualize this sacrifice, Christ the Healer had returned repeat-edly to this world in the shape of the lone exemplary man, a knight:

Who is he, this lord who comes from the fight,
with blood – red garments so terribly ordered?
It is I...the champion come to heal mankind
through battle...

Catherine of Sienna said of such a knight: "...the crown of thorns is his hel-met. His scourged flesh was his breastplate. His nailed hands were his gloves of mail. The lance at his side was the sword that cut off our death. His fas-tened-down feet were his spurs. Look how wonderfully this knight of ours is armed." *Letters of Saint Catherine of Sienna*, Medieval and Renaissance Texts and Studies, Vols. I and II (1998, 2001).

Claire Martin hated him.

He married many times. His madonnas, his Mamas, cooked for him and tried to coddle him; and one of them, standing on her *lino*, became a "kind of Buddha with cascading chins. The lovely brown eyes were mighty small, and no trace of thought enlivened them. The mouth was shapeless and looked more like a bad scar – and a scar that opens from time to time is abominable. Behind this, two cheap dentures clattered loosely and noisily. The body was like a cone standing on its point: the shoulders were massive, the breasts enormous, the waist bigger than the hips. The remainder dwindled down: thin hips, skinny legs. This precarious structure rested on a pair of uncommonly deformed feet. But the worst thing, I come back to it, was the chins. They were enhanced by long vertical wrinkles, and they trembled ceaselessly."

Scorned, isolated, treated by her husband as an obese slut, "This Mama knew, however, how to play Stepmother. She had been a nurse – not certified, she didn't have the cerebral equipment for diplomas – the doctor thought he could trust her with changing the bandages (of my sister's burned body) once a day. Instead of unbandaging and immediately rebandaging each burn in turn, she uncovered everything, the face, the two arms, the two legs. Then she would stand at the foot of the bed studying the wounds in a learned manner, taking her time, clucking her interest, while (my sister, lying) there between the open door and the open window, writhed in pain from the effect of the air on the raw flesh."

When the stepmother finally died after nine years, there was no weeping.

" 'I didn't make a very good choice,' my father said after several weeks of widowhood. 'She wasn't any too intelligent.'"

"For my father to say that – a man who didn't like intellectuals – anyway, he married again six months later."

Claire Martin, her priests, her nuns, those wives and that man, that *him* – all recoiling from tenderness – as if a kiss could cause only a wound encircled by lice – they lived with an awful view of sex and sin, a view seeded into the teachings of Jesus, seeded a very long time ago, seeded by the likes of Saint Anselm who said "the flesh is a dunghill." That dunghill, its heat, that heat between the thighs of the Madonna on her *lino,* may or may not be inherently wicked, but if it is wicked – it is wickedness – despite the obsessions of Jansenists – of a low order. As Claire Martin says, "real wickedness is quite an amazing thing. There are several varieties: intelligent wickedness, and stupid wickedness. Intelligent wickedness strikes me as being a rare thing, I have seldom encountered it, but (stupid wickedness) . . . . There it is, just like that, and one can't tell where it comes from, what its parentage is or how it comes to be there in one's path. It's just there, like some huge immobile and inexplicable monster."

Claire Martin has become, herself, a kind of storybook child monster. Intelligent, she is surrounded by stupidity. Her suffering is everything. Everyone else is seen through her pain; she is her pain; her pain allows her to feel superior. She emerges as an intelligent teller of truths, but for all that, she is unlikable; haughty, contemptuous, a woman of literary style and insight, yet snappish and provincial, easily wounded, capable of enduring monstrous suffering, capable perhaps of forgiveness, but incapable of forgetting *him,* or of letting the world forget *him.* She intends, with a vengeance, that we *never* forget *him.* That is her wickedness.

The Telegram, 1969-1979

A STOLEN KISS

A thief and his sister
lived in a hut.
She was very beautiful.
Crouching, she kept the fire.
At night, she went to the side of a road
and lay down. Men circled
her still body and then stole a kiss.
Her brother beat them to death
and stole their gold.
But one night a man gave her water from his flask.
The brother beat him but he did not die.
They carried him to the fire
and beat him until his cries fanned the flame.
He grew yellow, his eyes shining.
She lay near him, naked.
He said, "You are a dark flower."
She cradled his face, stole a kiss,
and crept away to kill her sleeping brother.
She came back carrying satchels of gold.
"Don't be afraid," she said.
"We are free."
He fell into the flames,
his arms on fire.

Hogg, the Seven Last Words, 2001

ARCHBISHOP CHARBONNEAU

In the dreary Québec mining town of Asbestos on the south shore of the St. Lawrence River, forty-five miles east of Montréal, there was a strike in 1949 against Canadian Johns-Manville. Five thousand workers walked out on the American-owned asbestos company, asking for a 15 percent raise of one dollar per day and protection against silicosis, the suffocating disease that came from lungs clotting up with asbestos dust. The mine itself was an enormous oval, an open gouge in the earth with huge lumbering rotators and slag trucks relentlessly moving from terrace to terrace, eating away at the side walls, a wound abscessing at its own edges, an incursion that undercut the streets and the houses of the town – so that the houses had to be demolished street by street, with company trucks hauling away the rubble of corner stores and homes and coffee shops and broken pavements as new sewers were put down and new houses were added to new streets on the outskirts, using old street names so that a sense of roots would not be entirely lost.

The vice-president of Canadian Johns-Manville, wearing a blue serge double-breasted suit and a regimental tie, said, "It is a strike against law, order and the entire social structure." The strikers had no social standing, no support in the law, no supporting press, no supporting worker priests, no strike fund, no worker rallies across the province. Many priests – who had visions of the Communist anti-Christ dancing in the bottom of their gardens – were only too willing to denounce the strikers from the pulpit and eager to condemn the strikers in the dark of the confessional. As well, their cardinals – scrupulous, narrow-minded, and ambitious for the Church – were up to their gaiters in debt to Premier Maurice Duplessis, dependent on him for government handouts, educational support, and tax favours. Duplessis, insolent and abrasive, boasted that the bishops ate out of his hand.

As for the provincial police, they were deep in Duplessis' pockets, too. They were his coddled henchmen and grifters, receiving $50 per day per man as bonus pay during the strike. Much of the working press was also on the take (the publisher of Montréal's *The Star* received, before every election, a cardboard box containing $100,000 for dispersal among "the deserving").

No one thought of the Asbestos strikers as deserving.

In Asbestos, as the workless days became workless weeks, the workers emptied out their pantries and emptied out their fuel bins, long before the oncoming hard winter. Tempers got raw. There were axe-handle fights in the streets and pistol-whippings in the alleys. There were family brawls, brother slanging brother. Creeping hunger, seeping despair. The company hired goon squads and brought in busloads of scab workers. But as the weeks became months (the strike lasted 141 days) – the strikers' refusal to knuckle-under to cop-law and bullying, drew several young, emerging political opponents of Duplessis to Asbestos.

It was not long before the strikers had a defence lawyer at their disposal, a callow Jean Drapeau (who would become Mayor of Montréal), and as an organizer, the amiably bluff but hard-nosed Jean Marchand (who would become a federal cabinet minister and senator), a flamboyant, moustached advocate for unionism, Michel Chartrand (who would become a Nationalist, a *séparatiste*), and reporting on the strike for *Le Devoir*, Gérard Pelletier (Duplessis, unhappy with his reports, arranged for an increase in the cost of newsprint to the paper), who would become Pierre Trudeau's confidant in his federal cabinet. And then there was Trudeau himself who, with other young intellectuals, founded in 1950 the journal *Cité Libre*, where he wrote in the first issue that he and his friends were men and – more importantly – women determined to "unshackle superstructures, desanctify civil society, democratize politics, break into economic life . . . ." Thus, the unlooked-for consequence of the Asbestos strike (in unintended tandem with the 1948 *automatiste* artists' manifesto, *Refus Global*) was not only the Quiet Revolution but the rise to power of the young men who supported the strikers, who wrangled with each other fratricidally in politics for a generation to come.

But one man – certainly the most engaging and moving of all – has been forgotten.

Deep into the strike, Archbishop Joseph Charbonneau of Montréal, a big-boned, energetic and able priest of piety *and* intellectual presence, said publicly: "We desire social peace, but we do not want the working class crushed. We are more attached to men than to capital. It is on this account that the clergy have decided to intervene. We wish to inspire respect for charity and for justice, and we desire to see less respect paid to the interests of money than to the human element."

He delivered a Mother's Day sermon from the pulpit of Notre Dame Cathedral, calling for food and cash collections for the strikers while condemning the Duplessis government and the directors of foreign-owned companies; they were, he said, creating a French-Canadian class of serfs, and he went on to imply that his fellow princes of the Church – who had buttoned their lips because Duplessis had not only threatened to let Protestants make inroads into education, but also to levy taxes against church property – were guilty of complicity.

Hard on the heels of the sermon, Premier Duplessis – who was his own Attorney General – sent 75 carloads of provincial police to Asbestos. He declared the workers' strike illegal. The families of 5,000 strikers were on the verge of starvation. The workers' ranks were on the verge of breaking as more hired thugs came into town to defend the company with crowbars. The strikers were entirely vulnerable to the predacious police.

Nihil homini amico est opportune amicius.

However, not long after his Mother's Day sermon – not long after some $200,000 to $300,000 had been collected at the city's church doors – Johns-Manville saw the writing on the church walls and ended the strike by agreeing to a ten percent wage increase, elimination of asbestos dust, and holidays for the workers with pay.

Premier Duplessis acted punitively. He knew who to hurt and how to hurt him. Two of his cabinet ministers appeared at the Holy See in Rome carrying a 184-page report on the Asbestos strike. In their report, they accused Charbonneau of being a Communist dupe. The Archbishop of Rimouski, Mgr. Georges Courchesne, in his own report to the Papacy, accused Charbonneau of being "no longer in communion with the hierarchy" – of "preaching an advanced social Catholicism" – of being hostile "to the legitimate government of M. Duplessis" – of making "too many concessions to Communists," and, worst of all, of promoting ecumenicism. Mgr. Courchesne was abetted in his attack on Archbishop Charbonneau by Mgr. Ildebrando Antoniutti, the Italian papal delegate to Ottawa, who disapproved of Charbonneau's forthrightness.

In 1950, in the Marian Holy Year, Joseph Charbonneau, after serving ten years as prince of the Montréal archdiocese, was relieved of his duties by the Vatican Secretariat of State. He wrote a letter to Pius XII, asking to be allowed to defend himself but the Pope did not reply. Instead, Archbishop Charbonneau was invested with the mock rank of "Titular Archbishop of Bosphorus." He was directed to report to a Home for the Aged in Victoria, British Columbia, and finally, to an obscure convent to act as chaplain to the Sisters of Saint Anne.

He seemed never, even at the time of his death in 1959, able to come to terms with Pope Pius XII's actions. He passed his years cut off from cosmopolitan society, cut off from his parish, a priest who – it seemed – had taken a walk "from breakfast to madness," a priest who ended his life hearing the confessions of nuns,

each mouth open and round,
breathing together
as fish do,
singing without sound . . .

The Telegram, 1968-1972

WHAT A MEECE

What did the Portuguese sailor say when he saw
the rat on board ship? — "Hézuz, what a meece."

THE WAR MEASURES ACT

THE INEVITABLE INCREMENT OF VICTIMS

The police came in the night. They broke down doors. They broke windows, they broke walls. They broke into bedrooms. They put personal papers into green plastic garbage bags. They broke up families, they took men from their wives and children and wives from their children and men. They would not say why. But they did say that there was a list of names and it was a list that had been given out in the night:

> *Why not burst in like a poisoned shell,*
> *Or steal in like a bandit with his knuckle-duster,*
> *Or like a typhus-germ?*
> *Or like a fairy-tale of your own invention*[1]

And so the body count began: twenty, sixty, one hundred and twenty, two hundred and twenty, three hundred and twenty, and more . . . .

---

[1] The poetry quoted throughout is from the work of Anna Akhmatova (translated by D.M. Thomas) who survived to write about the Great Terror of 1937-38 in Moscow and Leningrad.

IT WAS THEN THAT THE RAILWAY YARDS WERE ASYLUMS OF THE MAD

Poets, students, editors and civil servants, office boys and union officers, technicians and teachers, were jailed but never charged or allowed bail or counsel. The names of the arrested – "the disappeared" – were not given out.

The police had come in the night.

Federal regulations had been passed in Ottawa in pre-dawn secrecy, federal regulations that suspended the civil rights of every man, woman and child in the country, federal regulations that allowed for the arrest of those suspected of being about to commit an act in support of the FLQ. *About to commit!* This is the language of the War Measures Act. This is the language of Stalin: Article 58, the imprisoning of men for what they are suspected of thinking.

Within three weeks, four hundred and thirty-five innocent men and women were released without charge, not through their lawyers, but by the will or whim of the Québec Attorney General.

> *I should like to call you all by name,*
> *But they have lost the lists . . .*

Novelist Hugh MacLennan, trying to explain what it was like in Montréal during those October days of the Crisis, said, "The smell of terror was the same as I smelled in Moscow and Leningrad in 1937. It is worse than panic. Kidnapping and selective assassination touch memory traces on the subconscious; they go back to our primitive ancestors in their caves, knowing that at any instant the leopard may – or may not – come."[1]

---

[1] MacLennan says he smelled a terror far worse than panic in the streets of Moscow and Leningrad and he says he felt the same primitive fear of the leopard in Montréal, but his historical analogy is totally skewed: the citizens of those Soviet cities, during the Terror of '37, certainly lived in fear of a leopard but the leopard they feared was the police, those police with their lists who came knocking on doors in the night. In Montréal, the leopard MacLennan feared was not the police; he feared, among others, the inno-

The Province of Québec now acknowledges that the innocent were punished without cause, but mewling federal politicians still ask us to understand and accept what Lenin asked us to understand and accept – that there always has to be "an inevitable increment of victims."

But victims of what? Of whom?

HOW THE STORY BEGINS

On Monday morning of 5 October 1970, a crisp morning, James Richard (Jasper) Cross, the British Trade Commissioner, was kidnapped. He was hauled from his greystone Montréal house by four political thugs who were armed with submachine guns and dynamite. The leaves of sugar maples were turning to ochre, a tinge of red. A senior Québec cabinet minister, Pierre Laporte, meeting with other provincial ministers, said, "There is a wind of madness blowing across the province. I hope it won't last long."

The kidnappers, who called themselves the Liberation Cell of the FLQ, issued their demands.

Mitchell Sharp, the Ottawa cabinet minister, replied publicly that their particular set of demands was rejected, implying that another set of demands might be considered.

The Montréal police, inciting alarm, said they believed that the FLQ had 9,000 pounds of dynamite in its possession . . . they said the FLQ had machine guns, recoilless rifles, and mortars, all stolen from armories.

---

cents who were already in jail, and so like most English-speaking intellectuals and civil libertarians of Montréal, he supported the police. On the other hand (and in the other language), Victor-Lévy Beaulieu wrote in *Un rêve Québécois* of how "two cops were standing there terrorizing him…The hands grew heavier on his shoulders, the fingers dug into his flesh. A hand opened before his eyes and slammed into his cheek, lifting his head off his shoulders. He could feel the shadows pulling him from behind, bloody stars shot into his eyes…The cops must have felt provoked since one of them belched and the other muttered, a threat. Then they pushed him backwards as he wrapped himself into a terrified ball…"

If true, it was reason for fear and trepidation, but 9,000 pounds was a ludicrous figure, three times more dynamite than had been stolen from construction sites across the whole of Québec in almost two years.

A wind of madness, a swirl of confusion!

Premier Robert Bourassa, like a man startled out of a silence of snow, looked around and said, "Isn't it alarming, the people aren't concerned?"

Then, the Ottawa government increased the confusion. They allowed the reading, on radio and television, of the FLQ manifesto.

The manifesto is crude. It is a complaining screed, complaining about corrosive poverty, the crapulent slums, privilege and unemployment. Tonally, it had an authentic feel: it spoke to those workers who had been thrown out of their jobs at Vickers and Davie Ship; it spoke to workers who had failed to form a union at Murdochville; it spoke to the chagrin of green stamp families, and then it was laced with scorn for a litany of big-money names: DuPont of Canada, Senator Molson, university directors: *monkeys* and *slave-drivers;* men like Steinberg, Bronfman, Timmins, Thompson, Desmarais, *monkeys* and *slave-drivers*, Keirans, Drapeau the *Dog*, and Trudeau the *Queer*, they were all blamed as *monkeys* and *slave-drivers* for lousing up the lives of all working stiffs.

The Québécois had never heard such a public accusatory cry from the unlettered.

Emerging from Sunday morning mass, the elders of the towns and villages, when asked about the FLQ, stood on their parish church steps and pulled a disapproving face but then, when pressed a little, they allowed that what was said about poverty, welfare, the jobs lost . . ."*tabernacle*, those boys were telling the truth there . . . ."

Given this response to the manifesto, politicians – trying to get a handle on what was being felt among the people – said they noticed not only a certain confusion, they noted, they said, *an erosion of the will to resist.* Premier Robert Bourassa warned of a "dangerous apathy."

CAT-AND-MOUSE

Claude Ryan, the cautious, conservative, close confidant of important men in Québec, urged negotiation for the life of James Cross.

René Lévesque urged negotiation for the life of James Cross.

Lévesque, with his bobbing head and his fluttering hand as he held a cigarette, conveyed a troubled thoughtfulness as he recalled out loud how – on April 29 of the previous spring – the English voters of Montréal had deserted him and his Party at the polls, and he spoke of how bitter his supporters – getting nearly 25 percent of the popular vote but less than 7 percent of the province's seats – had been on that night:

"We were working our goddamned hearts out trying to keep these guys channelled in the democratic way. It was funny, during all the time of the build-up to the election, there wasn't one single explosion, not a bomb. But when that election was over, and they saw what had been done, a lot of them . . . well . . . how many of those, I thought afterwards became FLQ? I don't know."

Lévesque, with a disapproving snort, called the kidnappers, who almost certainly were among his supporters, *sewer rats.*

Lévesque had made his position clear: he was a democrat.

Hugh MacLennan dismissed Lévesque as "a Kerensky."

As for the kidnapper's demands:

Robert Lemieux, a lawyer acting for the FLQ's Liberation Cell, said: "The Federal Government is playing a dangerous cat-and-mouse game with the life of Mr. Cross. Mr. Sharp should have been more explicit as to what the government has to offer. He does not reveal everything in his mind."

A ROSE IS NOT A ROSE

The middle-aged Mrs. Rosa Rose and her two sons were parked by the side of a highway in Texas, looking at a Texaco map. They were in a yellow Valiant listening to AM radio. Mrs. Rosa Rose and her sons, Paul and Jacques, and a friend, Francis Simard, heard the news of the kidnapping of James Cross. They swung the Valiant into a U-turn toward home. Somewhere south of the 49th parallel they decided to give themselves a name because, after all, how could revolutionaries with no name be revolutionaries, so they named themselves the Chenier Cell of the FLQ. They paused in New York State to buy M-1 rifles and a shot gun and then crossed the Champlain Bridge into downtown Montreal on Saturday, October 10, at 6:18 pm, and kidnapped the provincial labour minister, Pierre Laporte.

The police came, the police went. They came and went. Night and day.

They were flummoxed. They had lists but no leads. They couldn't find James Cross and the Liberation Cell, and they could not find the Chenier Cell and Pierre Laporte. Premier Bourassa, safely ensconced if not barricaded in a bedroom suite in the Queen Elizabeth Hotel, received a handwritten note, a plea from Pierre Laporte: "Mon cher Robert . . . you have the power to dispose of my life . . . I had two brothers; they are both dead. I remain alone as the head of a large family . . . I don't see why, by taking more time about it, you would continue to make me die little by little in the place where I am held. Decide – my life or death."

Bourassa, harried and pale, spoke: "It is because we particularly want Mr. Laporte and Mr. Cross to live that we desire – before discussing the demands that have been made – to set up mechanisms that would guarantee, as Mr. Laporte says it will, that the release of the political prisoners will surely result in the safe release of the hostages . . . we ask the kidnappers to contact us."

Pierre Trudeau said acidly that the men in prison were criminal bandits. There were, he said, NO *political prisoners*.

He was right, but . . . .

It didn't matter, it didn't clarify: Bourassa had spoken of political prisoners, Trudeau had called them bandits; Bourassa had spoken of possible mechanisms, Trudeau had scoffed at possible mechanisms; Bourassa had asked for further contact, Trudeau had declined direct contact.

AND THE PORTUGUESE SAILOR SAID WHEN HE SAW THE BIG RAT: "HÉZUZ, WHAT A MEECE"

On Thanksgiving evening in Ottawa people looked up to the *thwopping* sound of troop helicopters. Five hundred battle-dressed soldiers, young grunts with fixed bayonets, took up defensive positions in the city streets of the capital. They stood guard by the stoplights. They stood guard by the curbs. Frightened drivers rolled up their car windows. Soldiers saw their own reflections in the window glass. Trudeau seemed surprised when he was asked if such military manoeuvres were reasonable. He talked disdainfully: "Well, there are a lot of bleeding hearts around who just don't like to see people with helmets and guns. All I can say is go on and bleed, but it is more important to keep law and order in a society than to be worried about weak-kneed people . . . ."

As public opinion swelled in approval around him, he preened – a man who had once written: "Public opinion seeks to impose its domination over everything. Its aim is to reduce all action, all thought, and all feeling to a common denominator. It forbids independence and kills inventiveness; condemns those who ignore it and banishes those who oppose it."[1]

---

[1] The principle of the tyranny of the majority was best explained by John Stuart Mill in *Utilitarianism, Liberty and Representative Government*: "The will of the people, moreover, practically means the will of the most numerous or the most active part of the people; the majority, or those who succeed in making themselves accepted as the majority; the people, consequently may desire to oppress a part of their number; and precautions are as much needed against this as against any other abuse of power. The limitation, therefore, of

Premier John Robarts of Ontario, stolid and florid, bristled with firmness. He said it was a time to stand and fight, he said it was a time of *total war*.

He was ridiculous but he looked pleased with himself.

. . . Only the dead smiled, glad to be at rest.

THE KNOCK IN THE NIGHT

In Québec, a remarkable coalition! Men who had squabbled, who had spoken rancorously of each other through the years, proposed a *countervailing force* to Pierre Trudeau (who had, of course, always advocated a politics of countervailing *forces*): Louis Laberge of the international unions, Marcel Pépin of the national unions, Claude Ryan, René Lévesque, and eleven others called for Ottawa to negotiate for the lives of Pierre Laporte and James Cross.

Life, they said, was the highest priority.

Instead, Pierre Trudeau spoke of the dangers of parallel powers, he spoke of the need for the maintenance of principle as the first priority.

In Ottawa, in closed cabinet, principle evolved into a plan.

Said Trudeau: "It is obvious that if urgent action is needed at some time in the middle of the night we cannot ask Parliament to approve it first."

Said a backbencher: "All these things happen in the middle of the night."

Said a television wag: "Maybe it's time to put aside principle and do what's right."

---

the power of government over individuals loses none of its importance when the holders of power are regularly accountable to the community, that is, to the strongest party therein. This view of things, recommending itself equally to the intelligence of thinkers and to the inclination of those important classes in European society to whose real or supposed interests democracy is adverse, has had no difficulty in establishing itself; and in political speculations 'the tyranny of the majority' is now generally included among the evils against which society requires to be on its guard."

Such is life, so it went.

In the dark hours of Friday morning, at 4 am, with Ottawa occupied and 1,000 battle-ready troops in the Montréal streets, the War Measures Act was imposed on all of the people of all the land. Men, women, children – all lost all their civil rights. Editorial writers spoke of the country losing its innocence[1] (one might remember, however, that only six months after Confederation in 1867, at the time of the D'Arcy McGee assassination, the country's first political killing, the federal government readily and immediately suspended all civil rights for all of the people, so that the police found themselves free and able to conduct a wholesale and indiscriminate round up of any and all Irish men *suspected* of being Fenian subversives and insurrectionists).

To justify enforcing the Act, the law said that there had to be an apprehension of an actual insurrection, and so Trudeau said: "Apprehended insurrection exists and has existed as of the 15th day of October."

"I recognize," Trudeau said, sounding on television uncannily like the sonorous Right Reverend Bishop Fulton J. Sheen, "that this extreme position into which governments have been forced is in some respect a trap . . . . The criminal law as it stands

---

[1] MacLennan, given entire pages in Montréal and Toronto newspapers to expound on the crisis, wrote: "What wonder, then, that the Canada only 20 years ago that seemed so innocent should now be in the vortex? What wonder that from coast to coast the sad cry goes up that our innocence is gone? The loss of innocence is an inevitable result of making adult decisions. We made no adult decisions in the two great wars, entering the first because the English-speaking majority was still Britain's child, the second because it was still Britain's adolescents. Step by step after 1945 we advanced into the isolation of maturity. We became suddenly too luxurious. Into our midst came the Mafia, the sexual revolution, the drug culture, the discovery by student and faculty politicians that propaganda was more exciting than truth...the collapse of religion and the collapse of human dignity in the slums, explains why the violent wing of the separatist movement is largely composed of students and young proletarians. Or am I being too intellectual?" He wasn't being too intellectual. His argument was of such a trite and simplistic order that it was useful only to local political opportunists, the emotionally overwrought, and the happily ill-informed.

is simply not adequate to deal with systematic terrorism . . . . This government is not acting out of fear, it is acting to prevent fear from spreading. It is acting to maintain the rule of law without which freedom is impossible. It is acting to make clear to kidnappers and revolutionaries and assassins that in this country laws are made and changed by the elected representatives of all Canadians – not by a handful of self-selected dictators – those who gain power through terror, rule through terror. The government is acting, therefore, to protect your life and your liberty." [1]

"It is my hope," said Justice Minister John Turner as the raids continued, "it is my hope that some day the full details of the intelligence upon which the government acted can be made public."

> *Yellow moonlight leaps the sill,*
> *Leaps the sill and stops astonished . . .*

An unleashed Jean Marchand ranted about subversive infiltration in high places. He smeared the FRAP party running against Mayor Drapeau in Montréal, calling it a front for the FLQ. In Vancouver, he identified separatists with the FLQ, as if he could not – in all reasonableness – distinguish between a legitimate opposition political party and thugs and criminals.

Jean Drapeau threatened that a vote against him in the upcoming city elections meant there would be blood in the streets.

There were warnings of selective FLQ assassinations.

Then the unthinkable happened.

On October 17, they found citizen Laporte's body in the trunk of a green Chevrolet, parked on the grounds of a private

---

[1] Jean Marchand described the insurrection as "an organization with thousands of rifles and carbines and machine-guns in their hands, with bombs in their hands, and with dynamite in their hands, some 2000 pounds of it, enough to blow up the heart of Montréal, people who are ready to kidnap and murder...how many? According to our more pessimistic information there are some 3000 of them in the FLQ."

flying club.[1] The body was covered with rags. Laporte's hands were folded in repose across his chest. He had been murdered with his own religious chain.

Strangled.

Politicians grieved on television. They spoke mournfully about the loss to the Laporte family, the loss of a Minister to the State.

The State? Certainly, but there was no State funeral. Not for citizen Laporte. The family would not allow it. The State had refused to negotiate for the man's life. The bitter family shut the State out of the funeral:

> *I shall leave you behind,*
> *O my dove, my sun, my sister,*
> *You will be my widow,*
> *And now . . . Goodbye. It's time.*

LET'S SKIP LUNCH

Several mandarins sympathetic to Trudeau spoke of his anguish at "having to impose" the War Measures Act. He denied this anguish. In an interview with Tom Buckley of the *New York Times* on November 10, he said it had not been a difficult decision to make. "Neither emotionally nor intellectually was there a great struggle . . . the question of timing was very important and I won't say we didn't discuss this a fair amount. It wasn't a question of whether we were doing something basically objectionable in our own consciences in invoking this measure. In

---

[1] The days and time sequences involved were: Monday, Oct. 5, 1970, just before 8:30 am, four armed men kidnapped James Cross. Five days later, on Saturday, Oct. 10, at 6:18 pm, four armed men kidnapped Pierre Laporte. On Thursday, Oct. 15, the army was ordered into the streets of Québec City and Montréal. On Oct. 16, at 4 am, the War Measures Act was proclaimed. At 6:18 pm, on Oct. 17, the FLQ claimed responsibility for Pierre Laporte's kidnapping and execution. On Sunday, Oct. 18, at 12:25 am police discovered Laporte's body.

my own mind, the importance of democratic movements not fearing to take extraordinary measures to preserve democracy – this importance has always been established."

The police raids dragged on, ragged, bullying, incompetent.

The troops did what troops standing in cities do: they stood around.

There was reckless talk among reporters, some saying that members of the FLQ had trained in Palestinian guerrilla camps. Talk of snipers, grenade launchers. Photographs of young men in desert camps wearing *kefiyahs*.

Victor-Lévy Beaulieu hallucinated the paranoia that was in the air: "He only wanted to see . . . his dreams marching into the future with raised fists, frost, or rather blood, on their moustaches, necks strangled by silver chains . . . buses overturned (wheels still spinning, fire causing the tires to explode, burning the embossed leatherette seats, sending the springs flying, leaving hideous, twisted, glowing-red hulks lying in the middle of the streets), looters walking among the debris . . . and those snipers on the roofs, those unrelenting machine gun bursts, those armed, invisible men in the doorways of houses where lying flat on their stomachs with chewed matches clenched in their teeth they awaited easy targets. And then sometimes it was screaming motorcycles and the disgusting *eee-aww, eee-aww* of armoured cars as they rolled over the dead, spewing forth tear gas, laughing gas, paralyzing gas . . . . Maybe it all belonged to the netherswirl of nightmare."

After fifty-nine days of *ee-awwing* in the streets and jawing on the airwaves they found James Richard (Jasper) Cross. He was haggard but healthy. His kidnappers agreed to cut a deal. The federal government did what Trudeau had said it would not do. It entered into negotiations, and when the negotiations were completed, the thugs, the twerps, who made up the FLQ's Liberation Cell, were liberated, and they flew to freedom in Cuba.

James Cross, taciturn, reserved, spoke of Pierre Laporte as "a brother" – he said he was bonded to him by death – but then he said dismissively, "It was a case of six kids trying to make a revolution." [1]

The politicians in Ottawa were not amused. Still, Trudeau, trying for élan, invited Cross to lunch, but Cross flew home to England, declining the Prime Minister's invitation to break bread.

The Chenier Cell, the feckless murderers, had dug themselves into a tunnel behind an empty farmhouse. They were down in a watery dark hole. They, too, at last were cornered and they straggled out into the slush – Catilinian *conspirators, agents of insurrection* – with an arsenal of one rusty shotgun, a starter's pistol and a clip of .22-calibre ammunition.

HOW TO SPELL CONFUSION

The only plausible explanation for the imposition of the War Measures Act remains the one given by Trudeau on October 26: "They are very clear facts. First, we had from the authorities of the Province of Québec and the City of Montréal a clear statement that they apprehended insurrection.

"Second, there had been the abduction of two very important citizens in the province of Québec, with an intention to murder them if the government did not give in to ransom.

"The third fact was circumstantial, if you wish, that approximately two tons of dynamite had been stolen in the province of Québec this year, as well as a sizeable number of small arms and other ammunition.

"Also, there was such a state of confusion and threats of violence in the province of Québec, we decided to act on these facts as we interpreted them, and on this the government will stand or fall."

---

[1] Hugh MacLennan wrote that it had been a conspiracy comparable to Catiline's failed attempt in Rome in 63 B.C. to murder a consul and kidnap and assassinate leading senators. Catiline failed, he said, because Rome was still a coherent state, and Canada, he suggested, had not yielded to terror because it was still a coherent state, and it was a coherent state because "political power had not yet fallen into the hands of people under 30."

Then the horses fell
And produced a sobbing echo . . .

The government did not fall.

There certainly had been confusion.

However:

Was the confusion lessened by the reading of the manifesto?

Was the confusion lessened by the Honourable Mitchell Sharp who suggested negotiations but never intended negotiations?

Was the confusion lessened by police raids in the night?

Was the confusion lessened by soldiers in the streets portending civil war?

Was the confusion lessened by talks of tons of dynamite and by the Honourable Jean Marchand, who spooked the country with his silly rant about subversives in high places?

Was the confusion lessened by the Honourable Jean Drapeau's warning that there could be blood in the streets?

Was the confusion lessened by tall tales of selective assassinations?

As for provisional plots to take over the province, therein lies a story . . . the story of Lucien Saulnier and the *coup d'état*.

Who were the men who gave the *coup d'état* story credence?

The men were:

Jean Drapeau, the loquacious mayor of Montréal.

Lucien Saulnier, the laconic boss of Montréal.

Their *coup d'état* story had its root in the 1969 Montréal police strike. After the rioting and the outbreak of smash-and-grab looting attendant to that strike, Saulnier, the Executive Director of Montréal City Council, delivered a report that outlined the causes of the strike. To avoid blaming the police for the strike and the consequent street violence, Saulnier said that he had discovered numbers of political subversives among – of all people – the Company of Young Canadians,[1] and these subversives, he said, were working conspiratorially to disrupt society.

---

[1] The Canadian equivalent to the American Peace Corps

Saulnier succeeded in shifting attention away from the disgruntled metropolitan Montréal police to "international forces" – those forces from abroad, he said – who were financing all the local labour trouble: "We had a beginning of revolution in the streets of our city."

> . . . the past is rotting in the future—
> A terrible carnival of dead leaves.

[An Interlude]

Going to meet Lucien Saulnier (this was *before* the kidnapping of James Cross) was like going to the heart of an onion: he was waiting for me in an enclosed room within an enclosed room within a closed room in City Hall, a stern big-boned man, he was sitting alone, waiting not just for me but for two armed detectives to close the door, to stand behind me, one with his hand on his exposed gun. Saulnier said of the police strike:

"Many parts of the country are subject to this kind of activity, pretty frightening kind of activity, subversion . . . . In Toronto, a very significant escalation in the wages of policemen was made. So one can understand that the policemen in Montréal made comparisons . . . . The very interesting questions would be: how did it escalate so much and why?

"The Prime Minister of Canada, the Prime Minister of Ontario, the Prime Minister of the Province of Québec, they do possess some information which is not in itself of a criminal nature, and which cannot be revealed. But they do have, nobody will doubt a moment that the Prime Minister of Canada has information which he cannot reveal . . . ."

He talked about information, information that could not be revealed – no one could doubt, yes, information about subversion, wage escalation, and no one will doubt the criminal nature of criminals . . . yes, their criminal nature . . . a tense wary man . . . a man seeding the air with suspicion. With mendacity. With complicity. That, no one could doubt. The more he talked the more confused he became – holed up with his holstered body-guards – Saulnier, the boss who had been on the phone to Tru-deau, the boss who had called for military powers to apprehend insurrection, the boss bunkered-in at the centre of his onion, he who had spoken to Ottawa of a *coup d'état* – a provisional gov-ernment plot – the boss, watching and waiting for the leopard.

But what of the plot, the *coup d'état*, and what of Claude Ryan?

Was Ryan the leopard?

MAGDALENA BEAT HER BREAST AND WEPT

The opposition demanded facts.

Into Ottawa came Peter Newman, reporter, ear bent to the powerful, ear open to the powerful. Someone – perhaps the Prime Minister – told Newman a story that, if true, not only jus-tified the War Measures Act but suggested a *coup d'état*.

The story, printed unsigned in the *Toronto Star*, could hardly have been more explicit: a group of influential Québécois had been working on a plan to supplant the legitimate government and this plan was part of the insurrection that had been appre-hended by the War Measures Act.

Mayor Drapeau, with all the bravado of the beleaguered tri-umphant, boosted the *coup d'état* story: he thanked his voters in the just-completed Montréal election for having helped "this gov-ernment resist not only known revolutionary attacks, but also resisted attempts to set up a provisional government that was to preside over a transfer of constitutional powers to a revolutionary regime."

. . . the age of dementia moves nearer.

Claude Ryan listened to this claptrap with something close to despair: he realized that a brief conversation he'd held one Sunday afternoon just before the imposition of the War Measures Act had become – in the *eee-awing* fantasies, or miscalculations of others – a plot to overthrow the Québec government, a plot to install himself as the FLQ prime minister.

In fact, Ryan had a) convened a Sunday meeting of his newspaper editors; b) they had agreed that the Québec Cabinet was in disarray; c) they had agreed that three possibilities presented themselves:

1. It was possible that hardliners in Ottawa, Montréal and Québec City might bring the War Measures Act into force. They had to oppose any such removal of responsibility to federal powers.

2. It was possible that increasing levels of terrorism would reduce the Bourassa cabinet to impotence. The answer to that would be a provincial unity cabinet made up of diverse political elements.

3. It was possible that Bourassa would succeed (they were convinced he intended to bargain the "political" prisoners for Laporte and Cross). If so, the Québec government would emerge as independent but it would be a good idea to take outsiders into such an independent cabinet as a sign of unity.

Ryan recommended the latter position directly to Bourassa, not as a threat, not as a plot to replace him, but in an attempt to reinforce him.

Ryan then went to Saulnier's office and explained the three possibilities. Saulnier said he did not think the situation was as yet so serious.

They parted amicably.

Then the story of the *coup d'état* appeared: it had weeviled its way out of the onion heart of Montréal; it had come from Lucien Saulnier and Jean Drapeau – "unimpeachable" sources.

Were these two men – an embattled paranoid and an inflammatory liar – behind the decision to invoke the War Measures Act?

Or, were members of the federal government, not caring whether the *coup d'état* story was true, trying to discredit Claude Ryan, who was Trudeau's critic? Or, were members of the federal government trying to provide, *ex post facto*, a justification for the Act?

Who knows?

[End of Interlude]

❦

This we do know:

The apprehended insurrection was never apprehended. It was not there. If Trudeau had not lied, he had certainly misled the people. Thugs, yes, bombs, yes, guns, yes, kidnappings and murder, yes, but never an apprehended insurrection.

Not surprisingly, "the full details of the intelligence upon which the government acted" were not made public.

So much for John Turner.

HOW FACES FALL APART

Pierre Trudeau is nothing if not consistent. On the eve of his 1968 election he wrote:

> The fact is that, at bottom, the Separatists despair of ever being able to convince the public of the rightness of their ideas . . . . So they want to abolish freedom and impose a dictatorship of their minority. They are in sole possession of the truth, so others need only get in line. And when things don't go fast enough they take to illegality and violence . . . . They want to be done with peaceful and constitutional methods. They proclaim to the newspapers that from now on they will go underground. These

terrorized terrorists will be led by Mr. X. And, on coura-
geous anonymity, they will sow their ideas while waiting
to set off their bombs.

They want to abolish freedom and impose a dictatorship . . .
When things don't go fast enough, they take to illegality and vio-
lence.

But that is not how history has played itself out. The sepa-
ratist Parti Québécois has moved like a snail. It has moved like
a snail because it is a legitimate political party. The FLQ is *not* the
Party. Is it possible that Pierre Trudeau, because of his convic-
tions, his antipathy to separatism, did not care to distinguish be-
tween a political party and criminals?

A conclusion, and for some it is inescapable, is that the Tru-
deau government – while trying to solve the kidnapping crisis
– sought to break the back of popular support for the Parti Qué-
bécois by linking it with the FLQ. Perhaps. Perhaps not. Myself,
I don't think we should forget how compelling it is for a man
to stand at the centre of his own panic – to stand like Edgar Allan
Poe's rational man whirling in a perfect stillness at the centre of
a maelstrom – to experience exhilaration while exuding the air
of utter control. "My fellow Canadians . . . this government is
not acting out of fear, it is acting to prevent fear from spread-
ing." I, of course, can not say that this state of panic – pinned
to the wall of calamity while conveying resolute calm – is what
Trudeau, with his excited cohorts in tow, went through. But we
do know that the police were turned loose, they were told to
take out their lists of *séparatiste* sympathizers. And they did
and so they came in the night. They broke down doors, they
broke windows, they broke walls, they broke up lives . . . they
acted as if they were in the midst of a cataclysmic moment . . .
but they were not in such a moment. This was not a time when a
president had been shot, his head blown away in broad daylight
in the back seat of a car, it was not a time when a black preacher,

Martin Luther King, had been assassinated in a motel, it was not a time when another Kennedy had been shot, live, on television in a crowded hotel, it was not a time when Malcolm X had been shot in a theatre and black city folk were firebombing and gutting whole city blocks and black city folk were sniping at police from the rooftops, it was not the time of the Chicago Democratic Convention when thousands of students and Yippies in the streets were beaten by rioting police, it was not a time when the Chicago police were murdering Black Panthers in their beds, it was not a time when the Weathermen, an actual organized terrorist underground, was setting off – over two years – some *one thousand bombs.*

We had two cases of kidnapping.

Our authorities, with unstinting support from our *clerks,* the intelligentsia, not only suspended our civil rights and put aside our legal privileges and gave political significance to Rosa Rose and her hapless sons, but they still advise us to accept the increment of victims as inevitable and they ask us to admire the political expediency involved in letting the Liberation Cell go free; they applaud Trudeau for having "stood tough," and shrug off our *traison des clerks.* Well, I say no, No – "the inevitable increment of victims" was a phrase used by Lenin, and, as for the *clerks,* the intelligentsia, the novelists and poets like Hugh MacLennan and F.R. Scott[1] and Irving Layton who scorned the few bleeding hearts in their midst, let us remember how Akhmatova put it:

---

[1] Within seven months, F.R. Scott – though still justifying the imposition of the Act – said: "In light of present knowledge it appears that the Government overreacted and that there was not really an emergency of such dimensions that the normal criminal laws would not have been sufficient. There was no revolutionary army, or infamous 'parallel government' ready to take over the country." Much of English Canada, it seems, has come to accept this view of the crisis – that the Act was an overreaction but was justified because it got the job done (whatever the job was) – and then they – unlike the Québécois – have chosen to forget about it.

Poets are blind to sin,
They must dance before the Ark of
The Covenant, or perish!

The Telegram, 1971-1973

FRAGILE MOMENTS

An early winter's white sun turns me to pure
white shadow in silhouette

Snow fell through my sleeplessness
so softly I heard
dry thunder whisper

Insomnia laid a hand on my brow
bathed in a sudden white sweat
someone beside me breathes

As twilight hollowed my heart
I strolled alone for hours
hoping to see the sun dip
like the night in dawn's undertow

As you leave like a dream in the wane of evening
wide-eyed alone facing the wall
I hear somewhere down by the river
a wild goose calling of loneliness

Strange pain   surprise twinge
stalled life   my head wilts
bloom of dandelion paling
strange pain   white lunacy
the burden of dying with little fuss
brittle childhood desire

to end up knowing nothing
strange pain unhinged eyes
nape on fire   fringe
of damp moss on the chest
strange pain   purified pulse
the hand feels   surprised
a hint of the face beneath my face

Translated from the Québécois French
of Jacques Brault

THE
PUBLIC ORDEAL OF
BRYCE MACKASEY

It was late in the afternoon and a winter sun cast a pale light across the St. Lawrence River. The island coves were filled with ice jumbled against the stone cliffs. It was a small, jagged island downstream from Île d'Orléans and old-town Québec, an island of disused fever sheds, graves, dwarf pines, and outcroppings of rock. On that February afternoon, it was covered in three- and four-foot drifts of snow. Grosse-Île used to be a quarantine station for diseased and dying men, women, and children. They had come in the coffin boats through the 1830s, 1840s, and 1850s, starving Irish sick with typhus and cholera, and they'd been forced ashore on this island, quarantined and condemned to die after the long crossing. A doctor who cared for the fevered for more than a decade finally fled the island and killed himself, leaving behind the dead stacked in unmarked mass graves close to Cholera Bay, the sickle-shaped shallows where the boats unloaded the living on their last legs. The sunken hollows are still marked by staggered white crosses, and up the sharp incline of the hill that faces the south shore of the St. Lawrence – a long walk from the old oblong wooden fever shed that is still standing – there is a tall, chiselled grey granite cross, a Celtic sign in the cold sky, facing away from the ship traffic, seldom seen.

A damp wind blew sprays of snow off the broken ice piled against the clefts in the stone along the shore. Bryce Mackasey, his solid, fleshy face red from the cold, stood at the foot of the hill rising up to the cross and, said, "Ugly, this is an ugly island, vicious-looking, austere indeed."

"It's worse than that," I said. "The ice along the shore, it's an asbestos colour, like there is sickness still seeping into it."

He let one shoulder slope the way a boxer does when he relaxes, and with a quick furtive glance, looked at me – his arms hanging – and then he smiled with the easy availability that is every politician's weakness. "You know," he said, "I've no enemies." He fumbled with his collar, blinked, lowered his head, and seemed smaller and paler, as if huddled in pain, but then he lifted his head with a broad smile, consoling himself. "Nope, no enemies," he said, a wounded man on a forbidding island talking to me, someone unknown whom he hoped to trust, after all those he knew so well had broken their trust and let him down.

"With your friends," I said, "I wouldn't want enemies. What about your old buddy, Brian Mulroney?"

"I love the guy," he said, laughing. "God's little fixer. We've been fishing together, we've been to the Beaver Club and through the La Presse strike, for God's sake. I arbitrated the last clause between him and Louis Laberge. I sang duets with him. My problem is that I regarded Brian not only as a friend but an extraordinary friend, almost a son." He took a step forward. "Poor old Brian. I can't face the reality that he has somehow let me down, okay?"

"Okay."

"I'll tell you one thing about Bryce Mackasey. I am not rolling over dead. I'm a tough old bird in a funny way."

"Yeah, I think you're tough."

"I said that to my wife the other day. She said, sure you're very tough, but it's your credo that's tough. I am loyal, see . . . Trudeau I revered. In his anger with me and often when I went into his office he was angry . . . he loved me. But if there'd ever been disloyalty . . ." he said quietly, his voice trailing away.

"Disloyalty to what?"

He looked at me and blinked. He was wearing borrowed low-cut snow boots, a well-tailored topcoat, a shirt and tie, and was bare-headed. The snowdrifts between the rock croppings and pines were four feet deep. There was no clear trail, no sure footing, and we sank to our knees, tottered, and fell.

"I wouldn't have missed this for the world," he said.

"I always wanted to come here," I said.

"It's where we begin, you and me, in this country and nobody knows the place, nobody cares about its sorrow."

We were squatting in snow, resting a moment, and then we went on past a clump of thorny bushes.

"You're still sure you've got no enemies?" I said, pulling him up over a ridge, his face flushed, and there was a flutter of panic in his eyes as he held his hand to his heart.

"You know my feeling all through this thing?" he said. "Bewilderment. I kept saying to my wife, what the Christ am I guilty of? I was bewildered and hurt, not defeated. That would be giving in. But the cruellest moment, the most degrading, wasn't in court. The goddamn RCMP guys, the bastards grilling me. After all, I'd been a cabinet minister. The fingerprints, that was the most humiliating . . . and then during the campaign, Mulroney called me an old whore. He phoned a friend of mine to apologize . . . not to me, but to a friend, and when Clark called to tell me I was out of the Portugal job, Mulroney was in Miami and he phoned a friend to ask him to ask me not to reveal the understanding we had behind the scenes."

"What understanding?"

"I won't tell you."

"Why not?"

"I'm wary by nature."

"But you were close with Mulroney!"

"That's right. He sat in the chair in my living room after I quit the cabinet in Ottawa in 1976 and spoke to me on behalf of Québec and Robert Bourassa in Québec. He had a message from Bourassa. Would I join his provincial team? He had the authority to speak for Bourassa, and he did."

"He was the fixer."

"I ended up in Québec. And I did think I could help. I did think English Québéckers were getting a bum deal. Somebody powerful had to be in the government and I was going to sit in the goddamn front row at the right of Bourassa. Bourassa offered me Industry, Trade, and Commerce and Brian was part of all that. My relationship with Mulroney has been very close."

"The go-between in your living room."

"Absolutely. And when Brian was settling the labour dispute that made him so prominent in Montréal, the guy who would get a call in the middle of the night was me, with Brian on one phone and Louis Laberge on another, because they trusted me and I trusted them. And when Brian came down to the convention floor after he lost the leadership to Clark, I went so far as to console him. I was quite surprised I didn't end up posted in Portugal. I don't pretend it was easy for him."

"It could have been easy. He could have let you have the job."

"Well, it wasn't. It didn't happen."

"And you're still sure you have no enemies?"

He smiled, took hold of the trunk of a small pine, pausing for breath.

"You won't tell me if your understanding with him was about Portugal?"

"No. Not yet."

The sky was a grainy grey with heavy clouds clustering over the north shore, up beyond Québec City. Around a hump of stone and down a sharp slope, a field opened on to a small bay, a white field with white crosses.

"A goddamn desolate place, isn't it?" he said, taking two more steps, sinking into a buried cleft and falling backwards, a sheepish, embarrassed smile on his face. As I turned back toward him, my hand out, he said, "No, no," too stubbornly self-sufficient to want help. There was a yearning in his eyes, the bewildered panic of a man who cannot understand why he has been treated with contempt and churlishness, the look of a man desperate for someone to help him regain his public honour. After all, he had been a political footsoldier of such charm and competence that he'd become something of an icon among Liberals in the early 1970s: a man who could white-knuckle it with longshoremen and bankers, a man who lived in a modest house with a Mercedes in the garage, a man who could clearly articulate the contradictions inherent in his kind of liberalism.

"Our so-called free-enterprise system is a model of compromise. A free-enterprise corporate structure that's wedded to a welfare state. Capitalist production and socialist distribution in a none-too-compatible marriage of convenience." The clustering storm clouds over the north shore looked as if they were gathering into thunderheads – strange for winter months. "And unless we resolve the conflict," he said, "and make the marriage work, I doubt that our kind of society can survive. Should that marriage fail and our unique mixed economy come to an end, replaced by a totally free-enterprise system, or one based on social democracy, then I guess the Liberal Party will have little or no relevance."

In fact, after the 1972 election when the liberalism he espoused stuttered and seemed about to fail – when the economy stopped growing and the head honchos in the private sector sneered at the welfare aspects of our state and demanded cuts in public spending – Bryce Mackasey teetered toward failure: he and his ambition turned aimless, he seemed suddenly to have no place, and even in his own party he became the poster prole for all that was wrong in public life.

In the paling light he pushed himself up out of the snowdrift and said, "Don't make this – what we're doing about me – too Irish. That's too easy. I'm more than that cockles-and-mussels crap they dump on me."

He certainly is. After all, he was a Verdun alderman who became a forceful cabinet minister, and, though he likes to call himself "a dumb bastard," when I met him he was reading Thomas Mann's *Buddenbrooks*. He can appear unassuming while completely self-absorbed, and he wears his ambition on his sleeve while downplaying any sense of destiny. He is a drinker and can be garrulous, but his serene moments come when he's standing alone in cold water, salmon fishing. He often ambles on in half-sentences, his memories leading him astray, yet he usually has a fixed idea of exactly what he wants. He has had heart trouble and has been in so much pain from arthritis that he has had to wear braces on his wrists, yet he will trudge through four feet of snow, totally unprepared, with startling stamina. He has the reputation of being reckless and yet he has an obsession with punctuality. He is a fine public speaker, yet he mumbles and whispers in private. And for all his capacity to charm and cajole and manipulate men of money and power, he ended up as a pawn, as a dupe in a shabby loan scheme, holding not the money but the bag. Pierre Trudeau, who seemed to love and hate all these contradictions, said, "I need a guy like that."

Mackasey stood hunched forward into the wind, close to a sharp drop down to the piled ice. Flat sheets of ice were moving with the current in the water, and they had a gunmetal sheen.

"You should have gone on one of Trudeau's camping trips," I said. "You should have been one of his Arctic kids."

"Not bloody likely," he said. "Too tough for me."

"Do you think Trudeau was too tough on you?"

"Pearson was a tough cookie, he was tougher than Trudeau. Trudeau's not tough. Trudeau's a pussycat when he's dealing with people. The secret with him was to quickly reassure him that any conversation was going to be civilized. If he was forced in any way, he got belligerent. That's what happened with Tim Ralfe [a CBC radio reporter to whom Trudeau had said, "Just watch me," during the War Measures crisis]. He was cornered and didn't know how to get rid of a situation. But Pearson, the old diplomat, he knew how to get rid of people, even his friends like Walter Gordon, and naturally he knew that it was necessary to avoid taking the blame. Pearson was a mastermind at that."

"So what about the image of Pearson as the bumbler who couldn't find the red phone in his desk drawer?"

"Bullshit. And there was something hard about how mischievous Pearson could be. I remember going to an Expos baseball game with him and before the game we went up close to the plate umpire, who looked seven feet tall. 'I've had one eye removed recently,' Pearson said to the umpire. 'That's too bad. I'm sorry,' the umpire said, looking puzzled since it was impossible to tell which eye was artificial, so perfect did the plastic replacement seem. 'Oh, don't feel upset for me,' Pearson said, 'I want you to know I can call balls and strikes better with one eye than you can with two.' Then the umpire, stunned, sees this mischievous grin on Pearson's face . . . ."

Mackasey laughed.

"I live in a riding that's got a huge mental institution, and back when I was just a guy learning where the washrooms were in Parliament, I found out Pearson used to correspond regularly with an old lady in the institution. And her letters to him were lucid, intelligent, full of advice, and he followed her advice."

"And he followed her advice?"

"Yeah. We went one morning to see her. Maryon [Mrs. Pearson], myself, Pearson, and he left a few hundred dollars for a party for the patients."

"Did he really listen to the advice of this woman?"

"He thought enough of her to spend about four hours there."

"With her?"

"Yeah, they had a big party and everything. I know the woman and they're prominent in the city."

"You aren't going to tell me the name?"

"It wouldn't add anything. It's just an odd little aside. Anyway, I've got some very, very lovely, sentimental, almost close, letters from Pearson. He liked me, for some reason. He wrote me to wish me well, to console me, to reassure me. 'You were a *good* minister, Bryce,' underlined. But he was no softy. He was tough, though he had his blind spots. Pearson was terrified of labour disputes. Terrified. He'd settle at any price."

Mackasey, of course, as Minister of Labour from 1968 to 1972, settled several seemingly intractable disputes, but not at any price. Mackasey was hard-nosed and knew how to get "leverage," as he calls it – pressing a nerve here, a little flesh there. And his dockside savvy and his union connections saved the federal government from a singular piece of silliness during the War Measures crisis when government officials found out that 100 rifles had been stolen from a ship. "The RCMP, everybody was running around and there were enough rifles and ammunition – you know how statistics go – to kill every member of parliament six times.

"So they wanted to know what to do, and I said, 'Wait a minute. Maybe I have better sources.' And I called one of the bosses on the dock, a likeable fellow, and whenever collective agreement time came I could always count on a fair deal with him, and I said, 'You're going to jail, you've stolen 100 guns.' He said, 'You can't put me in jail.' I said, 'Yes, I can, that's what the War Measures Act is for.' Two hours later, he called me. He said they're at the bottom of pier 49, and he said, 'There's not a hundred of them, there's ninety-nine, one got away.' He paused and said, 'After all, this is the hunting season.'"

"Did you report back?"

"Sure, it had nothing to do with the FLQ. No longshoreman buys his own shoes or other things. He waits for a shipment. It's kind of traditional bribery. Somebody turns their back, and it was hunting season, so somebody took a rifle for every longshoreman. They brought them back and left them in the water at the end of the pier.

"The only protection against panic," said Mackasey, "is to know who you're dealing with."

The man I was dealing with was born in Québec City in 1921, the son of a railroad foreman named Francis Joseph Parnell Anthony. All of Bryce's teachers had emigrated from Ireland. "They'd come here after the Rebellion of 1916 and the troubles of '21. They were like refugees from their history. They didn't have a vocation, they had an escape valve to Canada. And what they brought to my school was a tremendous love of literature. They had nothing else. I learned 'The Harp' and 'God Save Ireland' and 'Paddy Dear' before I learned anything else, and then Swift and Chaucer and the Irish warrior songs. They were Christian Brothers and brought us a high, hard standard: penmanship – the ink copy and the pencil copy – and literature and literary societies." His parish was in the spiritual hands of the Redemptorist Fathers. "God help anyone who's brought up by Redemptorists. Everything's heaven and hell. Mass at nine, retreat for eighteen days. If you came late you got a belt in the head."

"Like being in the army?"

"Right, I grew up on that. Though my father was an easygoing man, I remember he hit a Brother for hitting me. He was quite a man, badly shot up and gassed during the war. He was determined I was going in the railway because that's where the job security was."

"But you loved the books?"

"I was an avid reader. Rather than go play ball in the afternoon I'd get a book – Zane Grey or Tarzan adventure stories – and go up in the attic where it was cool."

"Did you read in French, too?"

"Oh, I read French like I read English. The English community was insulated but not me. I grew up in Sillery, and you had the Lamberts, the O'Briens, the McCormicks, the Clearys, and we'd be in the river at high tide, the river pure and clean. But everybody was bilingual and I was a good athlete so that, when our hockey team decided to play in a league five miles away, I played for the French team."

He paused and rubbed his arthritic wrists. Then he held his soft fleshy hands out into the light.

"Our neighbours had sixteen children," he said. "By Depression standards we had lots of dough and Mother used to buy maybe twenty pounds of hot dogs and put them in a big cauldron and I'd bring in the team and she'd feed them, and we'd all go to

Mass together and the priest would give the sermon, a very long sermon, in English and then in French, so Mass would be from 10:30 am until 1:00, and everybody, I mean everybody, went to church, and I didn't mind the long sermons because I loved to be told and taught things.

"As a matter of fact, my grandfather's second wife, she taught English to the royal family of Russia. This old lady used to play cards with me, we knew every card in Russian. She'd go on for hours telling me about Russian life, about Rasputin and the little child who was dying, and then the killing and she was in the carriage with the other servants and the coachman advised them to get out and hide in the woods and they saw him killed, and she somehow got right across Europe, back to England and Canada, around 1918, when she went to work in Québec in the Garrison Club."

"Where she looked after our aristocracy in their own little garrison," I said, trying to be droll.

"Right," he said, blinking, "except she met my grandfather there, and he was a character. He was selling meat to the army and I gather it wasn't always good meat. He was always in trouble, probably selling through some local politicians. He was always in something. He died in the Thirties but we made it through the Depression.

"But the Second World War came, and suddenly they closed the railroad plant in Québec City and transferred us all to Mont-réal, to Pointe Saint-Charles. Dad died within a year. It aborted the years I should have been in university. My sister died at seventeen, overnight almost. Suddenly the whole lovely thing of life was shattered. Maybe that's why I always wanted to know who I was dealing with, because that was all such a bum deal, a bum deal for my family."

Mackasey learned how to turn bum deals and backroom deals into good deals and public deals, and the most effective dealing of his political career was done when he revamped the national program for unemployment insurance in 1972. It was and is an enduring achievement, not only because it was necessary but because he actually imposed his policy on civil servants who were busy wiggling their legs in their own way under their carapaces. Trudeau had talked about a "Just Society" during the 1968 election, but there had been no consequent direction from him, no attempt to implement any such society, and so Mackasey had stepped into a social-policy vacuum and he had filled it, persuading and cajoling special interests, acting as the effective middleman. That was his place as he pursued his policy, and no other minister during the Trudeau years was so responsible for so progressive a piece of legislation. It is also true, however, that no one, including Mackasey, foresaw that spiralling unemployment insurance costs would become a burden to the Treasury. Mackasey still believes his original scheme was actuarially sound. "It was when they began bootlegging things into it that there were problems." After the 1972 election, when the Liberals won only a minority government, Mackasey – the depleter of the Treasury – became the easy fall guy. He was blamed for the Party's failures. Tarnished, and rather than accept a humbling shuffle to the side in cabinet, he resigned.

When he got to the crest of the hill so that we could see the great high stone cross, he was worn out. He stumbled over the wind-fretted snow at the base of the high cross. His boots were filled with snow. He slumped down, hacking for air, his lungs bursting. "I was with my dad when he had an angina attack," he said, and closed his eyes, letting the panic ease. "I was walking with him in the street and he just sat down on the sidewalk." Then Mackasey stood up, facing an inscription cut into the stone:

SACRED TO THE MEMORY OF THOUSANDS
OF IRISH IMMIGRANTS WHO ENDED HERE
THEIR SORROWFUL PILGRIMAGE
THOUSANDS OF THE CHILDREN OF THE GAEL
WERE LOST ON THIS ISLAND WHILE FLEEING FROM
TYRANNICAL LAWS AND AN ARTIFICIAL FAMINE

"You know what I thought when we passed the graves?" he said. "Maybe it's the mood I'm in, but the utter desolation of this place . . . . Suddenly I could see the futility of the struggle to get here, people saying, 'Thank God it's land,' but what a barren, grotesque place, jagged like the devil did it, an inhuman ugliness they had to face." There were flurries on the wind and the light was dropping quickly. "But you know, there's always got to be the redeeming gesture. I have come to believe that. Maybe it comes from being brought up by the Christian Brothers.

"When I was a kid, about six, I lived on Sillery Hill over there across the water. Father Maguire was one of the first priests who'd come here to Grosse-Île, when Boston had said no thank you to the Irish, and New York had said no thank you . . . and when they took the people off those ships, there were all the children whose fathers and mothers had died, orphans, and they put them in a pen and gave them identification and tally sticks and the bishop took one of these children to Québec City and mounted the pulpit and he said, 'Look at this blond child with blue eyes who speaks a strange tongue . . . if you hurry, if you get your cart on the road, if you rush to that island, there are hundreds there to be adopted.'

"But then the bishop – and if you're looking for human generosity of a special kind – he asked those farmers to adopt these children but he said to them, let the male children keep their names, don't let their names die out, so today there are Burns and Ryans and O'Neils who stem from that generous wisdom. And the surprising thing is no one ever asks today why those Irish names are here all over in Québec. For that matter, no one knows why you and me, why we'd be here, why we'd want to be here, or where this island is."

After Mackasey resigned from cabinet in 1972, he hunkered down in the back benches for eighteen months, defending his unemployment insurance act and, as the self-proclaimed "friend of the little guy," he dismissed his own government's economic policies, calling them punitive, saying they produced high unemployment. Several cabinet ministers were not pleased. Mackasey, as he waited to be called back to cabinet, had become something of a loose wheel on the Liberal left. As one MP put it, "He was on the Trudeau team, but he was on the bench." He did not stay on the bench long. In 1974, an election loomed. He was called back as minister without portfolio. "He speaks for a particular constituency in Canada," Trudeau said, "and I want to hear that voice."

His was a lisping voice, the measured throatiness of a man who could be affable even as he cursed those who thought and liked to say publicly that he had no standing, no place. After the 1974 election, he became Postmaster General and presided over the country's longest postal strike – forty-one days – with such affable reasonableness and yet such stern aplomb that his popularity soared. He collapsed from exhaustion.

The wheels, however, came loose again. More and more, his exuberance seemed merely erratic, his scrappiness petulant. Though the old stump speaker could mesmerize a crowd, he couldn't seize and hold the attention of cabinet. The government's middle-of-the-road policies distressed him. There were emotional outbursts in caucus. His role became uncertain. In 1976, after a holiday in Portugal, provoked, his temper got the better of him and he said he would resign. Trudeau accepted.

That was not exactly what Mackasey had wanted. "My whole world," he said, "collapsed after 1976." He began to flounder. Deeply involved in the growing social and political unrest in his Québec, he met with Mulroney – the fixer – resigned his Commons seat, and joined Bourassa. He made speeches on behalf of federalism, so striking and so innovative – asking that the rights of minorities be "enshrined in a constitution" – that novelist Hugh MacLennan wrote to him: "Your speech of October 21 was the most solid, necessary, clear and powerful of any political speech I have ever heard since the time of Churchill. God bless you for it."

But God did not bless him. Expecting to sit on the right hand of power, expecting to be the voice of English Canada in the crucible of Québec discontent, he became instead part of Bourassa's defeat. The Parti Québécois won the next elections and Mackasey was stranded on the opposition benches. He had parachuted into provincial politics seeking power and presence. He ended up twisting in the wind, impotent, with no real part to play. In 1978, he was given an award for the best national unity speech of the year – chosen for the honour over Solange Chaput-Rolland and Northrop Frye – but after eighteen months he resigned provincial politics and went looking for a federal seat, a place to position himself again. There was talk of Trudeau's retiring, and Mackasey let it be known that he might run for the leadership. Shrewd men lifted their eyebrows: he seemed unaware of how much ground he had yielded, how much ground he had lost.

Then, in 1978, on his own federal turf, he was defeated in an Ottawa by-election, placing third. Humiliations had begun to attach to him. And laughter, too. Then Trudeau, whose timing in such matters was often wanting, did him an inadvertent disservice, announcing just before the 1979 election that Mackasey would be appointed as the new chairman of the Air Canada board of directors. Men with scores to settle, backroom scavengers, wits, and caustic scribblers, made Mackasey the butt of abuse. It was true that the old footsoldier had been a cabinet minister, and he had been the political conscience of the Liberal left, but suddenly worthy men said he didn't measure up, he was not acceptable as Air Canada's chairman. It was too tony a job for his kind – and so, a certain opinion of Mackasey took hold – a ready willingness to agree that he was a greedy, low-flying buffoon who babbled and drank, a buffoon who was always on the lookout for a limousine in which to locate his limbo.

When Joe Clark came to power in 1979, he cocked an eye at Air Canada and fired Mackasey; it was easy and he did it with relish. "It's been a humiliating two months," Mackasey said shortly after getting the sack, lounging outside Air Canada's private box at Montréal's baseball stadium during a rain delay. But he knew how to take a punch; he has no glass jaw. "When I was a kid fighting Golden Gloves, I was knocked down on my can, and I got up crying, but I got up and beat up that kid."

In 1980, he came out sounding like his old self in the only place available: the rural seat of Lincoln in southwestern Ontario. "They say I'm greedy, but I gave up $350,000 severance pay with Air Canada to run in fucking Lincoln. Arthur Maloney, the lawyer, said I had a choice: possible severance pay for illegal dismissal from Air Canada, or elected office. And I said, 'No, Arthur, I've got something to prove to the Canadian people, to the politicians. I'm gonna run and win.'" He ran and he won and he told his friends with some confidence that he expected a place in Trudeau's cabinet.

He did not get it.

Within a year, Mackasey – who had been playing the small-chip stock market with some success – trying to provide for his last years – got stung in pursuit of a killing on a Vancouver stock. He had borrowed heavily from the Bank of Montréal. His collateral – surprisingly enough for a shotgun exchange like the one in Vancouver – was his stocks, and only his stocks, held under the control of the bank. In the early 1980s, the market had nosed down. Whereas the paper value of Mackasey's stocks had once been close to $600,000, by 1981 it was only $200,000. Interest charges were running more than twenty percent. As his debt grew, his capacity to cover it declined. Personal bankruptcy was suggested but that was not good for Mackasey and it certainly wasn't good for the bank, which would of course lose everything.

At this point, Mackasey's financial advisor, Robert W. Harrison, the president of the Montréal Board of Trade, offered the bank fresh collateral for Mackasey's $400,000 debt – a Harrison-controlled company known by its registered number, 109609 Canada Ltée. The bank seized this opportunity, turning over Mackasey's stock portfolio to Harrison in return for a note against 109609. The numbered company then went belly-up, sticking the bank with a $400,000 loss. The bank had been stung. Mackasey, having cashed in a retirement savings plan so that he could give $20,000 to the bank, plus another $50,000 borrowed from a friend, was financially wounded – as far as he was concerned – but clear of the huge debt. As *Le Devoir* put it later, "He did not demonstrate particular wisdom, but that's not a crime." Mackasey says now, "I never understood the bloody transaction until it was all over."

The real wounding was to come. He was fingerprinted and hauled into court and charged with trying to wheel and deal his way out of his debts by peddling influence. That was a real wound to his reputation but he was ably defended and found not guilty. However, just as these matters were being aired in the court and in the press, Trudeau – with insensitive timing again – announced that Mackasey was his choice to be the new ambassador to Portugal. His own party president, Iona Campagnolo, sniffed, "I don't approve of Bryce Mackasey." Richard Gwyn in the *Toronto Star* dismissed him as tired out and tiresome and suggested that Trudeau, by associating with the old labour minister, had taken to "shuffling along in the gutter." Mackasey's appointment, he also said, was "an insult to Canadians and . . . to the Portuguese."

Jeffrey Simpson of the *Globe and Mail*, not to be outdone, called Mackasey a public nuisance and a disgrace to the nation. Linking Mackasey and Eugene Whelan, who had been appointed ambassador to the Food and Agricultural Organization in Rome, Simpson said a friendly country had been irritated, Canada's foreign policy had been distorted, our professional diplomats had been kicked in the shins, the politicization of the public service had been furthered, and Canadians had been invited to view the goings-on in Ottawa with greater cynicism.

Stepping into line, Brian Mulroney – playing the wise guy while looking for a little easy familiarity with journalists – laughed off his old friend: "There's no whore like an old whore," he said. "If I'd been in Bryce's position, I'd have been right in there with my nose in the public trough like the rest of them." Of course – and there is no reason why Mulroney, who has since become the Prime Minister, should not be skewered on his own tasteless imagery – because, since taking office, he has led every friendly whore he knows snuffling and snorting to the trough.

Mulroney's scorn, however, and the possible loss of a posting to Portugal were the least of Mackasey's problems. The press was his problem. He was still on trial in the newspapers because, as Harrison's legal troubles ground on through 1984, he kept dragging Mackasey's name back into court.

In the beginning, the Montréal *Gazette*, reporting testimony given *in camera* by Harrison, chose to believe that Mackasey had been paid $400,000 for his stock portfolio, and that such payment could only have been for peddling his political influence. The *Gazette* assured its readers that Mackasey owned 109609 and they said they had a supposedly damning Bank of Montréal statement from 1981 showing the $400,000 deposit to Mackasey's account.

Mackasey took his case to the House of Commons privileges and elections committee, insisting that his reputation had been unfairly damaged by these allegations published in the *Gazette*. The committee suspended deliberations, saying they wanted to wait until Mr. Justice Benjamin Schechter had concluded his preliminary hearing. "During this time, the press crucified me," Mackasey said. "That whole time was hell." In August, 1983, the judge read his report to the courtroom in the Palais de Justice, exonerating Mackasey, dismissing the "flimsy evidence," chiding the Crown for its poor judgment, deriding the bankers involved, and deploring Harrison's manipulations. Of Mackasey he said: "There is not one iota, one shred of evidence in support of the three charges . . . I want to emphasize . . . that my decision to discharge Mackasey was not based purely on technical, narrow and legalistic grounds . . . . To assert that Mackasey received $400,000 from Bruyère, Harrison and 109609 is a preposterous, gross misstatement not supported by the evidence and a distortion of the truth." He described Mackasey's role in the affair as "passive . . . a man who was mauled, beaten and defeated by the exorbitant rates of interest . . . nothing more than a helpless pawn, a puppet, and quite impotent in their [the bank's] dealings with Harrison."

The judge's key point was this: the Bank of Montréal *controlled* Mackasey's portfolio; 109609 Canada Ltée was Harrison's "alter ego" and it "did not possess one cent, let alone $400, 000;" the bank officials, betrayed by their "gullibility in allowing themselves to be tricked" by Harrison, engaged in a transaction that was "merely strokes of the pen, cross entries, signifying nothing . . . no money really changed hands and certainly Mackasey did not walk away with one penny in his pocket."

Mackasey was free of the charge but not of the opprobrium, and awaited the report of the Commons committee, the MPs who were examining whether his situation had been fairly reported in the *Gazette*. The committee concluded that the *Gazette* had damaged Mackasey's reputation but they declined to censure the paper. Certainly, to be totally fair to the *Gazette*, a case could be made for the paper, and it was – by the NDP committee member, who argued that the *Gazette* had only given a fair, accurate, and responsible account of testimony delivered under oath by Robert Harrison.

But the Montréal *Gazette*, with a ludicrous if not shameless reference to "the supreme bludgeon of this committee's unusual powers," thanked God that the press had not been "muzzled." Bryce Mackasey, making the best of a miserable situation, said, "I'll be able to say I walked out of the House an honourable gentleman, which is important to me."

The *Gazette*, however, was not through with him, not through with "the Mackasey Affair." Its syndicated columnist – perhaps the most widely read columnist in the country, Allan Fotheringham – cried "codswallop." "It is hard to judge," he wrote "who was the most hypocritical in this astounding caper: the lily-livered members of Parliament or the unctuous three-piece world of banking." Fotheringham, too often long on the quip and short on depth, went on to ask: "How did Mackasey pay back the $400,000 to the Bank of Montréal . . . ? Harrison gave him a check for $400,000 for his faded stock portfolio . . . the whole thing defies logic. Why would 109609 . . . pay $400,000 for a stock portfolio that was worth less than half that?"

To use Fotheringham's phrase: codswallop. If he – in a column full of innuendo and misinformation – did not know the facts, then the editors of the *Gazette* did. Surely they had read the judge's statement. They published Fotheringham anyway, and when a Montréal radio commentator, Mike Donegan, took them to task, the editors sent him the Bank of Montréal record showing the $400,000 deposited to Mackasey's account, as if they did not know that Judge Schechter had already dismissed that paperwork as "cross entries, signifying nothing." Donegan then told his radio audience, "The *Gazette* has never challenged the *chef de jugement*. It just ignores it, publishing again and again the myth that Harrison purchased from Mackasey a stock portfolio at twice what it was worth."

It remained for *Le Devoir* to say that "doubt is unjustifiable" with regard to Mackasey: "In all fairness to the man and to truth, we have to recognize, without prejudice, that to this day Mr. Bryce Mackasey has been more victim than culprit . . . Judge Schechter, in a formidable decision of 139 pages, has concluded that there was not one iota of proof against Mr. Mackasey, that the latter had taken no illegal advantages, and had not participated in any reprehensible lobbying." Would that the *Gazette* had said as much, for there are still people who believe Mackasey is, if not an outright thief, a sleaze who got rich through shady dealings and special favours.

As we stood on Grosse-Île with our backs to the cross, the sun was just a dribble of light along the treeline on the far shore. It was time to go home, to get home before dark. Going back down the hill, falling forward in the snow, Mackasey said, "I've gone through a depression, and from that down to a disillusionment. I need to be vindicated, but the question is – vindicated against what? I need my honour restored. I haven't lost my inner sense of honour, but I want my reputation returned to me. This is a tragic thing."

The field of graves with the white crosses lay below a ledge, spreading out to Cholera Bay. Mackasey was hurrying, stumbling recklessly and half-sliding on his backside down the slope, as if anxious to get away from the field of the forgotten dead.

Then it was dark. The flurries had turned to heavier snow. We were standing beside the old abandoned fever shed, flakes of white-greenish paint still on the wood, looking in through the marbled old glass panes to a deeper darkness. "What's suddenly wrong with Bryce Mackasey's record," he pleaded, "that makes me a disgrace to go to bloody Portugal? Somebody said, 'This is a disgrace,' a cowardly unsigned editorial in the *Globe*, and because it's said like that, so it becomes a disgrace, but I think my goddamn record as a politician is twenty times Mulroney's."

"The guy who nailed you down was Mulroney."

"All right."

"Mulroney, by not appointing you, agreed with everybody. He laid his blessing hand on your ruined reputation."

"Right."

"And you still won't tell me what he promised you."

"No."

"But it's obvious. Why else would you have turned down the senate and held out for Portugal, if he didn't say you'd still have the job?"

"Yes," he said, with a sudden sadness. "He promised he'd leave me in the job. I think he meant it."

"He lied to you, and you still love the guy?"

"Sure, I don't forget, and I may not forgive, but I love him anyway. We were very close. Even when he said, 'There's no whore like an old whore,' I wasn't worried. I trusted him. You see what he's done to me and what they've done to me is what they don't understand. They've resurrected me, I'm no longer defeated. I've got things to say, they've got to be said; there are things to do; I'm outspoken but I'm not rude. There's no way I'm dead, and that's a fact. That's what they don't understand. I am not rolling over dead."

Saturday Night, 1985

CANADIAN WRY

I live in a perplexing country, a country that is a hotbed of rest. I find it hilarious, an exercise in deadpan slapstick at an undertaker's convention.

The first thing is this: Robertson Davies says, "our condition is stuporous; dully contented and stuporous." But we Canadians are never who we appear to be. Deception, sometimes self-deception, is our genius. We appear to be stuporous, we appear to be boring, but in fact, we're zany and make no sense at all.

I came to understand this several years ago, in the days of Leonid Breshnev, when I was in Leningrad trying to get to know a woman. She was watched by the secret police. I was watched by the secret police. It was grim. It was impossible. So I came home, and at the airport in Toronto, I had an epiphany. There, in front of me, was a Mounted Policeman, all in red and blue and yellow stripes. Like everyone in this world, we have our secret police, but suddenly I thought – what other people would dress up their secret police in scarlet coats, put campfire boy hats on their heads and have them ride around on horses wagging lances at the wind, calling covert action a musical ride? Then I thought, what other country's serious ideologues on the radical left would call themselves the WAFFLE, a word that means a total inability to take a position and hold to it, so that absolutely no one would take them seriously? What other country's serious ideologues on the radical right would form a new group and call it the Canadian Conservative Reform Alliance Party – CCRAP – meaning pure shit – so that no one could take them seriously? Then I looked at the roots of our history. What other country could dissolve into a duality – French and English – after a 19-minute musket skirmish 200 years ago on a ratty field outside Québec City and make both inept generals who got themselves killed into heroes? Such heroism is a deception. In fact, the whole land as it lies on the map is a deception: huge, bigger than the United States, but almost empty because the mass of the few million folk who live in cities strung like a necklace along the 49th parallel, cling to the border by their fingernails, as if the parallel were a window ledge on America, on the world.

So, that world on the other side of the window likes to think we're boring, likes to think we win more bronze medals than anyone else on the face of the earth. But here's the trick. Here's the laugh. We love people to think we're boring. We've raised being boring to a wacky art form. And why? Because it pays off.

Take our most successful prime minister, William Lyon MacKenzie King, our leader through the Second War. King held power longer than any other Western politician in the past century. How did such a pudgy, mundane-looking little man do it? And he was pudgy and parsonish. And little. The truth is, he did it deliberately. He was shrewd and self-effacing, and he told one of his friends in cabinet that the secret to holding power was to make every speech as boring as possible because then no one would ever remember what he had said and hold it against him. Twenty-two years in power, droning on and on over the airwaves, leading us through the war and the only phrase that stuck to him – a slogan thought up to define a domestic crisis – was "Conscription if necessary but not necessarily conscription." Seemingly balanced, nobody knew what it meant, so our soldiers went off to die. King smiled. Meanwhile, he was crazy as a loon.

He talked about economic policies to his dead mother, consulted his dog on matters of state, sought signs from Franklin Delano Roosevelt in his shaving cream in the morning mirror, and in the evening he did missionary work with local street prostitutes, trying to convert them to Christianity, and then – confronting mortality – he built his own little garden temple to himself from the stone remnants of old bank buildings. He was a choice one, *fol dol di die do,* but not so rare; after all, we're the only people anywhere who ever took the radical right-wing Social Credit economics of the poet Ezra Pound so seriously that we've elected several Social Credit governments – and we knew clearly what we were doing. We called them the Funny Money Party because when they went broke they just cranked up the presses and printed more dollars. When we grew tired of them we elected radical socialists, or rather, faux radicals, because they betrayed socialism by imposing wage controls on the very civil servants and teachers who had elected them.

So there we are, WAFFLING like mad one day, full of CCRAP the next, droning on in the middle of the road, telling the world that this is our special gift, a gift for the middle, a gift for compromise, a gift for running while standing still. What can anyone make of our chief droners and men of the middle over the years – moving as we did in Ottawa from a prairie populist prime minister, John Diefenbaker, whose national dream was to "green" the Arctic as the Israelis had greened the desert, to the lisping internationalist, Lester Pearson who – it's true – won the Nobel Peace Prize, but it's a good thing he never had to go to war because on the one day the Red Phone rang in his office, he couldn't find it. He was watching a baseball game and didn't know where the war phone was. He'd hidden it away in a desk drawer. Only to be followed by an expert canoeist, the ascetic and acerbic Pierre Trudeau who, after dating Barbra Streisand and Margot Kidder, took a flower child in tow to the marriage chamber. All seemed to be bliss, there seemed to be a fine monkish air of decorum in Bytown, until his wife showed up bra-less for supper with Fidel Castro, her nipples bare through a sheer blouse, and then she took to dancing at Studio 54 in New York and hung out for a weekend in a Toronto hotel with all the Rolling Stones. To inflict even more pain on the proud Trudeau, we tossed him out of office, making a man called Joe Who our prime minister – a man who'd never in his life had another job

– but then, cruel as we are, we let him keep the job for only nine months. Then we put Trudeau back in office. Before he quit, Trudeau the disciplined intellectual, the man of exquisite taste and manners, had actually given the Western part of the nation the finger, had told French taxi strikers to eat shit, and had told parliamentary back benchers that they were "nobodies" and one of them to fuck off ("fuddle duddle"), yet when he died, the people went into a paroxysm of praise and lament, even in Québec (where else but in Canada could you have a Revolution that was Quiet? Where else but in Canada would a federal government support a *séparatiste* party – the Bloc – whose only policy is to destroy federalism? Where else but in Canada would the leader of such a *séparatiste* party be treated as if he were a Right Honourable member in good standing and not Benedict Arnold?).

As for Québec as a whole . . . well, not even the French from France understand the Québécois, so scrupulously determined to preserve their *pure laine* culture – especially the pure woolliness of it all. They have enacted laws to guard their language, so that inspectors with measuring sticks go from store to store to make sure that the lettering on signs in French is larger than the lettering in English on English signs by at least a centimetre, and when the oh-so-secular Québécois cry *vierge, hostie, ciboire, tabernacle,* they seem to be chanting tidbits from the old catechism. In fact, they are cursing along the lines, in English, of *bugger off, suck this, my sweet ass.* The scatological is hidden inside the sacramental.

Who knows this? Do they want anyone to know? Not necessarily. Who else in the world can walk up to you and, as far as he's concerned, call you a suckhole to your face and smile as you cross yourself, believing you have just been blessed? Clever, we're clever as we cling to the ledge of the world, muttering that we have no identity, that we have no history. Again, so that no one will blame us, or hold us to account for anything, we never tell the Americans that they have tried to invade us twice – and tried through their whiskey merchants and cowboys to steal our

West. But we gunned down their booze merchants and defeated their federal armies. We chased those armies back across the border – and the second time (during the war of 1812) we marched south and burned Washington. To make things look good, like nothing had happened, Washington painted their charred government house white – and we have refused to rub it in – or give ourselves a belligerent history – by telling them that we're responsible for the White House.

Our determination to show a flat billboard face to the world marks our musical culture, too. None but a Canadian rock band – the greatest of all – would have called themselves – with simple, splendid, self-deprecating arrogance – The Band. Not surprisingly, the second greatest, as true Canadians, called themselves The Guess Who. No one but a Canadian would have carried on like Glenn Gould – the silver bullet among interpreters of Bach and Beethoven, a musician who was a great natural showman – seated on a dilapidated chair as if it were the edge of the abyss, wrapped in his scarf as he played with mittens on his hands. He was the toast of the concert halls, but what did he do? Dismissed it all as vaudeville, dismissed public performance as if it were as irrelevant as the appendix, and refused to ever play in public again, a recluse tinkling to no one but machines in closed recording studios, a true Canadian, a powerful presence, a studied absence.

So, what's the advantage of all this dodging, all this disdain for the glitter, let alone the glitz, of stardom? Well, we have – for all our need for law and order (and we have cities like Calgary in which brawling and free-booting businessmen will not cross against a red traffic light even in the emptiness of 3 o'clock in the morning) – a remarkable freedom.

In the United States, upright citizens suffer through a House Un-American Activities Committee because they not only know who they're supposed to be – good homogenized patriotic, hand-over-the-heart Americans – but they insist on it. Such a committee in Canada would be laughable. If anyone ever suggested a Senate Un-Canadian Activities Committee, the nation would fall on its face laughing. We still refuse to agree on what the words to our national anthem are. We don't know who we are and we don't want to. That way we don't have to be anybody's anything. It is a terrific freedom. People can curse us for being wrong, or vulgar, or stupid – but not un-Canadian. In fact, since we don't have to be anybody's anything, we can pretend to be everybody else, and if we make a mistake, *they* take the blame.

Our largest corporations got very rich during the Vietnam War, several have got rich in South Africa and are still getting rich in South and Central America, but when is the last time you saw or heard of an anti-Canadian demonstration in the streets of Santiago? We're so clean we squeak, the sound the sullen mouse makes beside the lumbering elephant. Haw! The Americans are our whipping boys, we blame them for our economic failures and cultural woes – while, if they think about us at all, it's to assure us that we are lucky to be out mingling among them.

And actually, we are: not so much lucky, but among them. We're insidious infiltrators inside their system. Do you know – do they know – that nearly 40 percent of their major television reporters around the world and commentators at home are Canadian? It's true. Every night we tell millions of Americans how to see the world, how to see their wars and their movie stars and heroes and bums, their dreams achieved and broken. And if Americans ever laugh at their own insanity, Canadians control the scripts. On the loneliest night of the American week, the television program *Saturday Night Live* is a joke conceived and produced by Canadians. Think of the Canadian comics – Jim Carrey, John Candy, Dan Akroyd, the SCTV Mackenzie brothers, Mike Meyers, Martin Short . . . the list goes on and on, Canadian laughter at American expense. As for expensive performers, think of the singer Celine Dion – who speaks French, who sings in English, who has become the Queen of Las Vegas with the Cirque du Soleil, the most imaginative circus in the history of the world, as her Court – and who knows or cares that she's Canadian, let alone Québécois? To the world, she's a nobody from nowhere except that she's a star, a celebrity, and if celebrity is now the opium of the people, then she – the perfect Canadian – is a citizen of the world.

As such, this archetypal Canadian – no matter how public – is invisible – he is that no one who is everyone from nowhere, a man like Rich Little . . . the most skilled show-biz impersonator in American history. Having no voice of his own, he has everyone else's – male or female – and he "does" everyone else, as they say, perfectly. Patrons in Las Vegas and the power folk in the White House prefer him to the real thing. In half an hour, when he performs in the intimacy of the White House, they get John Wayne talking to Richard Nixon, Sylvester Stallone talking to Ronnie Reagan, Bill Clinton talking to the Pope.

"Boffo," as they say in *Variety*, the American show-biz bible, because you see you pick up a few tricks while clinging to the ledge of the world. You learn how to amiably draw no public attention to yourself while secretly having your own way. Canadians (those Mounties, never forget those Mounties) could be the world's greatest secret agents. Who knows? A secret agent is secret. But remember our man in Iran during the Carter years, during the Iran hostage crisis, the biggest story in the world – and our ambassador, Ken Taylor, actually freed American hostages and got them out of the country. He explained to a flabbergasted and thankful America – when asked – that to get the Americans out of Iran he had only to "disguise them as Canadians."

Sound and fury behind a bland face.

But it was that global villager, Marshall McLuhan (what a perfect Canadian – the secret conservative adored by a New York advertising world that he abhorred), who came close to the point when he said that English Canada leapt directly from the eighteenth century into the twentieth century, skipping the romantic assertion of self so central to the nineteenth century, while Québec – as counterculture to the nation – lives in the self-aggrandizing nineteenth century as if that century were an *arrondissement,* dreaming of an independent national orbit, knowing such a state can never be. It's hilarious in its contradiction. Deadpan. Slapstick. We stand astride life as if it were a see-saw, balancing, waiting.

The prime minister, Wilfrid Laurier, who forecast that "The twentieth century shall be the century of Canada," was wonderfully Canadian in that he was right when he was wrong – and absolutely so. That is, he was right if Samuel Beckett touched any chord in the contemporary heart, and we know that he did. Being two cultures in one country, both waiting for the century to be ours, we are like Beckett's two tramps by the side of the road, watching in amazement as the Pozzos and Luckys of this world pass through our lives, and we wait. Bland-faced, we wait, and wait, and shrug and make self-deprecating jokes and sly probes – as McLuhan would have it. The probative Trudeau's most characteristic gesture, after completing a comic pirouette behind an august person like the Queen, was a shrug. You can't get any more contemporary – any more tragically comic – than that shrug, a shrug we take into the fire.

The defining saint in our history is the Jesuit, Jean de Brébeuf – who shrugged as he was tortured and burned to a crisp at the stake. His skull, saved from the ashes, is now an object of worship – but worshipped in a way that accommodates our divided, duplicitous Canadian mind. There are two Brébeuf skulls on display – one Brébeuf skull (right half *bone,* left half *wax*) in Québec, and another Brébeuf skull (left half *bone,* right half *wax*) in Ontario. Who's to know?

As for secret laughter, one of the Anglo-Saxon world's favourite humorists is our Stephen Leacock, master of the comic light touch, with a tinge of blackness around the edges, a little like a requiem mass card. Our own secret agent of small-town laughter. But almost no one in Canada – or anywhere else – knows how he went to his grave. It was, you see, the tradition in his family to be buried in a plain, good old Canadian pine box, but he'd bought a huge oak and brass-handled job. Heavy,

heavy, heavy, and burly men carried it to the hole not knowing – no one knew – that he'd had himself cremated. They sweated and heaved under the weight but inside, having the last laugh, Leacock was only ashes in a little glass bottle cradled on a satin puff. It is the final comfort we crave, ashes on a satin puff, watched over by a scarlet man, waiting, who may be the police.

Punch, 1985-2004

OF WINTER
AND OF LOVE

We endure the winter, but not in discontent. We are sometimes sluggish in the heavy heat of summer and we are too at ease with autumn, *mais, c'est la fin, c'est la fenaison,* the leap of the heart is always there. Sometimes, snow-blind, we forget that frozen apples on the bough are bells, but by and large we see how it is with clarity, because the light here casts sharp shadows. We live in *film noir* country and take on death directly, with delicacy and mordant laughter, as all great lovers do:

> *With Annie gone,*
> *Whose eyes to compare*
> *With the morning sun?*
>
> *Not that I did compare,*
> *But I do compare*
> *Now that she's gone.*
> —Leonard Cohen

We don't survive. We endure. Survival is a small idea, contrary to any notion of love. We are lovers whether we like it or not: ironic, with one foot in the grave, incubating in the gloom, and whimsical:

> *I should have begun with your toes*
> *with maybe just the little one*
> *so clean and succulent*

so tiny
it's no toe at all
but a spare nipple
    —Earle Birney

believing God loves us like catfish love the cut-glass glory of clear water, loves us with His own sardonic eye:

> *. . . loves us like earthworms love wood*
> *long after the body is dead.*
>   —Allan Safarik

  There is nothing sadder than those who say God is dead, God being our creation of our best sense of ourselves, forgotten and then discovered, giving us the Word, telling stories of hate turned to love or love turned to hate. Crucified and reborn into the cold in our sacks of flesh, we pursue the sacred and risk the mystical as lover follows lover "up the long stairway" to

> *where your body lies*
> *beside me, and you enter*
> *it as easily as breathing in*
> *I would like to be the air*
> *that inhabits you for a moment*
> *only. I would like to be that unnoticed*
> *& that necessary.*
>   —Margaret Atwood

  Of course, whether we are mystical, stealing music from the moon, or warthogs thrusting through darkness in search of the muse, we keep a poker face. We cultivate that poker face, that wry dry tone of the self-effacing snake – the accountant or the amiable after-dinner speaker – because we know from experience that "the nicest girls marry snakes." So, too, we cultivate a tone that masks our laughter, a laughter at love poetry itself:

The man who wrote 'twin alabaster mounds'
should have spent more time outdoors
instead of browsing in that musty old museum where
he pissed away his youth.
—Don McKay

In our outdoor moments, as we piss into the wind, we indulge in a verbal debauchery:

O Lunéthophyte
je ne penche et te cramuille
Ortie déplépojdèthe
Et dans le desert des marquemacons tes seins
obérent le silence.
—Claude Gauvreau

[*Oh Lunatophina*
i bend down and cramble you
Deplepodated sting-nettle
I agributt your rusplette
And in the desert of markmasons your breasts burden
the silence.]
—tr. Ray Ellenwood

With our roots secure in that silence we reach for celebration, for the "applaudisements and bravos bombinating along the Boulevard," or for things that go "BOING" in the nights, and we are never dull because we "know it ain't no sin to take off your skin and dance around in your bones." We shake those bones and rattle words at each other in two languages, Siamese twins pretending the other is not there – a "presence" that is always "absent." We have the blessing of double vision – the expected apocalypse, and the exuberance of *la marche à l'amour* as felt by two lov(h)ers bending into the echo of their own laughter across a lake fresh with snow:

. . . long temps longer nos corps encore à deux, à la faveur de la nuit. Folles et incompatibles comme deux hétérosexuelles avortées et qui ne peuvent se pénétrer mutuellement. La cicatrice doit cicatriser. Je mets ma bouceh avec ton sexe. Salive intérieure. Manger et penser à notre fin.

—Nicole Brossard

[. . . a long time lo(u)nging our bodies two-gether to pass under cover of night. Mad and incompatible like two aborted heterosexuals who cannot penetrate each other. The scar must form. I put my mouth with your sex. Inner saliva. Eat and think as though there were no end.]

—tr. Barbara Godard

Of course, there is an end, more final than *les petites morts,* there has to be, but indomitable – as we endure the winter, we do not do so in discontent – no, because we insist while we make love in *noir* country that

> *it is never over; nothing ends*
> *until we want it to.*
> *Look, in shattered midnights,*
> *on black ice under silver trees,*
> *we are still dancing, dancing.*

—Gwendolyn MacEwen

Lords of Winter and of Love, 1983-1990

A MOTIVELESS
MALIGNANCY

I was going in August to Saratoga for the horseracing season. I had packed my working manuscript of new poems, and my tinted prescription glasses so that I could read the *Racing Form* in the hot mountain sun. Claire had packed steel tools and oblong dark bars of beeswax so she could work for a fall exhibition of her sculpture in Toronto. I went out the back door, through our small wisteria-covered courtyard (we live in a lean 1880s refurbished house in Chinatown), and decided to move the car forward in the garage, toward the lane. I liked our car, the way it held the road. I turned the key and the Audi 5000 shot backward, taking out the whole stuccoed wall, dumping concrete blocks and broken cement into the garden. I stared through the rear-view mirror into an emptiness, wondering where everything had gone, and heard the whisper of malevolence and affliction on the air but did not heed it.

The car was fixed and we drove to Saratoga, where we stayed in the house of an old friend, a retired dancer who had been with Balanchine. He has a house of many rooms and gardens and a broad veranda. Not long after, my father came down and sat on the veranda, finishing his new novel, *A Wild Old Man on the Road*. We were doing well at the track, and then one morning the phone rang and it was Claire. She had driven downtown along the tree-shaded side streets; there had been an accident.

When I got to the intersection I found our Audi had been T-boned by an elderly, absent-minded man from California who was driving a Budget car; he had gone blithely through a red light, driving our car up over a sidewalk and onto a lawn; smashed to a dead halt against a steel fence, Claire had stepped from the car unscathed but stricken; the car's frame was bent and twisted and it was towed to a scrapyard where it was cannibalized and then reduced to a cube of crushed steel. The whisper of malevolence and affliction was on the air. I did not heed it.

Back home in Toronto I was sardonically amused by the gut-ted hole in my garden wall (nothing is what it's supposed to be: why shouldn't a car shoot backward when it's supposed to be standing still?), and we went on with life in our house and ordered a new Audi.

The house has always been open to writers who tend to drop in of a morning for coffee (and a little cognac in their coffee); sometimes I make pasta or a tourtière for two or three editors; and since Claire is a splendid cook, we have small suppers for poets from abroad, and we throw house parties, inviting forty or fifty people. It has been a friendly house, the walls hung with colour – paintings, drawings, tapestries – all our travels and some turbulence framed, but one afternoon the front door suddenly opened and a young man walked boldly in, his eyes bleary, his shirt torn. He stared sullenly at me, spun around and walked out without a word.

I felt a twinge, a warning.

As a punter or poet, you learn to feel for signs.

But I was busy. After Thanksgiving, I was to give readings in Rome, Zagreb and Belgrade, and then go on to Moscow, Riga, Leningrad, and stay for a month as writer-in-residence in Bo-logna before coming home in late November for Claire's exhi-bition. We decided to celebrate Thanksgiving at the family farm near Mount Forest, with our sons and Morley.

As we parked my Audi in the lane (Claire's car was in the garage), I looked back through the broken wall, the jagged hole. There had not been time to fix it. I felt a sudden vulnerability, as if in the midst of my well-being, I'd forgotten to protect myself.

I checked the locks on the doors. An old, fat Chinese woman stood in the lane watching me with a blank impassivity that made me feel strangely resentful. I knew she couldn't care what happened to me. I'd never seen her before, but she looked as if she and not I belonged there in the lane.

⊙⊙

Our farmhouse is on a hill surrounded by woods. The trees were red and gold. There were geese on the pond. We ate supper in a room that has old church stained-glass windows, under a candelabra that burns sixteen candles. For some reason, Morley and the boys talked about violence, whether it was gratuitous, or in the genes, or acquired, and whether there actually was something called malevolence, evil. Morley smoked his pipe, and we went to bed.

In the morning, the phone rang. It was my neighbour, the painter Charlie Pachter. He sounded incoherent, as if he were weeping. "Come home," he said. "Come home, something terrible . . . the house, it's been broken into . . . come home." I phoned my house. A policeman answered. "Yes," he said. "You should come home, and be prepared. There has been a fire. This is bad."

As we pulled into the lane behind our house (after two tight-lipped hours on the road), I felt a terrible ache in my throat: there, alone and in pairs and slumped in sadness, were several of our friends . . . . What are they doing there? How did they know? They came closer and then shied away, the way animals shy from the dead. The police were surprised. They were expecting Claire's red car (it was gone), and didn't know who we were, but then a detective, Sgt. Hamel, took me aside: "You should get ready before you go in . . . . I don't know if your wife should go in, it's the worst we've ever seen." He looked through the gaping hole in the garage wall. "She's not my wife," I said. "We've lived together for twenty years."

"Do you have any enemies?"

"I don't know."

"It looks like it."

"Why?"

"Because it looks like somebody's tried to hurt you."

"Really?"

"We'll have to go around to the front of the house to get in. They never did break the lock on the back door."

"I've got a key," I said.

"Oh, right, sure," he said, and another policeman tried to lead Claire away, but she broke free: "No one's keeping me out of my own home." In the kitchen, a long black-handled carving knife had been stuck into the wall; two fires had been set, one on the floor, the other on the gas stove, and the house had the sour reek of smoke; papers and broken glass and crockery covered the tiles, the television set was gone. In the dining room, the armoire door hung open, armloads of old family crystal and china had been swept out onto the floor . . . but I saw that a portrait of me by William Kurelek had not been touched, and I said warmly, "They're not after me, otherwise they would have slashed that."

"Don't be so sure. It doesn't look like you," a policeman said.

"The red car's been stolen," another policeman said. "It's just been reported in a hit-and-run accident."

We went into the living room with its high ceilings: the black sofa was hacked to pieces; an engraving by my old friend William Hayter in Paris was smashed off the wall and scorched; a tapestry I'd brought from Cairo, through the Black September War in 1970 when I was a correspondent, was cut open down the centre; the floor was littered with boxes, broken crockery, papers, broken frames, torn cloth, broken records and cassettes, a Chinese vase and ripped books, the curtains in the bay window had been set afire, blackened lace; in the vestibule, a turquoise funerary piece that had been in the pharaoh's tomb at the time of Moses lay broken and, beside it, a Phoenician bronze bull crushed under a heel, or at least there were worn black shoes beside the bull, and I realized my leather boots were gone.

"The son of a bitch," I said, laughing grimly. "He's not only smashed my house but he's gone off in my boots and he's left me his lousy Goodwill shoes."

"This is terrible," Claire said. We did not go near the grand piano. A fire had been set under it. I could see the charred veneer.

"It's worse upstairs," a policeman said.

"Well, lead on, Macduff," I said. He looked at me quizzically.

He was right: they'd torched a vase of silk flowers on the landing; my Philips word processor was stolen (a literary prize I'd never learned to use, didn't want to use, and was secretly glad to see gone); my library was overturned (they'd tried to set a fire using two books: *Child of the Holocaust,* by Claire's cousin Jack Kuper, and a *Dreambook for Our Time,* by the Polish novelist Tadeusz Konwicki); in the bedroom, they'd thrown a chair through one of Claire's drawings, *Earth Mother,* Chinese porcelain figures were smashed; and they had ransacked the bureau drawers for . . . all the gold . . . rings, charms, bracelets . . . all to be fenced and melted down by scumbag uptown swine who feed off junkie break-and-enter kids . . . melting down all our bindings of love . . .

The third floor was blackened: dozens of Claire's frames and drawings smashed; an enormous painting by her friend Robert Hedrick – a homage to John Kennedy on his death – slashed; the sofa bed burned; plaster casts carved open or broken; and the floor covered by a sludge of burned and scorched and then doused papers . . . they'd started a fire in an armoire . . . it had burned through the roof of the house, the heat blowing out the windows . . . and all those papers, so assiduously kept: letters, manuscripts, transcripts . . . twenty-five years of intimacies, words chosen with care, exactitude . . . .

"We were here three minutes after the alarm," the fire chief said. "When we got here the whole house was full of black smoke . . . luckily, the front door was open, luckily a woman across the road saw the smoke coming through the roof . . . ."

A policeman waited at the bottom of the stairs. "Your father's Morley Callaghan?" he asked.

"Yes."

"He had that boxing match with Hemingway."

"Yes."

I got a book from the library and gave him a copy of *That Summer in Paris.*

"That'll tell you all about it," I said.

"Thanks," he said, lifted his cap, wedged the paperback into the crown, and put the cap back on his head.

"Who would want to hurt you?" Sgt. Hamel asked again.

"I don't know. All I know is the Dom Pérignon is gone."

Claire came into the room. There were tears in her eyes. She does not cry easily. "It's the piano," she said. The piano had been given to her by her father before he died of cancer, a cancer contracted during the First World War, when he'd enlisted too young, lied about his age, been gassed at Ypres and buried alive. It is a 1912 Mason & Risch, a rich mahogany grand with a beautiful fiddleback grain and carved legs.

A fire had been set under it, burning into the hardwood floor, climbing up an antique silk shawl draped from the lid. When the lid was lifted, the piano was a burned out, warped, gutted box.

"It's gone forever," she said.

"No, it's not," I said.

A whalebone shaman, a drummer figure by Ashevak – the finest of the Inuit carvers – was standing on the piano, the drum broken, the beater scorched black.

"Don't you feel violated?" a woman, a friend who'd come in from the lane, asked. "Don't you feel raped?"

"No," I said.

"You don't?" she said.

"No, and as a woman you should know better. This is a house. No one has entered my body, no one has penetrated me. This isn't rape . . . ."

"Yes, but . . ." She was offended, as if I had been unnecessarily difficult, when all she intended was sympathy. I was being difficult, because I believe – especially in times of trouble – that exactness is how we make a last stand in the ditch against sentimentality, self-pity, falseness.

"But the rage," she said. "Someone attacked your place in a state of rage."

"It looks that way."

"How do you account for such rage?"

"I don't know."

"Any ideas?"

"Motiveless malignancy," I said. An officer took me by the arm. He was smiling, a tight little angry smile. "We've got one of them," he said.

"You have!"

Police, driving down a lane behind the El Mocambo tavern, had seen a shabbily dressed man clutching two bottles of Dom Pérignon. "We knew something was wrong," they said. They handcuffed him in their cruiser. Strung out on drugs, he said he'd show them the house he had broken into that morning, and now he was in the backseat of the cruiser in the lane.

"I don't know whether I want to see him," I said.

"Oh, you can't see him."

"Why not?"

"I don't want an assault-and-battery charge on my hands, too."

But I did not want to beat anyone. I felt only the torpor that comes with keeping an incredulous calm in the face of brutality. Rage, imprecations, threats, were beside the point. In fact, having seen what skilled and sanctioned thugs can do to a house – in Belfast, Jerusalem, Beirut – I felt curiously thankful that so much had survived. . . . But people, and certainly some policemen, have their expectations: I learned later that for a while I was a suspect . . . . I was too cool, too detached; I had to be in on it, a policeman had told Sgt. Hamel, who tried to explain to him: "No, no. He's a writer. Writers stand back and look at things."

The suspect was named Lugosi ("a cousin of Bela Lugosi," a detective insisted), "of no fixed address." He'd fought in the cruiser, kicking out the rear window, punching, biting and spitting. He fought with them at the station. He seemed driven by rage. The officers went to the hospital for shots for hepatitis.

Sgt. Hamel, a quick, yet reflective man – who does not, like most cops, look at you as if you must have a criminal secret – opened the trunk of his cruiser. "They set seven fires," he said. "It *is* the worst we've seen." He reached into a bag and took out several small bronzes . . . more funeral ornaments from a pharaoh's tomb; a grotesque Phoenician clown's head, an alabaster fertility monkey from a scent dish . . . .

"These yours?"

"Yes."

"It's terrible, things like this being broken."

"Yes. Lasting this long, smashed on Sullivan Street."

"I want you to think about your enemies."

"I'm not sure I have any."

"You've written a lot."

I did not think about it, not that night or the next morning, when we woke in the Hotel Admiral, on the waterfront. "We've got to go where there's water," I'd told Claire, and in the morning, with the dawn flaring red across the water as we sat up, we were suddenly full of the light on the water. "I had an old philosophy professor," I said, "and he talked with his eyes closed, and when he forgot where he was going he'd open his eyes and say, 'Well, we'll lick the lips and start afresh.'"

We went back to the house. Standing alone in the sooty squalor of the rooms, I knew I had lost things that connected me to the past, but they would be nothing compared to the loss of the future. I wanted to sit at the piano, as I had on other morose days, and play in a minor key, on the black notes, singing, "*If*

Beale Street could talk, married men would take their beds and walk . . ." but it was charred, and then the expert piano restorer, Rob Lowrey, came into the house, shook hands, and then shook his head as he lifted the lid. "Burned to a crisp. It'll cost more to fix it than it's worth, it'll cost $30,000 if we can do anything, and we can't."

I talked, he listened; he hung his head and then opened his hands.

"The insurance people will never pay for it," he said.

"I don't care," I said. "We'll work out something."

His men carried the piano out of the house. Lowrey said, "If we come back, it'll be in a year, and if we come back at all, it'll be a miracle."

"You bring the loaves, honey," I said to Claire, as I closed the door, "and I'll bring the fishes."

We lived in the hotel for over two months. It is small and elegant, charmingly run by young women, and one wall of our room was glass facing over the water. Every day we came back to the room after sifting through rubble and refuse in the house, and we sat and stared as the sun leaked out of the autumn sky; and then we dressed for supper . . . a determined elegance of spirit, a determined refusal to yield to the lethargy of dismay, regret or self-pity, or blame (all questions asked by the police or insurance adjusters or oneself – even the simple question, Why? – contain a hint of blame, of accusation . . . it was even suggested by a friend that we had asked for it: our house had been too open . . . and another friend wondered whether we wouldn't at last learn that expansiveness was a vanity that was always punished), but we did not blame ourselves. We ate and watched the island airport lights on the dark water. There was a pianist in the lobby, out of sight, the ghost of our piano playing, our piano being rebuilt, and ironically, before our house could be rebuilt, it had to become the ghost of itself.

Walls were washed down, the quarry tile floors stripped, the broadloom ripped out, the hardwood floors sanded . . . as if a deep stain had to be eradicated, as if cleansing had to be done (and all the while, we went through the dreary listing of each broken or missing thing . . . each thing the ghost of a moment from the past – like counting little razor cuts on the skin though the wound is deep in the bones). Papers had been hosed down by the firemen and letters turned to sodden ash in my hands; rolled drawings were scorched funnels that fell apart . . . a fingertip, a lip . . . all stacked in a hundred boxes piled in the basement . . . two lives, boxed and stacked, in stasis, and then, shortly after the police told us they had arrested a second man named Costa, in a gesture of dumb normalcy we put a new television set in the kitchen, a dead grey eye but a promise of sound . . . .

Then, on a crisp December morning we ate breakfast and watched the long, lean harbour police boat leave on patrol. The lake was icing over but there were still geese on open patches of water. We went to the house and discovered the back door open, the television set gone, some jewellery and a fox fur jacket gone. We had been robbed again (when a house has been hit, the word goes out on the street: they know television sets will be replaced, and an empty house is a sitting duck). So we were being watched, we were a word on the street, the word a whisper of affliction on the air again.

A policeman came by to dust for fingerprints. He was wearing a narrow-brimmed hat, a suit with narrow lapels. He was lean and close-mouthed, gruff and meticulous. Yes ma'am, no. Dust and fingerprints. For a moment I thought I was losing my mind, except I couldn't stop laughing quietly, and I mumbled to Claire, "Go ask Jack Webb if he thinks we'll ever catch these guys."

"No," he said. "Not likely."

This affliction and folly was going to go on, I could see, for a long time. I went down to the water and sat by the hotel window, watching single-engine planes take off from the island airport. I worked on *Hogg* poems:

Grace

The light
inside
a
stone
is
like a dream
refusing
to be
revealed
or
the voice
of
God
concealed
in
the heart.

As I drove around the city, a rankling awareness grew in me. This tawdry, soft mockery of our life was going to last at least a year: we would, of course, outlast it because we could still laugh (grim men fear laughter because laughter dispels fear), but I was suddenly alive to all signs and signals of affliction: at Dundas and University, I saw through the car window the memorial monument to the poor dead airmen of the Second World War. I was suddenly enraged. I heard myself hissing: Hal Jackman . . . the monument so contrary in every aesthetic sense to the lives and deaths it presumed to honour, to celebrate – a monumental exercise in banality stuck in the city's eye. I could rebuild my house, and someday – if Rob Lowrey could work his miracle – I would play our piano, but I was going to have to look at this cretinous piece (which the kids call *Gumby Goes to Heaven*) for as long as I lived in the city. It was a permanent offence, a tin-

soldiering view of life and death. What galled me was that Jack-
man, who would never understand my weary sorrow, and cer-
tainly not my pity for those two addicts sitting in jail, had been
able to have his sentimental ignorant way on our city streets
just because he was rich . . . a monument had been put up in
violation of city laws, a monument that by its very existence
breaks the law, but nobody cares.

Just before Christmas, on a cold, clear day, we drove over to the
old City Hall for the preliminary hearing. I had not thought
much about the two men doing dead time in the Toronto Jail
(my own contacts on the street had told me that six men had
been in the house, that six men had been in Claire's stolen car).
I wondered about their faces and pondered the old questions:
was this a hired hit? And, if so, who hated me so much? And if
drug money were the motive for the break-in, was the raging
destruction of the contents a malignancy without motive?

We sat in an overheated room with the fire chief, detectives
and officers, a woman who said she was Lugosi's girlfriend, a Viet-
namese bricklayer who had come face-to-face with Costa as he
hauled suitcases full of our things out the front door, the woman
who had seen the smoke, a stout woman who was the desk
clerk at the Waverley Hotel on Spadina Avenue . . . .

As we went up the marble stairs to sit and wait outside a
courtroom, a courtroom next to the marriage bureau, I was told
several things by several people: that when they were looking for
Costa, two officers cornered a man in a cappuccino bar on Col-
lege Street and the man flattened them both, driving one into the
street through a plate-glass window . . . the cops felt sheepish
about that, they said; also, Lugosi had checked into the Waverley
Hotel before breaking into the house and he had checked in
under my name; the house had been cased by a man, a mulatto,
named Bo . . . and Bo had probably been in the house at least

once before it was hit; Bo worked for any "interests" who would hire him; Lugosi had come back into the hotel after leaving the house waving a blowtorch, threatening to set fire to the hotel "just like he had torched a house" on Sullivan Street; several men were waiting in a blue car at the hotel and they got into Claire's car without Lugosi and drove off; Costa had made several trips to the fence during the night using Claire's car; Lugosi's old girl-friend, saying he had done her harm, not only wanted to testify to that harm but also said she could explain why he had savaged our house; it was all, she said, because of an incident in August when I was taking the ferry to the island and Lugosi, who worked with a punk rock band, had spoken to me and I had snubbed him: "He said he would get Callaghan for that." The only problem was I hadn't been on the ferry to the island for four years and in August I had been in Stockholm and then in Saratoga.

Why this determined fantasy? Were any of the little stories told to me true? Did it matter? Weren't all these people suddenly onstage for a moment? Wasn't this their time, not ours?

As the afternoon passed, as we waited to be called into the courtroom to at last look into the faces of the two men, to say to them and to the court what we had been through, what we had lost inside ourselves, what music had been stilled, we listened dryly to the sullying confidences of the street while very young couples – most of them black and surprisingly alone, without friends or family – strutted by, beaming, untarnished and newly wed. Then, after all the witnesses had been heard in the closed courtroom and the afternoon had waned, we sat alone on the bench, uncalled in silence, the doors opened and Sgt. Hamel, looking pleased as a newlywed, explained that everything had worked out, we were unnecessary. "They're being sent to trial." Lugosi was led to the elevator, slender, head bowed, penitential; Costa, less shrewd, smirked with bravado and stared brazenly at Claire. The elevator doors closed, so, with nothing left to do, we went Christmas shopping, and then on Christmas Eve, after the sanded hardwood floors had been stained, we stood at midnight in the vestibule, pleased with the wet, dark sheen. "It'll go beautifully with the piano," Claire said.

On Christmas Day, though there was no furniture in the house, we moved out of the hotel. Two old Chinese women stood in the lane watching me unload books and papers and clothes. They said nothing. I realized that in four years of living in Chinatown not one Chinese neighbour had ever spoken to me, not even the people who run the corner store, who sell me cream and paper towels. We had handed change back and forth, but I didn't even know if they could speak English. I was angry at Lugosi and Costa but loathed a political culture that encouraged people to close in on themselves like that.

Separate trials took place in February. The Crown attorney, a pert young woman, was eager. She had a solid case – break-and-enter, theft and arson, fingerprints and a witness. She thought she could get a substantial sentence. A plea bargain was struck: Lugosi would not contest his guilt if I would agree to five years. Yes, I said, I suppose five years will do. (But what did five years mean? – this curious attachment of penitential time to a crime . . . not the inflicting of corporal pain, but the religious notion of "serving time" in a monkish cell; and I recalled the idiotic notions of my childhood catechism and the confessional – two years off purgatory for going without candy for a week; four years off for . . . five years off for . . .). We sat in an almost empty courtroom. A couple of men I'd seen around the Waverley Hotel sat beside me, and a lone woman, and a detective. Lugosi sat in the box, head down. I looked at him for a while and felt little or nothing: no witnesses were called before Judge David Humphrey. Police photographs of our house were entered as evidence of willful havoc and the seven fires.

At the court's request, I had written a note about what it was like being a victim. It was for the judge to read. Time, I told him, was our punishment, too. Guilty of nothing, we were being punished. Time was the real bond between criminals and victims. "Having survived three months' dislocation we realize how disruptive the devastation has been . . . the endless sorting through drawings, papers – charred, destroyed, these are the tissues of our life, our spirit. We have been robbed of time, it is a robbery that goes on and on . . . . Creative time, insights – those fleeting moments of inspiration – they are gone forever . . . . The dispiriting loss of time – and we cannot help each other – for Claire, as an artist, has suffered exactly the same loss as I have. We are doing time, and we get no time off for good behaviour. The terrible irony is that these two men may well do less time than we will. For us, the loss of time spirals . . . each week implies a month of lost writing, sculpting . . . every two months a half-year, a half-year two years, a year will become five. Together, we may do more dead time than they will. There is the real crime committed against us . . . ." The judge expressed his stern dismay; we said nothing; Lugosi said nothing. He was sentenced to five years.

A few weeks later, Costa was tried. His defence was hapless: he said that all the damage had been done by Lugosi after he'd left the house for the last time at 9 o'clock in the morning. The fire alarm had been turned in at 9:03. That meant Lugosi had savaged the house and set seven fires on three floors in under three minutes. The judge shook his head, embarrassed by the ineptness of the argument. Costa was a young immigrant man, a drug addict, his life ruined, on his way to the brutality of prison. I wanted to say something but there was nothing to say. He was sentenced to two years in penitentiary.

"At last," Claire said, "I feel safe." She stopped thinking about them at night. But we took no pleasure in the sentencing. It had to be; the arson demanded it, the police – for their own morale – needed it; as victims we were witness to it; but we took no pleasure. Vengeance, like jealousy, is a second-rate emotion, which is why I have always found the old Jewish tribal stories of an "eye for an eye, tooth for a tooth" – charged with self-congratulatory moral delight – so twisted.

I am no pacifist, but vengeance gives me no pleasure, no satisfaction.

We felt only a hollow in the house, and the need to fill it with laughter, meditation and music. But every morning, all day, there was only repairing, hammering.

Drilling.

Waiting for workmen to show up.

Waiting. Life as repair.

Nothing on time, time meant nothing, till in the summer we went to Rob Lowrey's to see the piano: it had become, in our imaginations, more than scorched fiddleback veneer and charred legs; after opening the lid on its inner parts, so scarred and warped and twisted by fire and supposedly beyond repair – it had become the embodiment of our own renewal. Mahogany can be turned and trimmed, as we had turned ourselves out for dinner every night at the hotel, but only we knew the ashes, the soot we could still taste on our breaths. So the piano had to be cleansed and brought back to life. The stillness that lies between the struck key and the string, the stillness that contains the note, had to sound.

Rob Lowrey, who had said in dismay that restoration would require a redeeming miracle, greeted us with a subdued eagerness, a caution that comes from dealing with damage. But he had a solid, rounded playfulness as he moved quickly and soundlessly into the aroma of varnish and glue in his workroom, standing in his white apron, obviously relishing his young workers' bashful way of laying their hands on wood. There were men at several pianos, each striking a note, listening, head half-cocked, then malletting a tuning peg into a pin plank, threading thin wire through the peg . . . slowly tightening, tuning the treble and then the heavier bass strings . . . twenty-four tonnes of tension in those strings, all our anxiety struggling toward the inner harmony that is always the mystery of the piano . . . the piano in tune with itself.

I stood staring into the hollow guts of our piano as if I were looking back into the months that had passed, the veneer peeled down to the glue-stained frame and new wood held by vises, the bridges and ribs, the pin planks all laid out . . . and Lowrey, smiling, said: "September. We've had to send the legs to Cleveland. No one here can carve those old legs . . . ."

"September?"

"Don't worry," he said. "It'll play like a charm."

"I'll have a party, then, open up the house."

"Why not?"

We felt safe: the lane and the garden were floodlit at night, the garage door could be opened only from inside, the garage wall was rebuilt, all the glass doors had jam-bars, the rooms had all been wired to an alarm system of motion detectors, and we were three: we had a young, powerful golden retriever who chewed our shoes as we retrieved our losses. We had been fortunate to have a good man – fair and accomplished – as our insurance adjuster: John Morris. His efficient cheerfulness puzzled me: more than a priest, it seemed to me, disasters rolled across his desk . . . an endless array of mishaps and malevolence that he adjusted. In his middle years, he had heard every story and dealt with every scam, yet, for all his rigour, he had been fair and sympathetic, and the insurance company had accepted all his recommendations. We would never recover our losses, but the company was going to honour their obligations without argument.

But as we prepared to drive again to Saratoga, to renew the ritual, the hammer fell. Our insurance company, Trafalgar, announced it would not renew our coverage. They were shedding us, leaving us completely vulnerable. So be it, I thought. Our agent tried to make arrangements with other companies. To her astonishment, to my rage and sudden fear, no one would insure us. Not Trafalgar, not Wellington, not Guardian, not Laurentian, not any company approached. At the same time, the mortgage company wrote asking for confirmation of fire insurance, a condition of the mortgage. Without insurance the mortgage would be called. We would be broken by debt, driven out of the house. "Because," I was told, "you're high profile, you're a controversial journalist." This was worse than any street thuggery.

Even our insurance adjuster, unbelieving, tried to get us insurance with his contacts: the answer was no. There was nothing to be done. Though I had paid house insurance into the industry for twenty-five years, as soon as I was hit – as soon as what I was insured against happened – those companies all closed down on me. These men weren't junkies, strung out and hooked on crack; no, these were the close cousins to the auto insurer for Budget Rent-a-Car in the U.S., Zurich – which still, a year later, owes us $1,200, and refuses to pay . . . bigger thieves than any dipso break-and-enter kid: these were men who intended to leave us twisting in the wind defenceless. I knew where I was. I was in the land of Erewhon, Samuel Butler's *Erewhon*, where "ill-luck of any kind, or even ill-treatment at the hands of others, is considered an offence against society, inasmuch as it makes people uncomfortable to hear of it. Loss of fortune, therefore, is punished hardly less severely than physical delinquency." We had committed an offence by becoming victims. The insurers – and who sits more at the centre of our society than insurers? – were going to punish us more than any druggies had ever dreamed of . . . the motives behind this malignancy were clear. "The insurance companies are protecting themselves," a woman said with disarming openness. "If you weren't who you are, there'd be no problem."

"If I wasn't who I am," I said to myself, standing one afternoon in front of Gumby, "I'd blow you up."

Then, after talking to a sensible, experienced woman in the insurance business – who reminded me of the way good bank managers used to be: unafraid of their own judgment – the problem was solved.

"No, I am not a public personality," I agreed, as she winked at me. "I write here and there and do a little television, but I am a professor. I have been a professor for twenty-two years."

The house was insured by Chubb.

❦

On a September Saturday afternoon, two men levered the leg-less and lidless body of our piano onto a sling and lowered it out of a truck onto a trolley and rolled the trolley into the house. They malletted the pins that hold the legs and set the piano in the bay window, all the light catching the grain, so that Rob Lowrey's brother, John, could tune the strings, and then in the early evening, Al Cromwell and Doug Richardson – friends for more than thirty years from the days when I used to go to the black dance halls – came in. Al is a guitarist. Doug plays flute and saxophone, and they had two pianists with them, Connie Maynard and Carlton Vaughan. "You get to christen the keys," I said, as Connie sat down and worked through several songs, and then stood up, beaming: "Very nice. Beautiful sound. Quiet touch."

"Quiet, I like quiet," Doug, who has an impish wit, said. "I hate noise, noisy cars most of all. Expensive cars are noisy. Who'd want a Ferrari? How could you ever hold up a bank in a Fer-rari?"

The house began to fill with friends carrying flowers and wine, crowding into conversation in all the rooms, friends who were writers and newshounds and gamblers, editors and the two carpenters who had meticulously trimmed the house, pro-fessors and maître d's and film producers, and after Claire said, "This'll be strange, being hosts at our own resurrection," I drifted happily from room to room pouring wine, all the slashes on the walls healed, hearing – I was sure – each note as it was un-locked from the stillness between struck key and string. Before reading one or two of my poems, which had just been published, I introduced Sgt. Hamel. Doug, playful as ever, stopped honking on his sax and spread-eagled himself against the wall. Everyone laughed, and curiously for me, it was a bonding laughter, an acknowledgement that there is a little larceny in all of us, and in a cop, too. Thinking of the druggies who'd bung-holed our house, I read in the voice of a character of mine, Sisyphus the Crack King,

Git down, git down,
you got to git down
on your hands and knees
and keep your ear close to the ground.
There are druggies
who honey-dip around parking lots
playing the clown
instead of the clarinet,
looking for
peddlers of high renown
as in H,
or dealers doing sap of the moon plant,
crack and smack.
I used to dial a vial
myself,
a little digital digitalis,
the speed I dropped
absorbing the absence
in the air
with a light so rare
it baked
the shadow of despair
on a wall that wasn't there.
God almighty, it was a time
in fields of asphodel . . .

and then Al led us into a chant of "Stone Blind Love" in answer and call with Doug's sax, Vaughan on the piano holding it all together.

In the early morning hours, after everyone had gone home and Claire had gone to bed, I stood on the upstairs back porch staring down into the darkness of the back lane, the dark split by a shaft of light from the new high-beam lamp on the garage. The two thieves had come up onto the porch out of that darkness to break and enter into our lives, but as I stood there staring at the light I remembered my childhood and how, at night, when the light from a kitchen door fell across an alleyway, I'd crouch on one side of it – as if I were a mysterious traveller – and then I'd leap through the light and go on my way, unseen, unscathed. The year had been like that light; we had leapt through it and with our secret selves intact, we were now travelling on.

Toronto Life, 1988

SUICIDE

Some years ago, of an afternoon, the telephone rang. A woman said, "Hello, my name is Helen."

"Yes?" I said.

"You don't know me. In fact, I picked your name at random out of the telephone book."

"And . . . ?"

"Yes. Well. It's this, I want you to give me one good reason why I shouldn't kill myself."

"You what?"

"I'm serious. I'm going to kill myself."

"You're not doing that to me, not outta nowhere!"

"What d'you mean to you, I'm going to kill me."

"Not with me you're not."

"All I want's one good reason."

"I'm not playing that game."

"It's no game. I'm going to do it, and you won't even try, you're . . . ."

"You're not going to dump that load on me, lady, not a chance."

"I'M SERIOUS."

"So am I, goodbye," I said, and I hung up.

I couldn't believe the gratuitous, crass self-indulgence of such a call, the grotesque skewed selfishness of such an act. I have, ever since, had a clarity when it comes to how I feel about suicide and men and women who commit suicide.

Then, the wife of my friend, James Clarke, killed herself. He is a judge, a Justice of the Ontario Court, and a poet, who has since been compelled to remember over and over that one afternoon that had seemed like any other afternoon when his wife had

> *got up from the sofa,*
> *left for the corner store*
> *to buy a pack of cigarettes*
> *and had never come back.*

She had driven for ninety miles to the Honeymoon Capital of the World, Niagara Falls, and jumped. He wrote these poems:

> *After she left that Palm Sunday*
> *the police searched the house,*
> *powdered for fingerprints.*
> *They took out their notebooks.*
> *"Tell us everything," the Sergeant said.*
> *And so he told them everything,*
> *which wasn't much, but they kept*
> *returning to the question:*
> *"When was the last time you visited the Falls?"*
> *Finally they said they had to go,*
> *but promised to be back.*
> *The next time they took*
> *furniture, books,*
> *letters, old postcards,*
> *even clothes,*
> *left him rattling around the big,*
> *empty house, naked and alone,*
> *with the thought:*
> *"Maybe I did kill her."*

•

. . . Four witnesses
had seen her climb, camera in hand
and jump. The woman from Wisconsin
thought she was a tourist, said she looked
almost peaceful as the white current swept
her on her back toward the Falls. Did she
panic, want to call the whole thing off?

•

"Remember," she'd said in the hospital
when the black dog howled in her mind,
"You've been a good husband and
a good father, never forget it,"

preparing him for the hour
when he would stand before their children,
mouth stopped . . . the "ifs"
twisting like a dull blade.

"I forgive you husband, father
and when you look
into the beautiful dark water of my death
forgive me too, and learn to love
the face you see."

For fifteen years, her suicide – her face, her forgiveness, her kiss, her black hair, her rage, the black dog howling in her – for fifteen years her "her" has been in his thoughts, before sleep, and in his thoughts in the morning.

Then, James Clarke wrote a memoir, or rather a prose meditation, a series of prayers reflecting on fifteen years of struggling to come to terms with her suicide, fifteen years of trying to accommodate his determination to live to her decision to die. Though I'd never known her, he asked if I would write a preface to his prayers.

⊙⋙⊙

Preface To A Mourner's Kaddish

Suicide is an end for the person who has jumped to her death, but it is a beginning for those left behind. It is a terrible beginning because – as Plato said somewhere – staring at death, staring into the black hole of nothing, is the beginning of philosophy. Since we can know nothing about being dead, we can only try to know something about being alive . . . .

To know the play of perspectives, the play of possibilities: life as a cankered rose, or life as a rose in a canker.

But suicide is the utter and complete rejection of perspective and possibilities. The suicide is a killer.

Unlike any other killer, the suicide gets away with murder while the lovers left behind get punished for the crime.

Since suicide is an act that is inexplicable – that is, the killing of one's self – the achieved deadend ends up as beginnings:

The beginning of horror, of guilt, of remorse, of mourning, of blame, of tenderness, of renewed love but a love to be forever unrequited, of resentment, of anger – unrelenting anger, at oneself, at the suicide, at God – the interminable questioning of God while resurrecting past joys, past passions, past affections, followed by repeated penances, and perhaps most painful of all, the silences – the silence of the suicide, the silence of God.

In other words, suicide is the beginning of a consuming obsession – the hour by hour, day by day asking of the question:

Why?

And so, suicide, for all its seeming surrender to death, is a defiant, angry act against the living.

This is what James Clarke's prayers are about.

Clarke has tried – as a judge, poet, loving husband, lover of God – to not only defend life but to affirm life, to redeem life, to redeem even God.

He's done this by turning to the only thing we have, memory. Out of memory he has made anecdotes and stories, and out of anecdotes and stories he has made prayers – prayers for his wife, of course, but prayers mostly for the living. Those prayers have often become poems. Songs. He has tried his best to sing life. To celebrate life.

But he is not just a singer.

He is a judge and that has complicated matters for him.

He is in the habit of passing judgment.

He has, of course, done so in the most expected of ways – he has passed judgment on himself.

The loved one blames himself, convicts himself of a crime he did not commit, shows a mercy to the murderer that he does not show to himself . . . is even ready to forgive – but then, he can't quite do that. He knows that to forgive there must not only be a crime, but an acknowledged crime.

And who is the criminal? His beloved wife.

It has to be said: the loving judge has to judge her of a crime against that which he loves most, life.

He has to, among all his prayers, turn judgment into a prayer, but before he can do that he has to convict her.

Her, not himself.

And so, here is the revelation: whether life is a cankered rose or a rose in a canker, the great mystery at the heart of Christian experience is being played out. In the end is the beginning – and perverse as it may seem – the closer James Clarke comes to that moment when the unforgivable is to be forgiven, the more everything about life seems to come alive for him. Through her death and his loss – a death and a loss he would have done anything to prevent – not just his love of life and his love of her and his readiness to love anew, but even his faith in God is refreshed and made large, is renewed and made large, and is begun again.

2004

THE BLUES

in this climate of cold sweat
sore gums the dry heaves
the head twined in tenderness denied
all breakage in the voice
those stifled words
this rancour in the lungs
as fatigue whittles the senses
the things that hobble us
fish bones jammed under the armpits
this surcease of small moments
everything oozing out of the walls
the hunt for flies in the month of May
this allusion to memory
an aftertaste of almonds
among cyanide eggs
everything eluding our understanding
the day as it enshrines itself
with plastic vestments
in our artificial respirators
the night our nerves are eased
everything that aspires to oblivion
coffee bowls sugar fix
fillings
too much time poor-mouthing
this weariness this trepidation
all that rustles in the rooms
percolators cats

rarefying the silenced slumber shed
all this coddling of the self
the coming day full of foreboding
bound up by its own perfumes
too much aching in our bones
oratory tattooed to the corners of the soul
vibration of telegrams
the brow bent on worlds elsewhere
shunted from hand to hand
when you thumb through telephone books
leaving unloaded messages
so it goes so
it goes so it
goes so

Translated from the Québécois French
of Michel Beaulieu

MUHAMMAD ALI

Stronger than a man, simpler than a child, Muhammad Ali, said, "Man, I ain't got no quarrel with them Viet Cong . . . ." It was February 17, 1966. As a young boxer, he was bright, he was quick, he couldn't spell very well and he could barely do his sums. His mouth was where his wisdom was:

What a beautiful swing
And the punch raises the bear
Clear out of the ring
Liston is still rising
And the ref wears a frown
For he can't start counting
Till Sonny comes down . . . .

He had no idea how to be all things to all men; he only knew how to be himself, and so he had talked his strut as Cassius Clay and then strutted his talk as Muhammad Ali until the U.S. Army, short of poor black soldiers, lowered the IQ requirements for the Vietnam draft and Ali woke up one morning to find that he was no longer "too dumb for the draft." Officials said that he would do just fine. He was going to be inducted. Gung-ho patriots said they were "going to induct his Black Muslim ass into the army."

Though he had changed his name to Muhammad Ali and he had converted to Islam, they were going to send him to boot camp as Cassius Marcellus Clay, nominal Christian.

The day after Ali said he had no quarrel with them Vietcong, he was vilified by American sportswriters:

Red Smith: Squealing over the possibility that the military may call him up, Cassius makes himself as sorry a spectacle as those unwashed punks who picket and demonstrate against the war.

Murray Robinson: For his stomach-turning performance, boxing should throw Clay out on his inflated head. The adult brat, who has boasted ad nauseam of his fighting skill but who squealed like a cornered rat when tapped for the Army should be shorn of his title. And to the devil with the old cliché that a ring title can be won or lost only in the ring.

Jimmy Cannon: Clay is part of the Beatle movement. He fits in with the famous singers no one can hear and the punks riding motorcycles with iron crosses pinned to their leather jackets and Batman and the boys with their long dirty hair and the girls with the unwashed look and the college kids dancing naked at secret proms held in apartments and the revolt of students who get a check from dad every first of the month and the painters who copy the labels off soup cans and the surf bums who refuse to work and the whole pampered style-making cult of the bored young.

On April 18, in Houston, Texas, Ali – now the cause of anger and slanging wherever he went – refused to stand in response to the public calling out of his induction order. His name had been given as Cassius Marcellus Clay. He did, however, respond in writing to the order as Muhammad Ali: *"I refuse to be inducted into the armed forces of the United States because I claim to be exempt as a minister of the religion of Islam."*

Following his induction, broadcaster Howard Cosell said: "Muhammad Ali is a figure transcendental to sport. He's important to the history of this country because his entire life is an index to the bigotry lodged deep within the wellspring of this nation and its people. The only other person to come out of sports who might be as important as Ali is Jackie Roosevelt Robinson. And Ali has the advantage of coming in the 1960s. Look at what was happening then: the birth of the drug culture, the birth of the pill, riots in the streets, an ugly unwanted war, assassinations . . . . That time period was incredible, and Ali understood it; he was at the heart of it; he helped shape it all."

Ali was indicted and on June 19, after a jury had deliberated for twenty minutes, an old conservative Texas judge sentenced him to five years imprisonment and a fine of ten thousand dollars.

His lawyers entered into a long process of legal appeals.

He was berated, he was vilified, he was stripped of his heavyweight championship title, and then he was barred by America's boxing commissioners from the American ring.

The FBI put him under constant surveillance.

Howard Cosell said: "It was an outrage; an absolute disgrace. You know the truth about boxing commissions. They're nothing but a bunch of politically appointed hacks. Almost without exception, they're men of such meager talent that the only time you hear anything at all about them is when they're party to a mismatch that results in a fighter being maimed or killed. And what they did to Ali! Why? How could they? They took away his livelihood because he failed the test of political and social conformity . . . . It's disgusting. Muhammad Ali was stripped of his title and forbidden to fight by all fifty states, and that piece of scum Don King hasn't been barred by one. What does that tell you about government and boxing . . . ?"

As opposition to the war and to the draft erupted on college campuses and not only continued but intensified, he cobbled together an income by talking his talk and rambling and signifying and chanting his rhymes for SNIC students and the Negro Ladies of Abernathy Hall and Peace Now Sit-Ins, plane-hopping from town to town, though he was terrified of flying.

Attorney General Ramsey Clark said: "Muhammad's conflict with the draft board was a great concern of mine, although I'd have to say, not as great as the concern I had for the poor young black kids from the ghettos or the rural poor from the South who never had a chance to question whether or not to go to Vietnam and who got brutalized and killed. My own personal view was that a person should have a right to conscientious objector status without professing a specific religious faith, and that one should be able to base it upon what you might call philosophical rather than religious grounds. But that of course was not the law then, nor is it now."

In December of 1968, Ali was sent to jail for ten days in Dade County, Florida, for driving without a license.

He said: "Jail is a bad place. I was there for about a week until they let us out for Christmas, and it was terrible. You're all locked up; you can't get out. The food is bad, and there's nothing good to do. You look out the window at cars and people, and everyone else seems so free. Little things you take for granted like sleeping good or walking down the street, you can't do them no more. A man's got to be real serious about what he believes to say he'll do that for five years, but I was ready if I had to go."

All compasses were spinning.

One day he called a press conference and said that he had hired on, with top billing, as a song-and-dance man for a Broadway musical. The musical was called *Buck White*. He was Buck.

On a cold December day, I stopped by his small residential suite in a modest midtown Manhattan hotel.

"What's your story?" Ali said at the hotel room door, "man, 'cause I got mine."

"I got no story," I said.

"Too bad for you," he said.

Solid through the shoulders, sleek, boyishly slender in his tight jeans, a plain white shirt and tie, he was wary, abrupt, his eye quick on me for the least hint of edge. "The world want to whup me the only way they can." He thrust out his jaw. He could take a punch. But it was clear that he was bewildered at having been belittled by politicians and pugs alike. He had tried to make it clear – he was *clean*, he was not only no coward, he was *clean* of meanness, avarice, calumny, *clean* of vengeance . . . or, in the words of Drew "Bundini" Brown, his cohort in signifying talk, *he still do float like a butterfly, sting like a bee, an' America is where he want to be.* ("To me the U.S. is still the best country in the world," he'd said. "You may have a hard time to get something to eat, but anyhow I ain't fightin' alligators and livin' in a mud hut.")

Still, even Jackie Roosevelt Robinson had denounced him. And Joe Louis, too.

He pawed the air . . . *jab jab* . . . *pitty-pat pitty-pat* . . . his lip running loose: *I'll say it again, I ain't got no quarrel with those Viet Cong* . . . as his girl-child hung on to his pant leg. "Think of all the hangers-on who have clutched at this man," Bundini said, draping his arm around Ali's shoulders. Ali turned to the mirror on the wall, lowered his shoulder, feinted a jab and a hook and *bam bam* combinations to the body. He told the child – so quietly I could hardly hear him – to go to her mother, Belinda, in the bedroom, and then he called out, "How you doing?" glaring at me from out of the mirror as I stood staring at him in the mirror. I said, "What's happening, man? What you been doing?"

"Since when?"

"Since whenever. When we talked."

"Singing my songs," he said, doing a playful *bang bang* of fist-to-palm, fist-to-palm, the outcast *champeen* of champions, standing in front of me, punching the air, scraping a living out of nothing so that he could live three-to-a-bedroom in a drab hotel. But then he stepped back and assumed his wise preacher-man tone, saying "Some men complain because they got no shoes. Some men complain because they got no feet."

Ali wasn't complaining.

Ain't gonna lope through Texas like no mule.

He had feet. He'd been so fast on his feet that he'd been there and gone with his hands by the time a man knew he'd been hit.

He had fast hands.

Zora Folley had said: "The moves, the speed, the punches, and the way he changes style every time you think you got him figured. The right hands Ali hit me with just had no business landing, but they did. They came from nowhere. Many times he was in the wrong position but he hit me anyway. I've never seen anyone who could do that. The knockdown punch was so fast that I never saw it. He has lots of snap, and when the punches land they dizzy your head; they fuzz up your mind. He's smart. The trickiest fighter I've seen."

He had been sly, he had been a dandy in the ring, and he had played the trickster when it had come to the exigencies of promotion, but there was one thing he would not put up with – he would not be called "Clay." Floyd Patterson had insisted on calling him "Clay." There was nothing he could do. Patterson hadn't been up for a fight.

But when he and Ernie Terrell had met to sign for their fight, Ali had demanded, "What's my name?" Terrell had said, "Cassius Clay."

Ali had promised he was going to give Terrell "a whupping and a spanking and a humiliation. I'll keep on hitting him, and I'll keep talking, and here's what I'll say. 'Don't you fall, Ernie.' *Wham.* 'What's my name?' *Wham.* I'll just keep doing that until he calls me Muhammad Ali. I want to torture him."

And that's what he had done.

By round three, Terrell had a fractured bone under his left eye, the eye was pushed down to the bone: "The bone broke," Terrell said, "and the muscles that turn the eye got caught on the bone, and the eye wouldn't turn. It was jammed straight ahead. So the other eye would follow him around, but the hurt eye stayed straight and I had double vision . . . . So I fought walking straight toward him till I could see which one he was."

He had walked straight into the vicious one, the Ali who seemed to be possessed, the Ali who had taunted him, shouting, "What's my name?" and then had beaten on his broken eye-bone, crying, "Uncle Tom. What's my name?" and by the fourteenth round, as described by Tex Maule, "Terrell could no longer control his tormented body. Instead of reacting normally to a feint, he flinched instinctively with his whole being, and when he ventured to lead with his left, his recovery into a protective crouch was exaggerated and somehow pitiful. It was a wonderful demonstration of boxing skill and a barbarous display of cruelty."

"What's my name?"

Ain't gonna lope like no mule . . .

❦

"Buck White, how you doing?"

"Singing 'bout big black balloons."

Watching him sing on stage, I had cringed. As one of the ring's most fluid men, he had looked like he was doing chores, like he was *walking* by numbers . . . keeping busy by being busy. As a church basement performance, it was surprisingly competent, but as a Broadway performance it diminished everything beautiful about him. He hadn't been reduced to playing Steppin Fetchit, he wasn't playing the *boon coon*, but he had been reduced to pretending that he could croon and dance while draped in a long blue robe, wearing a goofy little Afro wig-hat on his head, signifying from a podium, *Get down, get down* . . . the ring's most elegant boxer coming on to the world as a campy Father Divine, stage-whispering *We'll fill the street with dancing feet beneath big black balloons* . . . . He had showed bravery, but there had been a sheepishness to his stage strut, a sheepishness that was seductive: he'd given off the scent of shame.

❦

"Belinda," he called.

Bundini, wearing a camel's hair coat, whispered a word in Ali's ear. Ali nodded.

"Belinda. Try an' not have no noise in there with the child."

"Bring the child back in," I said.

The toddling child, Maryum, came into the room and stood facing the television, the picture on, the sound off. The child peered into the dead zone screen, and so Ali sat and watched the silent moving shadows, too, until Bundini, without a word, went into the bedroom and the child turned to Ali, who was sitting on a chair, and climbed up on Ali's knees and into his lap and put her child's eye on me.

"She's play-acting," he said. "Everybody in this family is play-acting now."

We both lowered our heads, as if miming a moment's silence for the dead.

Then: "I know it doesn't matter, I mean my saying so," I said, "but you made a mistake being in that play."

"I'll tell you about that play," Ali said. "This was really a *black* play, the way they talk, certain words they have in their language only they understand. The play carried a message, it was clean and all profanity was out of it, and no nudism. Each character represented the typical *black* man in all walks of life, you know, one militant, one a pimp, a hustler, one a dope peddler, one talks like a militant leader, you know, and the songs and the beat, the rhythm . . . ."

As he spoke, he was playing *patty-cake* on his daughter's knees, *pitter-PAT, pitter-PAT*, keeping the jive-talking beat behind his patter . . . a rhythm rooted in the old 'delta talkin' blues, "Saturday Night Fish Fry" talk, Louis Jordan and Daddy Cool talk . . . .

"The word on the street is the play's going to close . . . ."

"No black man, no black woman who's watched that play has said they didn't like it. They just laughed, they jumped, they wanted to see it again. But whites, I can see where you'd just sit there, like I watch TV all the time . . . ." He hunched forward on the chair, a little red rooster coming up in his eyes, an' *Pow Pow* the popping sound of his lips, the whites of his eyes glistening, a glimpse of cunning in the whites, and maybe a hardness, too, his hips held to his chair by the child as he said, "This is a song the man who wrote the song got from watching a rat." He began to perform, reciting the rhyming words to one of Buck White's songs, his voice toneless, a schoolboy's recitation, no verve:

> *We came in misery,*
> *now all our pain*
> *and suffering is a*
> *part of history . . .*

His plump-cheeked daughter looked up and began to rock in his lap as he talked his song:

> *We came in chains,*
> *we came as livin' loot,*
> *so you could boast*
> *slave-gotten gains . . .*

He went on testifying to the room – to me and his daughter – instructing me in the Buck White story, playing his part while saying, "They's people, they just don't see no hope, they don't see no victory [*a furled brow*], they just not thinking. They just really ready to die, they don't care. [*pause*] The reason many of them got guns is because being peaceful never helped them, and they were shot and killed just for speedin', and saying something back to a policeman. It's savage out there. There are a group of people who are hot [*his tone flat*], but they got no chance. They got guns but militarily they got no airplanes, they just don't understand." He lifted the girl off his knees and said, "There in the play, they think we're all gonna buy machine guns but instead we're gonna buy big black balloons . . . *in the sky so light it seems snow white . . . on one bright morning, soon dancing in the sky, you're gonna spy up high a black balloon,*" and he rose up, reaching out with his free hand as he held his little girl against his hip, calling out, "*You niggers don't talk like this in Georgia . . .*"[*a glimpse of laughter in his eyes as he entered into the conspiratorial telling of a joke*]: "Take this white fellah [*small pause, to confide*], he was standing next to this black fellah in Georgia at the airport and he said, 'Are you a Blackstone Ranger?' [*pause*] The black fellah said, 'No.' He said, 'Are you Rap Brown?' The black fellah said, '*No.*' [*his voice rising up*] '*No,*' and he said, 'You follow Stokely Carmichael?' The black fellah said, 'No.' He said, 'Do you believe in the Black Bosuns?' The fellah said, 'No.' [*quickening*] 'But you like the late Malcolm X?' The fellah said, '*NO.*' [*menacing pause*] He said, 'Well, *nigger*, get offa my damn toe.'"

Bundini, leaning out of the bedroom, collapsed in laughter.

"*See,*" Ali said to me, "if he'd said, I *am* a Black Panther, or a follower of Rap Brown or Stokely Carmichael, he'd have got more respect . . . ."

And as he'd said: "We've been brainwashed. Everything good is supposed to be white. We look at Jesus, and we see a white with blond hair and blue eyes. We look at all the angels; we see white with blond hair and blue eyes. Now, I'm sure there's a heaven in the sky and coloured folks die and go to heaven. Where are the coloured angels? They must be in the kitchen preparing milk and honey. We look at Miss America, we see white. We look at Miss World, we see white. We look at Miss Universe, we see white. Even Tarzan, the king of the jungle in black Africa, he's white. White Owl Cigars. White Swan soap, White Cloud tissue paper, White Rain hair rinse, White Tornado floor wax. All the good cowboys ride the white horses and wear white hats. Angel food cake is the white cake, but the devil's food cake is chocolate. When are we going to wake up as a people and end the lie that white is better than black?"

He went into the mime of a cowering, shuffling black man, flapping and knee-knocking. He laughed hard at himself and the child laughed, and then he pointed at me, singing:

We see you lookin' cruel
with your cold blue eyes,
you think we're just your fools
and only you is wise.
We see you with your greed
[several shuffle steps]
while we are down here

in dyin' need,
but it's all over now,
Mighty Whitey,
it's all over now.
[again shuffle steps]
We can't bear no more,
we don't care no more,
and you see where

we don't scare no more.
We declare therefore
just as sure as we are black,
till our roles are reversed
and the last are first,
and our colour is no longer a curse,

you can do your worst,
but we are not turnin' back.
[several shuffle steps again]
Call out your National Guard,
call in all the po-lice,
tell 'em to come down hard,
ain't gonna be no peace,

'cause if you think
I'm gonna Uncle Tom,
you might as well go in

and get your bomb,
'cause it's all over now,
Mighty Whitey,
[several shuffle steps]
it's all over now.

Maryum, who had slid down between his knees, began to squeal. He sat down and lifted her to his lap. With a cradling gentleness, he put a nipple in her mouth. "Here's your bottle. Come on, come on, get your milk, gotta keep her quiet, she loves the bottle, there you go. There you go, woman." She sucked. Then she offered him her bottle. He took the nipple, sucked on it, slurped, said *Ahhh,* gave it back, she slurped, said *Ahhh* . . . she slurped and smiled . . . *Ahhh* . . . *Ahhh* . . . .

"No nation is greater than its females. A man's woman, don't you see," he said, "a man's woman is the field which produces his nation. And if he don't protect his woman he loses his nation. A farmer will protect his fields, but how much more important is a man's woman than his cabbage, his corn? In America, a black woman is allowed to walk the streets, any strange man can come and carry her to the motels and use her, but only because men are not *men,* because if men be *men* they'll fend and take care of their own women. We must care and protect our women. How can we invite anyone to respect us if we don't even protect our women? The woman is the one long step to freedom, we got to control and protect our women, because from this little girl comes our future generation, and if she's nothing, then the nation will be nothing."

"When this is all over," I asked, "how are you and the guys who run the nation gonna come out of this, I mean, how are you going to find yourself?"

"I don't know. I might be in jail, with no bail."

His body flexed, he had gone taut.

"A complicated guy like you, you don't calculate . . . ?"

"I plan, I may go to jail, but I don't care."

"You don't feel any bitterness?"

"Everybody pays great prices for stands. The Jews were put in the ovens for what they believe, the Christians were fed to the lions for refusing to deny their faith back in the olden days . . . I'm just paying for my stand. I'm not mad at nobody."

But he looked truculent.

"Maybe you're already a martyr in the minds of black people."

"I don't know. I'm just trying to do what I'm trying to do."

"Don't you see, sometimes, that you set out to become a boxer, and you're already a legend. You're not even through fighting yet, and your next fight – whenever that will be – is part of the legend."

"I don't really know what a legend is," he said. "I'm just myself, honest in my beliefs. Some people may wantta die for me, some wantta shoot me. I'm just an ordinary person doing my best."

Jab bip bam bam.

"There's various people coming to me saying, 'I'm sure we can get licensing in Nevada,' but I'm too proud to beg to go where I'm not wanted. I was wanted on stage. I never got beaten in the ring. They can't take that. There are people who got no ideals. I understand we're supposed to fight Joe Frazier in Florida, in a studio."

"It's been a long time since you've been in a fight, the timing goes."

"Yes, yes, I have to build up my heart, my lungs, my legs . . . ."

"You think you can do it?"

"I really don't know. I know I'll never be the same. I'll never be the same as I was when I quit. But that's just the gamble I'm gonna have to take."

"I'm getting the feeling that you're tired, weary?"

(Here I had in mind a blow to his sense of self that he would not talk about! – he had been abandoned by the Nation of Islam newspaper, *Muhammad Speaks*. Upon hearing that he intended to box again, they, too, had cast him out:

We tell the world we're not with Muhammad Ali. Muhammad Ali is out of the circle of the brotherhood of the followers of Islam under the leadership and teaching of Elijah Muhammad for one year. He cannot speak to, visit with, or be seen with any Muslim or take part in any Muslim religious activity. Mr. Muhammad Ali plainly acted the fool. Any man or woman who comes to Allah and then puts his hopes and trust in the enemy of Allah for survival is underestimating the power of Allah to help them. Mr. Muhammad Ali has sporting blood. Mr. Muhammad Ali desires to do that which the Holy Qur'an teaches him against. Mr. Muhammad Ali wants a place in this sport world. He loves it. Mr. Muhammad Ali shall not be recognized with us under the holy name of Muhammad Ali. We will call him Cassius Clay.)

"I don't know what I am," he said.

He rose up, caught sight of himself in the mirror, went *jab jab bip bam bam.*

"You really believe, if you get to fight again, that you can take Frazier?"

"I'm beat, I'm so beat. But I believe I can win, right, but, mentally, you know, there are a lot of things you want to do but you can't, your body won't allow you. It's the hardest sport in all sport is boxing, and it takes condition to win for fifteen rounds. Sonny Liston, he was beaten once for six or seven rounds easy. But then Liston caught his man. So, I could probably beat Joe Frazier for seven or eight rounds real good, maybe going into twelve, but I have three more to go, which is a long time. If I'm tired enough and exhausted enough, and dazed, and shook enough – he could win. It's a rough thing, it ain't easy. I was so good when I was fighting that people just can't believe that I couldn't do it easy, but, it's not that easy. It's not easy."

"By the way," I said, as he walked me to the door, "Chuvalo says to say hello to you."

"The washerwoman," Ali said with a nod of affection. "He gave me a fight and he fought me a fight. I give him that."

"How come you call him the 'washerwoman?'"

"Because of the way he moved his shoulders. He fought me a hard fight, but he moves his shoulders like he's scrubbing floors."

Jab jab bip bam.

"I don't scrub no floors."

CBC Weekend, 1969-1991

CRIME AND REDEMPTION: RAMSEY CLARK

We lock men down in a black hole. We lock men in prison cells – 2, 4, 6, 8, to a cell – to punish them until they do their *black* penance *crawling in their brain* and their penance is toted up by time – 2 years less a day for assault, 5 to 10 for murder-2 – but with time off it could be 3, though if they do not act like penitents – *crawling* as the clock ticks, if they do not *do* good time, then they will do hard time – and we will lock them in higher security prisons, lock them into a warehouse degradation where there are *black* drugs, *snake* rapes and *crawling* suicides.

In 1969, a young black fellow, Ronnie Brown, was arrested for robbery. A teen boy, he had never been convicted of a crime. He was locked in jail for 19 days, though no grand jury had indicted him and no lawyer had advised him, and then he was discovered to be dead, hanging from a light fixture, his own belt looped around his neck. Ronnie Brown had written to his mother, "Dear Mom. This is not the life I want. I am not really bad . . . I want to get out and work and do something good." He told his mother he "was afraid to go to the bathroom." He did not tell why. But his wardens knew why. He did not want to suck cock. So, presumed innocent, he hung himself dead.

Under President Lyndon Johnson, the Attorney General of the United States was a self-effacing laconic, raw-boned lawman, Ramsey Clark. In 1968, his hard-nosed Justice Department indicted 1,166 organized-crime hoodlums. Clark was a crime-buster – but now he is retired – and he has turned out to be a strange breed of lawman. Soft-spoken and self-assured, he castigates and cautions hard-line cops and congressmen, he castigates and cautions J. Edgar Hoover, he castigates and cautions the wardens of prisons and penitentiaries.

Though the FBI says that crime in our time has risen by 148 percent, though police chiefs and citizen committees plead for more police, Ramsey Clark warns that what they will get is more law and order but less justice. Instead of punishment, he wants to talk to us of charity (not to be confused with mollycoddling), a charity to be extended towards student protesters, pot hustlers and minor hoods like Mafia shakedown men, and he is always demonstrating – like a good lawyer – through bold statistic after bold statistic that punishment as a mechanism – as an end in itself – breeds nothing but desolate, desperate men in prisons that are crime factories – demonstrating that what is wanted is not more punishment, not more lock-downs, but a respect for the individual, a respect that approaches redemption.

Clark sifts through the contentious mounds of information and misinformation surrounding crime; he sifts and combs through what can be deduced statistically about poverty, slums, racism, court delays, technological change, bail procedure, marijuana, laws that cannot be enforced, underpaid prosecutors, underpaid and undertrained police, prison squalor, bondsmen, the Supreme Court, capital punishment, manipulated crime statistics, the mushrooming arrests of the young, *made* goons in the Mafia, public defenders, confusion among judges, inept judges, overpopulation, invasion of privacy, hamstrung rehabilitation programs, plea bargains, the unregulated sale of guns, cross-border crime, the need for alien conspiracy laws, dope addicts and drunks and hookers, law and order lobbyists, the National Guard and the Army, protest movements, the National Rifle Association, civil-rights leaders, preventive detention and parole . . . dada data dada data pointing toward one inescapable conclusion: that our attitudes toward the *black snake crawling* of crime and criminals, and the system of justice that reflects those attitudes, do not work.

Clark attacks the current ethic of punishment: he asks – who among us has the power, how do they wield it? For him, power is a closed circle, a little wheel turning within a big wheel. The big wheelers, the elect, are those who not only think of themselves as the elect because they have the power but, because they are powerful, they are able to condemn small-time wheelers and dealers, the dispossessed, to the lawless life of the criminal repeater (80 percent of all crimes in the U.S. are committed by repeaters, boys and men who were arrested at an early age and who were then schooled and reschooled in the prisons). Clark says there are so many proven criminals in the prisons and so many impoverished who are incubating as criminals out on the streets that powerful men, fearing an increase in chaos among the powerless, demand that we spend more money on enforcement and they insist that we spend less money on poverty; they want us to pack the prisons with more blacks from the ghettos; they want us to become more repressive – they want to wire-tap and bug us, they want to listen to our thoughts, they want to be able to detain those whom they merely *suspect*, they want to *not* inform us of our civil rights.

Above all, they want to build more prisons.

Clark is adamant: none of this can work.

His solution seems visionary though he is in fact a data man, data being a basic, if limited, perspective on the story of what men have actually done. Given how he reads what has been done, man to man in our institutions, Clark is seeking a revolution in sensibility or at least a major readjustment, where the formula – Time = Punishment – is not a defining mechanism. He suggests, for example, that the criminal, once he is convicted, should not be sentenced to a fixed time, should not be sent away for a proscribed number of years. Rather, he should be given a particular sentence and then he should be offered incentives to progressively rehabilitate himself – he should be offered an incentive to not only achieve a sense of dignity, but to merit early freedom through singular good hard work – an incentive to not only progressively reduce his time in prison but to, in effect, redeem his person.[1]

Such redemption is to be accomplished through the practical application of indeterminate sentences. That is, once the public is protected, once the man convicted is taken from the dock to his cell, he should be allowed – through hard work – meditative and reflective, perhaps, but mostly productive – to merit early release (of the thousands who have recently been afforded temporary freedom in the federal work-release program, only one in twenty failed to comply and tried to escape, and all escapees were caught).

Clark's approach and his admonitions (though he does not go into this) are rooted in the commentary of those French intellectuals who wrote about prison reform in the opening decades of the 1800s. It was a time when cellular imprisonment – based on the medieval monastic model of isolation and silence – was established at the Petite Roquette prison in Paris. In the spirit of monasticism, Tocqueville, among others, had argued that the penalty imposed on a convict should not only be individual to the isolated man, but the penalty should be individualizing: "Thrown into solitude, the convict reflects." And so, it was argued, the convict, alone in his cell, could well become aware of his capacity for shame, and therefore, his capacity for dignity. The

---

[1] To get some perspective on how radical Clark's argument is: consider the Catholic idea of Purgatory, a place – a holding prison, if you will – between Heaven and Hell where the individual soul, in anticipation of his death, can reduce the length of time he is to be punished for his sins by doing good works. In the Catholic scheme of things this meriting of salvation is usually associated with acts of charity. Clark, it is true, urges a charitable approach toward the individual but he has brought his Protestant sensibility to bear on the Catholic idea of merit, associating good works and a salvation to be achieved not with charity but with the Protestant ethic of productive labour.

obvious threat, therefore, to such individualizing of the isolated prisoner lay (and still lies), as Tocqueville said, in the "general criminal population (where) there exists at this moment among us an organized society of criminals . . . . They form a small nation within the greater. Almost all these men met or meet again in prison."

For the French reformers – members of the *Société pour L'amélioration des prisons* or the *Société des prisons* – incarceration, if it was to serve any intelligent purpose, had to be more than punishment, it had to be more than a "finalizing mechanism" – it had to be more than keeping a man locked up for a proscribed period of time. A. Bonneville – in *Traité des diverses institutions complémentaires* – argued that the length of a man's penalty should be adjusted – as if on a sliding downward scale – to the "useful" transformation of the inmate during his term of imprisonment – that is, "expiation ought to end with the complete reform of the prisoner; for, in such a case, all detention (if he has reformed himself) has become useless, and from then on (detention is) as inhuman to the reformed individual as it is vainly burdensome for the State." In making much the same case as Bonneville, and to put that case in theological terms, Clark is not only rejecting our puritan system of predetermined prison sentences for the damned who have confirmed their damnation – first, by being poor – and then, by committing those crimes that the poor, and especially the poor who are black, commit: – store theft, drugs, public drunkenness, assault and battery, drugs, break and enter, drugs, etc. – but he also is arguing that such an inmate, since he was actually born "in liberty" should be able to rebel against his damnation and return to that condition of "liberty" through meritorious work.

Prison should not be a Hobbesian warehouse, a place of punishment, perversion, idleness and crime schooling, but a confessional experience in which a man alone in his cell might, out of a sense of his potential goodness, his potential redemption, opt to begin again. This is, for Calvinist, punitive America, a wildly optimistic view of human affairs.

And the practical, statistical problem for Clark is, of course, that with 2, 4, 6, 8 men to a cell, with arrest piling upon arrest, with thousands upon thousands of idle prisoners living in controlled areas of chaos where murder, drugs, rape and the suicides of terrified innocents like little Ronnie Brown are commonplace – people at large, knowing that the system has failed, believe only in punishment and more warehouses and more punishment:

> *Mean black snake*
> *been crawling round my brain*
> *been crawling round my brain*
> *I betcha my bottom dollar*
> *I'm gonna kill . . .*

The Telegram, 1970-75

LEROI JONES:
DEATH,
HE GRINNING

If ever America undergoes great revolutions,
they will be brought about by the presence
of the black race on the soil of the United States;
that is to say, they will owe their origin, not to the
equality, but the inequality of conditions.
                              —Alexis de Tocqueville, 1840

Yet do I marvel at this wondrous thing,
To make a poet Black and bid him sing.
                              —Countee Cullen

Newark, New Jersey: in the dilapidated tenements of the Central
Ward – in the dilapidated part of the ghetto – under yellow
smog – if a black man walks east to take his pleasure, then his
main street in the ward will be Springfield Avenue – low-rent
shops, package stores, the steel mesh-work of designer burglar
bars, the fluttering light of half-dead neon signs, furniture bar-
gain houses (plush sofas and arborite), cheque cashing joints,
laundromats (way-stations for daytime hookers) – and dives –
Jefferson Cut-Rate Liquors and *Pabst Blue Ribbon* at *Popular Prices.*
Child-girls get laid up against walls or give head in the hallways
or in the back seats of stripped-down cars, their babies breast feed
on snow-milk because absolute drug addiction in the ward is

seventh highest in the nation, population density is second, as is infant death.

"Death be just around the corner in Newark, just around the corner. And he grinning."

When Newark erupted this summer, when snipers crawled out of the rooftop pigeon sheds and started firing and when the police turned into hunting packs and gang squabbles became a four-corner shootout and when ten square miles of the city were barricaded by 3,000 National Guardsmen, the Mayor, a man named Addonizio, announced with an aplomb that was appalling, "If I had it to do all over again, I would follow the same policy and program I followed for the past five years."

⊚⟨⊙⟩⊚

After the Harlem Rent Riots across the river, James Farmer, from the Congress of Racial Equality, said, "I saw a bloodbath. I saw with my own eyes violence, a bloody orgy of police . . . a woman climbing into a taxi and indiscriminately shot in the groin . . . police charging into a grocery store and indiscriminately swinging clubs . . . police shooting into tenement windows and into the Theresa Hotel . . . . I saw bloodshed as never before . . . . It is the duty of police to arrest, not indiscriminately shoot and beat."

In Newark, evening curfews were set because several precincts had run out of ammunition.

A kid wearing handcuffs in the Newark courthouse, after listening to a judge bemoan the situation, said, "Love them honkie crocodile tears."

H. Rap Brown told reporters, "Violence is as American as cherry pie."

Stokely Carmichael, having a cigar in Havana, said only urban guerrilla warfare could "meet the savagery of these white United States."

Senators and congressmen demanded that Carmichael be tried for treason and Governor Lester Maddox, looking as if all

219

compasses were spinning behind his eyes – blathered on about "savages, rapists and murderers."

The Reverend Billy Graham offered to kneel down and pray with Lyndon Johnson.

Norman Podhoretz, the Manhattan intellectual, cold-cocked his white friends by cosily confessing in a *Commentary* essay that he had – as he put it – a particular Negro Problem: "I know it from the insane rage that can stir in me at the thought of Negro anti-Semitism; I know it from the disgusting prurience that can stir in me at the sight of a mixed couple; and I know it from the violence that can stir in me whenever I encounter that special brand of paranoid touchiness to which many Negroes are prone."

Lorraine Hansberry, who wrote the play, *Raisin in the Sun*, said, "There's something horrible, that Norman Podhoretz can sit down and write the kind of trash that he did, being disturbed at the sight of a mixed couple . . . . And somehow, anti-Semitism from a Negro apparently upsets him more than anti-Semitism from a German fascist . . . . We have to find some way . . . to encourage the white liberal to stop being a liberal and become an American radical."

LeRoi Jones said,

> *Cold air batters*
> *The poor (and their minds*
> *Turn open*
> *Like sores).*

❦

LeRoi Jones was born in Newark in 1934, his father a postman, his mother a social worker. He came up through the Depression, and the War, and he became a writer and now he is a collegial poet teaching *American poetry since 1945* at the New School at Columbia University: ". . . MY POETRY is whatever I think I am. (Can I be light and weightless as a sail? Heavy and clunking like

8 black boots.) I CAN BE ANYTHING I CAN. I make a poetry with what I feel is useful and can be saved out of all the garbage of our lives . . . . ALL are a poetry, and nothing moves (with any grace) pried apart from these things. There cannot be closet poetry. Unless the closet be wide as God's eye . . . and all that means that I *must* be completely free to do just what I want, in the poem. 'All is permitted': Ivan's crucial concept."

Newark: four days of fire and four days of looting, and during the killing, Jones, doing what he wanted to do, was arrested by National Guardsmen and hauled from a Volkswagen Beetle carrying two loaded .32 calibre pistols in his pockets. He was taken to jail and beaten up, and clubbed about the head before he was set free. He needed seven stitches to close wounds to his scalp.

Though slight of build, thin, and hunched at the shoulders, though he speaks softly and walks with a boy's bounce in his tan desert boots, Jones is full of bristle – he's got a mouth, a mouth that's quick to run upside any white man: "The Black Artist's role in America," he told me, "is to aid in the destruction of America as he knows it." Since he's no goof, and no roll-me-over for the police, what's surprising is that he was not killed or crippled by the cops. They had death on their minds, he had death on his – verbal inflammatory violence seems to possess a potency, a magic for him: "The dead are what move me. The various dead," to whom he has

talked tenderness . . .
their nothing
grown to sounds
the deaf take for music

This is a bleak music – night dreams on a fire escape – the music of a stern moralist – plague has broken out in the city of his imagination – yet the music is somewhat derivative. His play *Dutchman* has been to bed with Jean-Paul Sartre's *Respectful Prostitute*. Céline is in his prose line, Charles Olsen is in his verse line, and he keeps Oswald Spengler under his thinking cap: – Céline and Spengler shacked up in Newark:

Dark cold water slapping long wooden logs jammed 10 yards down in the weird slime, 6 or 12 of them hold up a pier. Water, wherever we'd rest. And the first sun we see each other in. Long shadows down off the top where we were. Down thru gray morning shrubs and low cries of waked up animals . . . . Chipped stone stairs in the silence. Vegetables rotting in the neighbor's minds. Dogs wetting on the buildings in absolute content. Seeing the pitied. The minds of darkness. Not even sinister. Breaking out in tears along the sidewalks of the season. Gray leaves outside the junkshop. Sheridan Square blue men under thick quivering smoke. Trees, statues in the background of voices. Justice, Egalité. Horns break the fog with trucks full of dead chickens. Motors. Lotions . . . . Night queens in winter dusk. Drowning city of silence. Ishmael back, up through the thin winter smells. Conked hair, tweed coat, slightly bent at the coffee corner . . . .

He takes a deep breath. He hasn't been walking and he hasn't been talking but he takes a deep out-of-breath sigh, and gives me a wan smile and then his

> *mind*
> *turns open*
> *like a sore*

"Ishmael Reed and I ain't got no time to truck or trade," he says, looking hard at me, "I ain't got no time for offay liberals." All liberals do, he tells me, is confuse the issue, confuse the times by encouraging integration because all they want, by hook or by cunning, is black accomplices in crime. "What the liberal white man wants is for the black man somehow to be elevated in Martin Luther King style so that he might be able to enter this society with some kind of general prosperity and join the white man in a truly democratic defence of this cancer, which would make the black man equally culpable for the evil done to the rest of the world . . . . But these are the Last Days of the American Empire. Understand that Lyndon Johnson is a war criminal of the not-so-distant future . . . there are wars of national liberation going on all over the world, wars that will push these sadists and perverts into the sea."

⊙⊙⊙

He preached upon 'Breadth' till it argued him narrow.
—Emily Dickinson

We are stool-by-stool in an under-lit bar on University Place in New York, The Cedar Bar, famous among painters, abstract expressionist painters who've been living off "the whimpering pigment of a decadent economy," Jones has said. The white bartender calls out, "Hey LeRoi, where you been? I miss seeing you." I am surprised at how slight he is, how delicate his bones, how soft his eyes, and surprised at how his heavy rust-coloured corduroys and the bulk-knit sweater he is wearing make him seem stooped, even fragile, a fragile man whose plays are possessed by a big-boned rage, an implacable rage . . . a rage so free of nuance that it seems no more than strident and finally, small.

We talk about blues singers and laugh a little at the white boys in our time who "have caught the blues like it is the clap," and I feel loose enough with him to sing out Lou Reed's wry lines: *I wanna be black/have natural rhythm . . . . I don't want to be a fucked-up middle-class college student* but he doesn't laugh so then I tell him about my friend blind Sonny Terry and how he one day hunkered down in his west side flat, sitting in a chair facing the door, holding a gun, and by mistake he almost shot me dead in the doorway, looking (as only an angry blind man can) to shoot someone, and an hour later, sitting in the same chair, he nearly shot his partner, Brownie McGhee, which reminds me of how years earlier Sonny – when he "was just comin' up" – had gone into a bar in a tobacco town in one of the Carolinas, trying to shoot the owner who had refused to pay him for his playing, and when he started firing a woman had cried out, "Get down, get down, this blind man gonna kill us all."

Jones laughs, but I know by the tilted look in his eye that he's not laughing at what I'm laughing at . . . and because I don't know what exactly he's laughing at, blind Sonny shooting at the woman yelling or maybe my being shot, we leave off the blues and talk about the cold and the cutting winter dampness in New York.

And guns.

The eyehole end of it all. "Cold steel, a black that feels blue."

And almost in a whisper, Jones says, "If it was summer here all year round, there'd be civil war. The winter cools the blood," but nothing seems to cool his yearning for retribution, or at least his yearning for the thrill of giving threat:

> *Plastique, we*
> *do not have, only thin heroic blades.*
> *The razor . . .*
> *Come up, black dada*
> *nihilismus. Rape the white girls. Rape*
> *their fathers. Cut the mothers' throats.*
> *Black dada nihilismus, choke my friends*
> *in their bedrooms . . .*

We walk to the Eighth Street bookstore. There, too, they seem glad to see him, as if he is an old school friend or poet friend who hasn't been in the store for a long, long time, this pistol-packer padding along in his collegial desert boots, who can look me cold in the eye and say the word kill like he means it and then admit,

> *We take*
> *unholy risks to prove*
> *we are what we cannot be. For instance,*
> *I am not even crazy.*

I wonder if he is even cunning. Two loaded .32s in a Beetle! We putter through the shelves making hesitant but friendly small talk, and he is helpful about contemporary poets he admires (all of them, strangely enough, white – Ed Dorn, Denise Levertov, Frank O'Hara, Robert Duncan . . .) and then we agree to meet the next afternoon at the Cherry Lane Theater.

To begin. There. Where it all ends. Neon hotels, rotten black collars. To begin, aside from aesthetes, homosexuals, smart boys from Maryland. The light fades, the last earthy blue, to night. To night. Dead in a chair in Newark. Black under irrelevant low stars. On a hill night fades, behind the house. Silence.

At the Cherry Lane Theater, where his play, *Dutchman*, has just closed, we amble down the centre aisle to the small stage and hoist ourselves up onto the apron, and he says, shoulders hunched, head thrust forward, giving me no warning, "You know, white society is not just sterile. I say more than that. They are evil. Not only do I know that America, in its official image, is a country that goes around killing people. The one cure," and he leans back, spreading the palms of his hands on the stage, staring up at the ceiling, "would be to have white America altered, you know, like you do to dogs. You just alter them. That's what would have to happen to America. I've thought sometimes about leaving. I used to think that all those Jews that stayed in Germany after a certain time were fools, but now I see that I don't really want to leave. I want to see what happens, even though it might mean that I get killed or somebody else I love gets killed."

I had forgotten to run . . . . An ugly middle-class Negro bitch laugh-
ing in the hot kitchen in my red wool shirt and new jeans: a bucket
of coal. She shouted that from her stairs . . . Dolores, who said to me
behind her pimples: My brother is dumb, my mother is dumb, my
father is drunk, but you're beautiful. Will you be a doctor and take
me to the doctors? The movies? The ball games? And later we will
watch television on our linoleum and throw apple cores out the
window . . . . I went home in the afternoon and fucked Beverly.

⟪◦⟫

About his play, *The Slave*! In tone, it is apt for the apocalyptic
moment: so many downtown city blocks are in flames, it is apt in
its dreaming anticipation of a purging violence.

 The story: the white citizens of a large American city are be-
sieged by massed black armies. Machine gun and artillery fire
are heard as a black Commander forces entry into the home of
his former white wife. She has married a white professor and has
brought to that marriage two children by the black Commander.
He is about to kill the professor (he has already killed the chil-
dren). After an exchange of insults, he does kill him – as a
bomb hits the house, fatally wounding the white woman. The
Commander – who survives the bomb – tells her, to shock her
into death, that he has already murdered their two children.

 That's it.

 Curtains. All fall down.

 Jones shrugs, saying, "Well, it's a possibility, 'cause I'm mar-
ried to a white woman. We have two children. The play was an ex-
periment with my own feelings, with my emotions."[1]

---

[1] In the *New York Post*, Langston Hughes suggested an experiment of his
own: "Every other night let all the present Negro characters be played by
white actors, and vice versa…. Let a bullying white man kick, curse, brow-
beat and shoot a nice liberal black professor and his wife in their suburban
living room…since some critics…claim that LeRoi Jones may not really be
writing about colour at all, but instead is concerned with no group smaller
than mankind. God help us all!"

There's shock in them thar hills!

The shock is not in the action. The action is too trite for shock. The shock is in the language, in the verbal violence of the black Commander and the white professor as they threaten, castigate, and slang each other. Of course, it is the Commander – not the white professor – who tries to affirm himself by reaching for a kind of verbal grandeur (as with his distant cousin, Marlowe's Tamburlaine, beneath the roiling adjectives and tumbling verbs, the Commander's brain pan is a killing floor: the Commander is one of those men that Oswald Spengler called Fallaheen – grandiose brutes knee-deep in the rubble of civilization).

"Your plays, like this one, they're about murder and rage and violence and hate and loathing and contempt and insanity, and you've said in *Dutchman* that if Charlie Parker had walked down the street and killed the first ten white men he'd met, he'd never have had to play the blues, so what is that all about? That's barbarism . . . ."

"No," Jones says, "it's just artistic compensation. If you become an artist you somehow compensate, even if you feel you should kill the first ten white people. I feel every day like doing it. Well, maybe every other day . . . every three days . . . ."

"Where's that muthafucka." . . . "I'm gonna kill that muthafucka." Waved the cleaver . . . "I'm gonna kill somebody." Now the blood turned and he licked his lips seeing their faces suffering. "Kill anybody," his axe slid thru the place throwing people on their stomachs . . . .

We leave the theatre and go around the corner to a dark narrow bar. I am struck by Jones' reserve: he makes no *sound that the deaf could take for music,* no gesture that could encourage a reciprocal gesture. Yet he seems to be asking that I be reasonable, that I understand what he is saying, that I believe he speaks with a genuine concern for the sacredness of life, that his concern requires strength, and that his concern *has* to be filtered through death, and that it *has* to be filtered through death because of the criminality of white men.

We talk of the riots.

"I've been on symposiums," he says, "and everybody asked me will there be riots, and I kept saying, Yes, and all the other people kept saying, No. Now we've had the violence. There'll be more . . . just a kind of disorganized reaction, anything could set it off."

"Why disorganized, when there are so many leaders? What about Martin Luther King?"

"Most blacks would never follow Martin Luther King because most blacks are not college graduates nor are they middle-class. Most blacks are, like . . . poor."

"Well, who is going to lead the poor blacks?"

"The first really intelligent man to actually preach a holy war."

"Come on, Christianity's worst years were when men dragged little children across Europe, fighting for God."

"Well, we've had it – my people have had it for three hundred years. I know that there is nothing that will stop white America from killing people except force. I'm saying that this country is going to be ravaged by force, by racial violence. Look, this is weird . . . because the classical revolution, what the West has known, has been a minority oppressing a majority and then the majority rises. In America we have the reverse. It's a majority, the white middle-class, oppressing a minority. So other things have to happen. I don't know exactly what it will be, but I know that as white America becomes more and more repressive and begins to take on the exact characteristics of the kind of police state that Germany was, people will find it necessary to fight back to preserve any connection with human dignity."

"A head-on clash?"

"It's difficult to say. When the white West triumphed it was because of machines, because of industrial culture. They subjected all those peoples. Now the thing is starting to swing back. Now the East is confronting the West. China is the giant. China is a giant again. And the black, the American black, represents energies within white society which would destroy it, just as there are energies outside the society which want to destroy it. Those two energies are coming together as a pincer movement. The blacks are not alone in wanting to see this society fall. You whites are gonna make it difficult for the rest of the world for some years to come, but look, the majority of the people in the world – now get that – the majority of the people in the world want to see this society fall – and it will fall – absolutely."

As we part, Jones holds my hand, but only long enough so that I can feel him let it go. I am a white man. He is a black man. He pads off down the street in his desert boots, and it may be that Death be grinning in his head – and it may be that he'd like to beat on the first white man he meets, but he is also a black man who knows – no matter what he says – that when the talk is over and the beating gets done, more than likely – day to day – it'll be done "at the curb/of the dead white verb," it'll be one black man beating on another black man – so that white men – sepulchres to the core and liberal to the quick – will be able to stand back and bemoan – on behalf of blacks – the blood-lettings and the police orgies, bemoan – on behalf of blacks – "the savagery of these here white United States."

Three tall guys were coming down the hill I didn't see until they got close enough to speak to me. One laughed (at the way I looked). Tall strong black boys with plenty of teeth and pegged rayon pants. I just looked and nodded and kept on. One guy, with an imitation tattersall vest with no shirt, told the others I was in the Joint last night "playing cool." Slick city nigger, one said. I was going to pass close to them and the guy with the vest put up his hand and asked me where I was coming from. One with suspenders and a belt asked me what the wings stood for. I told him something. The third fellow just grinned. I moved to walk around them and the fellow with the vest asked could he borrow fifty cents. I only had a dollar in my pocket and told him that. There was no place to get change. He said to give him the dollar. I couldn't do that and get back to my base I told him and wanted to walk away. And one of the guys had gotten around in back of me and kneeled down and the guy with the vest pushed me backwards so I fell over the other's back. I fell backwards into the dust, and my hat fell off, and I didn't think I was made but I still said something stupid like "What'd you do that for?"

"I wanna borrow a dollar, Mr. Half-white muthafucka. And that's that." I sidestepped the one with the vest and took a running step but the grinning one tripped me, and I fell tumbling head forward back in the dust. This time when they laughed I got up and spun around and hit the guy who tripped me in the face. His nose was bleeding and he was cursing while the guy with the suspenders grabbed my shoulders and held me so the hurt one could punch me back. The guy with the vest punched too. And I got in one good kick into his groin, and stomped hard on one of their feet. The tears were coming again and I was cursing, now when they hit me, completely crazy. The dark one with the suspenders punched me in my stomach and I felt sick and the guy with the vest, the last one I saw, kicked me in my hip. The guy still held on for awhile then he pushed me at one of the others and they hit me as I fell. I got picked up and was screaming at them to let me go. "Bastards, you filthy stupid bastards, let me go." Crazy out of my head. Stars were out. And there were no fists just dull distant jolts that spun my head. It was in a cave this went on. With music and whores danced on the tables. I sat reading from a book aloud and they danced to my reading. When I finished reading I got up from the table and for some reason, fell forward weeping on the floor. The Negroes danced around my body and spilled whiskey on my clothes. I woke up two days later, with white men, screaming for God to help me.

CBC Show on Shows, 1964; The Telegram, 1964-68

MOJO

My skin is brown, my manner is tough
I'll kill the first mother I see
——Nina Simone

It was late morning in Berkeley. Because of the smog and a slip of a wind, the sun was a blurred peach. We were sitting on the porch of a small house, talking about *mojo* and talking about dreams – the young novelist, Ishmael Reed, author of *The Free-Lance Pall-Bearers* and *Yellow-Back Radio Broke Down* – and I said, "*I got a black bone, I got a mojo tooth*, what's that mean, what's the dream in that?" and he said, "Everything in America turns to dream, man, but everything, even including the Panthers. Dig it, they are black, man, tough black, and where it's at, but they have turned likewise to take their place in the white dream, like, all American history is tough, but also a dream. Those Panthers have the baggage of white Europe on their bodies, the berets and sunglasses and the jackboots, dig it, the trappings of white revolutionaries, so they can truly have reality in the white dream, being the Big Bad Nigger decked out in Redneck Regalia and white America gets off on that.

"White America has always got off on the black man, like Jane Fonda would like to get off on Angela Davis, or Pigs get off by killing Panthers. That is the white man living his dream, but dig it: the Panthers, under that Parade Dress, they are proud black, and they, my man, get off on that. They got their *mojo* working. That's outside the white dream. Pride, my man, Pride."

James Baldwin, as an elder black storyteller, has written *An Open Letter To My Sister, Miss Angela Davis*, a young imprisoned black woman – who is a professor of philosophy, a declared Communist – a lady who is in lockdown in solitary in a jail cell, on trial for her life.

Her story is, as all such things are, complicated.

On January 13, 1970, three black prisoners in Soledad in California's Salinas Valley, who were known for their aggressive black power politics, were murdered by a prison guard. Shortly after that killing, the guard was found dead. And shortly after he was found, three other black activist prisoners – who've come to be known as the Soledad 3 (George Jackson, John Cluchette and Fleeta Drumgo) – were indicted for the guard's murder.

As those three, the Soledad Brothers, waited for trial, there was yet another killing – on August 7, 1970 – that took place during hearings for another activist – a James McClain – and during those courtroom hearings there was a shootout at the Marin County Courthouse – a shootout caused by George Jackson's younger brother, John, who had come to the courtroom carrying guns.

McClain, John Jackson, and the presiding judge were killed in the consequent crossfire.

The police then learned that Professor Angela Davis, over a period of two years, had purchased four of the guns that Jackson had brought into the courtroom. The FBI issued a warrant for her arrest, charging her with unlawful interstate flight to avoid prosecution for murder and kidnapping. J. Edgar Hoover pronounced that she was a terrorist and *Wanted* posters were distributed across the country and she was declared one of the ten most dangerous criminals in America.

She was arrested in New York, held in quarters for the mentally deranged and then extradited to California (flown coast-to-coast in a requisitioned National Guard aircraft) where she was charged with the capital offences of murder and kidnapping, and also conspiracy.

President Richard Nixon and Governor Ronald Reagan (James Baldwin had called him "a *King's Row* basket case") went on television and praised Hoover and the FBI for so promptly arresting such an egregious threat to the State. Davis appeared in shackles on the cover of *Newsweek*, Aretha Franklin offered to put up $250,000 bail. Bail was denied. Davis was confined to a small cell in the Marin Country Jail.

In his letter to Angela Davis, James Baldwin told her:

When I was little I despised myself, I did not know any better. And this meant, albeit unconsciously, or against my will, or in great pain, that I also despised my father. And my mother. And my brothers. And my sisters. Black people were killing each other every Saturday night out on Lenox Avenue, when I was growing up; and no one explained to them, or to me, that it was intended that they should; that they were penned where they were, like animals, in order that they should consider themselves no better than animals. Everything supported this sense of reality, nothing denied it; and so one was ready, when it came time to go to work, to be treated as a slave . . . .

But that particular aspect of our journey now begins to be behind us. The secret is out: we are men![1] *What has happened, it seems to me, and to put it far too simply, is that a whole new generation of people have assessed and absorbed their history, and, in that tremendous action, have freed themselves of it and will never be victims again. The enormous revolution in black consciousness which has occurred in your generation, my dear sister, means the beginning of the end of America . . . we must fight for your life as though it were our own – which it is – and render impassable with our bodies the corridor to the gas chamber. For, if they take you in the morning, they will be coming for us that night. Therefore: peace.*

[1] "When Cassius Clay became Muhammad Ali and refused to put on that uniform," Baldwin says, "a very different kind of instruction had begun."

In this time of napalm, of street killings and assassination killings going on inside dreaming America's mind, Bobby Dylan has stood up and sung *God said to Abraham, kill me a son. Abraham said, where you want this killing done? God said, out on Highway 61,* the highway that runs due north out of the *mojo* town, Muddy Waters' hometown, all the way up to the Chicago of August of 1968 when the Highway 61s of the country all led straight to the Democratic Party National Convention – straight to thousands of student and hippie and Yippie protesters out in the streets – especially in the Loop and in Lincoln Park – causing the bullying city police, as seen for hour after hour on national television, to break heads and break the law.

After that street bashing and scuffling was done, after Nixon had gone back into the White House, after General Westmoreland had seeded the overseas rice paddies with more dead soldiers – in the Fall of 1969, eight activist men from across the country were arrested and charged with having conspired to create the '68 Chicago riot – seven white men and one black man.

Tom Hayden, one of those seven white defendants, while out of jail and free on bail, wrote about his six months in the courtroom of the feral judge, Julius Hoffman, and particularly about the *eighth* defendant before that Judge, Bobby G. Seale, Chairman of the Black Panther Party. Chairman Seale, Hayden says, like all other Panthers who are presently in jail, is not a political prisoner:

> He is a prisoner of war . . . . Bobby was seized on the Berkeley streets, indicted on a Connecticut murder charge, secretly driven in chains to Chicago, denied his right to representation, chained again, gagged (in Hoffman's courtroom), and severed from the case, shipped back to California and then off to Connecticut, where he now faces the electric chair . . . .

234

(His) case is not unique .... Nearly all members of the original (Panther) Central Committee have been suppressed: killed, jailed, or forced into exile .... During the (Conspiracy[1]) trial ... Bobby Seale remained in jail every day, while we were free .... Bobby was the one who experienced the gagging. We asserted our unity with the Panthers but could do nothing to prevent Bobby's sentence and the murders of (Black Panthers) Fred Hampton and Mark Clark .... (During the trial) not one major demonstration occurred to protest what had happened to Bobby .... The Panthers correctly criticized whites for not moving rapidly enough to deal with the special repression inflicted on blacks ... the U.S. government ... concluded that the Panthers were isolated and therefore easy targets.

On April 1, 1969, 21 members of the New York chapter of the Black Panther Party – an "easy target" – were accused, in a 30-count indictment, of conspiracy to bomb a Manhattan police station, to bomb a section of the New Haven railroad, to bomb four Manhattan department stores, and to bomb the Bronx Botanical Gardens.

Of the 21, seven went underground and 14 were arrested. The 14 were then split up by the police and moved from jail to jail – shifts in time and shifts in location that denied them the right to adequately confer with their counsels. Then, bail for 10 of the

---

[1] Under American law, the existence of a conspiracy – which can be defined as an agreement by two or more people to commit a crime – may be *inferred* – not proven as to intent and fact – but inferred by a jury from a suggested similarity of purpose shown by defendants, and such defendants not only need not have met each other in secret to plan a crime, but they do not need to have known each other. The statute under which the Chicago Eight were tried is the so-called Rap Brown Amendment to the 1968 Civil Rights Act which makes it a crime to cross state lines to incite a riot, inciting a *riot* (my italics) being defined as an act by an individual in a group of three or more to threaten the property or safety of a fourth person.

14 was set at $100,000 each and they were incarcerated in New York's dreaded Tombs, among them, a young man named Lee Berry.

Berry, an epileptic, had been hauled out of his hospital bed and carried across town and walked in chains to a vermin-ridden cell where he was kept in solitary confinement with a bulb burning over his head for four months. He was returned to hospital but he was too ill to appear in court. The 13 other Panthers could not raise the extraordinary bail money that had been set by the court. Many New York Liberals of substantial means thought that this was an intolerable situation and they decided to hold a Park Avenue fundraising social, not as support for particular Panther political positions, but to try to ensure that the justice system would not be used – as it had been used in Chicago[1] – as a political weapon in and of itself.[2] The fundraiser's host turned out to be the impresario and composer, Leonard Bernstein, and he and his wife invited many persons of wealth, and a handful

---

[1] During the Chicago Eight trial, former Attorney General Ramsey Clark (1964-68) had been scheduled to testify in open court before Judge Hoffman and the jury. When it was learned that he was going to say that Mayor Daley's "shoot-to-kill" order during the demonstrations was "unlawful and unthinkable"; that he, as Attorney General, had opposed the pre-positioning of 5,000 troops one week before the Democratic Convention; that he had called Prosecutor Thomas Foran and suggested that there be an investigation of police brutality (some called it a "police riot") but no investigation of the demonstrators; and, that he had turned down an FBI request to wiretap the conversations of the Chicago Eight, Judge Hoffman not only refused to let him testify before the jury but did so on the grounds that his opinions would constitute "a mockery" of the proceedings. He also instructed the defendants' lawyers to say nothing about his refusal to let Clark appear before the jury, under penalty of contempt of court.

[2] There is a history in the U.S. courts of men being sentenced to death for crimes they manifestly did not commit, and sentenced on grounds that were not only political but political only by association. In the 1930s, Judge Webster Thayer sentenced Sacco and Vanzetti, two immigrant anarchists, to death for murder and robbery, saying of Vanzetti during the robbery sentencing, that "this man, although he may not have actually committed the crime attributed to him, is nonetheless morally culpable, because he (as an anarchist) is the enemy of our existing institutions."

of Black Panthers, into their posh home for an evening of drinks, canapés, and conversation. Not invited to the fundraiser was the writer, Tom Wolfe, but he came anyway, in his usual guise as the Man in the White Flannel Suit. It is telling that when he wrote about the evening affair, this benefit for the Black Panther Party – he did so by describing – not the Panthers – but a *white* fantasy about the *black* Panthers set in the head of a *white* man.

Tom Wolfe's pamphlet has now been reprinted in a small book, *Radical Chic & Mau-Mauing the Flak Catchers*, and it begins with that dream:

> He could see himself, Leonard Bernstein, the *egregio maestro*, walking out on stage in white tie and tails in front of a full orchestra. On one side of the conductor's podium is a piano. On the other side is a chair with a guitar leaning against it. He sits in the chair and picks up the guitar. A guitar! One of those half-witted instruments, like the accordion, that are for the Learn-to-Play-in-Eight-Days E-Z Diagram 110-IQ fourteen-year-olds of Levittown! But there's a reason. He has an anti-war message to deliver to this great starched white-throated audience in the symphony hall. He announces to them: 'I love.' Just that. The effect is mortifying. All at once a Negro rises up from out of the curve of the grand piano and starts saying things like, 'The audience is curiously embarrassed.' Lenny tries to start again . . . .

Of course, there was no such concert: but the Bernsteins had, in fact, opened their home to the rich so that the rich, while pressing the flesh of a Panther Field Marshal, might raise bail and defence money for the Panther 21. Otto Preminger was in the library, Peter and Cheray Duchin in the living room, along with Frank and Domna Stanton, Gail Lumet, Sheldon Harnick, Cynthia Phipps, Burton Lane, Mrs. August Heckscher, all the old zircons among the sapphires – and all of them were there to meet the Big Black Bucks, especially "the one with the black leather coat and the dark glasses and the absolutely unbelievable Afro, Fuzzy-Wuzzy-scale, in fact – is he, a Black Panther, going on to pick up a Roquefort cheese morsel rolled in crushed nuts from off the tray, from a maid in uniform, and just pop it down the gullet . . . ?"

Wolfe, casting his wry eye upon the rich, said he could actually hear them think inside their "upholstered skulls" (a neat reportorial trick): "What a relief it was – socially – in New York – (that) the leadership (of the Black Movement had) seemed to shift from middle class to *funky*! From A. Philip Randolph, Dr. Martin Luther King, and James Farmer . . . to Stokely, Rap, LeRoi, and Eldridge! This meant that the tricky business of the fashionable new politics could now be integrated with a tried-and-true social motif: *nostalgie de la boue.*"

The chief minister *de la boue* that night was Don Cox, the *funky* Panther Field Marshal from Oakland. He was cast in "the role of black militant *mau-mauing* the rich white liberals . . . slowly backed into a weird corner. Afro, goatee, turtleneck, and all, he has to be the diplomat . . . the house guest trying to deal with a bunch of leaping, prancing, palsied happy-slobber Saint Bernards . . . ."

The *egregio maestro* was the half-manic Lenny who kept insisting in conversation that it's STEIN and not STEEN, allowing Wolfe to do a little tap dance on the cultivated parvenu Jews of New York and then to drag Otto Preminger on to the parlour room floor to speak in phonetics: "Dats not *trdue* . . . . Dere are many people wid wealth all over . . ." but *trdue* or not *trdue*, there was Lenny, good old Lenny, bobbing up, bobbing down, pejorative, questioning, operating like he was all alone on the 13th floor of his mind, Lenny – the *maestro* who had become, in Wolfe's catchphrase, the Impresario of Radical Chic – the rich geek in charge of the "new wave supreme" – that urge among the rich to not only slum among poor blacks, radicals, and revolutionaries, but to clothe themselves in the spectacle of outlaw ghetto paraphernalia: in other words, to send badass white matrons out into the world wearing wig hats and high-heel sneakers. This was farce, this was ludicrous, this was very funny in a sneering way; there's no question – palsied white people, seen through Wolfe's gimlet lens, are stupid, shallow, and very vulgar in their *nostalgie de la boue*.[1]

Wolfe concludes where he began: in the dreaming head of that Parlour Panther, Leonard Bernstein. He is on stage, and he hears *boos*!

"Fools, boors, philistines, Birchers, B'nai B'rithees, Defense Leaguers, Hadassah theatre party piranhas, UJ Aviators, concert-hall Irish men, WASP ignorati, toads, newspaper readers – they were booing him . . . . They weren't clearing their throats. They were squeezed into their $14.50 bequested seats, bringing up from out of the false bottoms of their bellies the old Low Rent raspberry boos of the days gone by. *Boooooo*. Newspaper readers! That hair-brained story in the *Times* had told how he and Felicia had given a party for the Black Panthers and how he had pledged a conducting fee to their defense fund, and now, stretching out before him in New York, was a great starched white-throated audience of secret candy-store bigots, greengrocer Moshe Dayans with patches over both eyes . . . . *Boooooo Boooooo*. It was unbelievable."

So ends the debacle.

Perhaps those "greengrocer Moshe Dayans with patches over both eyes" were foolish. Perhaps the Bernsteins were guileless,

---

[1] Wolfe feels he has to explain that romanticizing proletarian primitives, *une nostalgie de la boue*, is a nineteenth-century French term that means, literally, 'nostalgia for the mud.'

and even a little gauche. Many thought them so, and many relished Wolfe's happy ridicule of them, but it is interesting that Wolfe does not speak, given all the words that pirouette upon his page, with any persuasively felt concern for the *mud men*, those blacks – those Panthers – who are *actually* imprisoned.

Tom Wolfe is unable, so it seems, to believe that the Impresario, whatever dog-and-pony show he was conducting, might have acted out of good faith, that he might have wanted to see justice done by helping to pay to get justice done.

Wolfe must demean them all.

Boooooo.

James Baldwin believes that he has lived to see the *mojo* moment when a *nigger* has become a man. Tom Wolfe can only envision a nightmare among the sapphire and *foie gras* set. James Baldwin believes that he has lived to see men and women being punished – shot or jailed – solely because they have escaped *niggerdom*. Tom Wolfe belittles the escapees and belittles their would-be benefactors. James Baldwin concludes his letter with a call for conciliation. Wolfe ends his pamphlet on a note of slapstick: Boooooo. James Baldwin remembers those black men locked in the Tombs – and asks to be understood by Angela Davis who is sitting in her cell, facing the electric chair. Tom Wolfe – wise about the pecking orders of Park Avenue but forgetful of the Black Panther prisoners – turns the situation of the moment to farce, which is a convenient way to keep yourself well-suited in white.

During the 1968 Democratic Party National Convention in Chicago, Jean Genet, the playwright, ex-con, and black-eyed susan among the flowers of Paris, wrote about the Police and Panthers, and then wrote about the Panthers and Palestinians:

Both the Black Panthers and the Palestinians are without land. Their two situations are not completely identical, but they are alike in that neither group has any territory of its own.

So where can these virtual martyrs prepare their revolt *from*? The ghetto? But they can't take refuge there – they'd need ramparts, barricades, bunkers, arms, ammunition, the support of the whole black populations. Nor can they sally forth from the ghetto to wage war on white territory – all American territory is in the hands of the American Whites.

The Panthers' subversion (therefore) has had to take place by other means . . . . Spectacle . . . . The tragedy of their situation – the danger of death and death itself: physical terror and nervous dread – teaches them how to exaggerate despair. But spectacle is only spectacle, and it may lead to mere figment, to no more than a colourful carnival; and that is a risk the Panthers run . . . heading for either madness, metamorphosis of the black community, death, or prison.

Alabama's got me so upset;
Tennessee made me lose my rest;
And everybody knows about Mississippi – Goddam!
—Nina Simone

Angela Davis is in prison, in the Marin County jail in California. She is in solitary. But she is notorious, her face has been posted up and down Highway 61 – those soft mournful eyes, her head haloed by nappy blackness, Black Power taken as a natural sign (Larry Neal, the poet, has said: "For a sister to wear her hair natural asserts the sacred and essentially holy nature of her body. The natural, in its most positive sense, symbolizes the sister's willingness to determine her own destiny. It is an act of love for herself and her people. The natural helps to psychologically liberate the sister . . .), and though she has the *mojo* working, she is slender, 145 pounds at 5'8" – a small scar on both knees – as the *Wanted* poster says, and she is incarcerated.

At the Marin County jail, on a cool but sunny January day, all is calm: a young deputy, his hat tucked under his arm (ash-blond hair shaved above the ears, a boot-camp crop), led me along a narrow brightly lit corridor,[1] and then he stepped aside to let me into a small room where Angela Davis, "terrorist," was waiting, dressed in a long-sleeved black sweater, a black skirt, black stockings (convent-school black!) – with no eyeshadow, no

---

[1] I have told the story of how this meeting with Angela Davis took place in prison – the only such conversation that she gave during her incarceration – in my memoir, *Barrelhouse Kings*. I did not, however, in telling that little

lipstick, looking not so much shy as wary – yet sure of her singularity. She glanced at the deputy who mumbled that he had to remain in the doorway so that he could overhear our talk (we had given separate assurances that we would not discuss the particularities of her case), and so she sat down, her elbow on a small table (Styrofoam cup of water, and an ashtray), and she said, "You've been with the Palestinians . . . ."

"You've been told."

"Something . . . ."

"They arrested me," I said, laughing.

"Really!"

"Put me on trial, in Beirut."

"I wasn't told you'd been arrested."

"It all worked out. So what I'd like you to tell me – is – what was it like for you when you were arrested in New York."

"When I was arrested, I was isolated first in the psychiatric ward and treated as if I were someone who had profound mental problems. There was a guard on 24 hours a day, either inside the room, or sitting on the outside. I couldn't talk to any of the other women. In fact, I couldn't talk to any of the matrons."

Earnest, quietly intent, not flustered by the closeness of an unknown white man, she kept a measured tone, had a nasal pitch to that tone, and at moments of exasperation – when she had to recount certain facts – that nasal pitch rose and was saved from

tale, quote the telegram that awaited me when I arrived in San Francisco the night before the conversation was to take place: "CBC (Canadian Broadcasting Corporation) policy decision has forbidden us to do the Angela Davis interview. Have been instructed by John Kerr to tell you that the contract you have for her is not to be conducted under any circumstances." That policy decision, agreed to by John Kerr, was initiated by Eugene Hallman, Vice-President of the Corporation. Hallman, in conversation with me prior to the proposed Davis interview, had told me angrily that he disapproved of the critical tone taken by reporters toward President Richard Nixon and toward the Vietnam War and that he found the increasingly critical attacks on Nixon's Attorney General, John Mitchell, "inconceivable." Since I was fired on orders from Hallman after this conversation was broadcast, I had no chance to ask him what he thought when Davis was freed, with Nixon impeached and Mitchell indicted.

being a girlish whine by her gentling drawl, the refinement of her diction.[1]

"Once we went to court and got a federal injunction, that stopped. I became another sister who was trying to cope with being in jail. The situation in the jail, physically speaking, was of course, horrible. There were mice and roaches everywhere you turned, even in your food. There was practically no medical care. And it was dirty, filthy, the whole place."

"One more form of oppression?"

"As a black person who grew up in the South, oppression was always all around me, it was everywhere I turned. Then, of course, there's this myth that black people did not resist till Watts, or until Malcolm, or until the Black Panther Party. It's just not true. My father participated in armed patrols, they'd get out every night, and in shifts of course, with their weapons, and they'd drive around the community. My earliest childhood memories are bound up with sounds of dynamite. W.E.B. Debois, who was the greatest American black scholar and teacher, and also a member of the Communist Party, he carried a gun all his life, he carried a shotgun, he carried a pistol all of his life."

"Surely solitary confinement has been a shock to your emotional and philosophical sensibility – to be alone – for so long."

"I've understood very well that the Marin County officials wanted to break me. They wanted me to feel the burden of the solitude, and I just had to make up my mind that I was not going to let it affect me that way."

---

[1] At 15, Angela Davis had left her hometown of Birmingham, Alabama, to take a Quaker scholarship at a New York City high school. At the end of her senior year, she was awarded a scholarship to Brandeis University, where she majored in French literature – going for her junior year to study at the Sorbonne in Paris – and then, after her senior year, after entering into philosophical studies under Herbert Marcuse and graduating *magna cum laude* with honours, she did two years of graduate work in philosophy at Goethe University in Frankfurt, West Germany. She then returned to the University of California at San Diego to complete her doctoral program under Professor Marcuse. She was appointed – though she was a declared Communist and was working closely with the Black Panther Party – UCLA professor of philosophy in the fall of 1969.

"You're not suggesting you are no different now from when you came in?"

"I think that what George Jackson said about life in prison is very appropriate. He said that prison either breaks a person, or makes the person stronger. I would like to think that I have become stronger because of this system, which is a model in brutality, it's a model in repression. The current head of the repressive California Department of Corrections has said that they are going to 'experiment in dealing with violently prone prisoners,' they are going to remove a part of their brains."

She folded her arms, as a bird folds its wings, folding into herself.

"Is prison a logical extension of capitalist America?"

"Well, of course, capitalism implies prisons. You can't perceive of a capitalist structure without prisons. In a capitalist society, you have two contradictory things at work. On one hand, so many people are shut out of all that capitalism has to offer, and therefore, they are often forced to resort to crime in order to survive. On the other hand, crime in a capitalistic society is almost inevitably an unconscious desire to become the capitalist, to become he who owns the property. In the prisons and jails today, men and women are beginning to realize that the correct political approach (to capitalism) is to begin to build a collective mass movement which can make demands upon the system, and perhaps bring about a revolution.

"However, the room for meaningful political activity in prison is so narrow that obviously, as soon as prison officials become aware of any movement (toward politics), they confront the new developments with the most devastating repression imaginable. At Soledad Prison, it was January 13th, today, two years ago, there were what I call political assassinations. Three prisoners who were known to be political activists in Soledad, for no apparent reason, were shot down, murdered."

"Prison crystallizes everything that is ruthless in the capitalist structure? Is there no give anywhere?"

"I think it was Dostoievsky who said that you can generally determine what the nature of any given society is by taking a look at its prisons. I think that that is a very fitting way to understand what American society is all about, today."

"Many blacks have said that the prison guards represent a fascist force, that America is a fascist society. You have pointedly disagreed, though you see prisons having a central role in capitalist America."

"I think," she said, holding out her right hand, a hand open but cupped, "we are closer to fascism than we've ever been before. However, I would not say that this is a fascist society. According to my analysis of past fascist states, and the dynamics of fascism in general, fascism is something which moves and develops, and eventually consolidates itself. Once it consolidates itself, it can no longer be torn down from the inside. It can no longer be destroyed internally. If you look at history, there is not one example of a fascist country having undergone a revolution from within, not once fascism had reached the point of consolidation.

"Some say that what you have to do in a fascist society is extend its contradictions to the point where everything is completely polarized: a totally fascist state on the one hand, and then, because you have this very intense repressive fascist society, they say you're automatically going to have resistance from within on the other hand. That's just not true, that's not historically true. The objective situation will not allow resistance. If you look at Germany, it's tragic to see the attempts at resistance which failed because there was no longer any real room for individual acts. There were assassinations and so forth, and so on. But those could not break the fascist society."

"A lot of people take solace out of the way recent black trials have worked out. The Panther 13 trial in New York, Bobby Seale and Huey Newton, are free, and so people say that if the process of the law is allowed to run its course, then justice will be done."

"Well, I was incredulous when I read the *New York Times* editorial saying that the American system of justice is still the keystone of American democracy. There were 13 individuals, 13 men and women, most of whom had been in jail continuously for two years, one of whom, Afeni Shakur, had been forced to live in a New York women's house of detention while she was pregnant, living alone with the rats and the roaches. It would be foolish to attempt to maintain that the New York 13 were the recipients of justice when they had two years wrested from their lives. This is the real nature of the political trial. It doesn't matter, in the end, whether the person is free. The repression has already run its course.[1] The State has succeeded in silencing those sisters and those brothers who are the leaders in our struggle."

"Jimmy Baldwin wrote to you and said that when he looked back to his father he saw that he was just another *nigger*, and when he looked at his own life, he saw himself separated from your generation, your kind of political awareness, your political activism . . . ."

"James Baldwin is a writer, and his comments have to be seen in a literary context. I don't think he meant that his father was just a *nigger* who kowtowed to white people, I don't think he meant that he was removed from us. I think he was saying that, through time, there's been a constant development, an increasing militancy among black people, and it's impossible for us to see ourselves, as to who and what we are, without our mothers and fathers having done what they did, and without their mothers and fathers having done what they did, and on and on and on, until you have to talk about what our people did during slavery, the revolts and their resistance, without which we wouldn't be what we are today."

---

[1] On May 13, 1971, all 13 defendants were acquitted of all charges by a jury which deliberated for 2 hours. Also, all murder charges against three activist Soledad prisoners – James Wagner, Roosevelt Williams, and Jesse Lee Philips – were dismissed in May, 1971, after the prosecution's star witness admitted on the stand that he had given perjured testimony in exchange for an early parole. But George Jackson, still under indictment for the murder of the Soledad guard, was killed by guards during a prison uprising at San Quentin on August 21, 1971.

"Have you confronted the fact that if you are convicted, it is your life?"

"If I were truly alone, if there weren't a movement to free me, to free the Soledad Brothers, to free the San Quentin 6, then I would be in really bad shape because there'd be no one to relate to, no way for me to break the spell of these walls. But when I decided that I was going to devote my life primarily to the Movement, to the struggle for socialism, I decided that my life belonged to that struggle. And to my people. Anyone who makes a commitment to continuously engage in the liberation struggle – and remember, I have seen many of my friends shot down, my friends killed – anyone has to be aware of what the risks are. My life is my risk."

I'd been talking with Ishmael Reed about the Panthers and Davis and Baldwin, too, and the 12-bar backbone to the blues, and how, behind it all, behind everything that is going on, the lurch toward freedom, the blues is both its own world and the whole world at the same time, a great song cycle of stories that, by being told, are a freeing up of a people who have been trapped by bad love, by the needle or *niggerdom*, or by jail time – but it's when you're telling the story, any one of those stories, that the *mojo* is working, which is exactly how Reed has explained *mojo*: "It's Mandingo, man . . . *ma-ma-gyo-mbo* . . . the old grandmother's got the magic so she can make the ghosts of your unhappy ancestors go away. *Mojo* sets you free."

Angela Davis was acquitted of all charges in March of 1972.

The Telegram, 1971; *CBC Weekend*, 1971-75

DEAN ACHESON

Immediately after the Second World War, when Harry Truman was President, Dean Acheson became his Secretary of State, became his advocate for an international American order. He writes in his memoirs: "Only slowly did it dawn upon us that the whole world structure and order that we had inherited from the nineteenth century was gone and that the struggle to replace it would be directed from two bitterly opposed and ideologically irreconcilable power centres." Acheson and Truman, doughty men not given to bouts of contemplation or remorse, turned a cold war tactic into a strategy and called it containment – the Truman Doctrine. First, they contained Soviet military forces in Greece and Turkey and then they force-fed several continental economies, calling it the Marshall Plan. Soviet influence in Europe and in the Middle East was thwarted, it was held in check, except for one breach in that curtain of containment – but more of Acheson's view of that later.

There is about Dean Acheson the primness of the man of moral principle and the ruthlessness of the man who is in service to power. I do not mean the vulgar power of the pimp or the commonplace power of the prosecutor or the bullying power of an Alabama police chief like Bull Connor. I mean power that has about it the air of the anointed, power that has been assumed with a disarming candour by a patrician, power that is exercised with political vigour but also with a disdain for that art that is so essential to the elegance of politics, the art of betrayal.

Acheson, assuming that he was one of the chosen (he was the son of the Episcopal Bishop of Connecticut), also assumed, as a consequence, that he had a societal obligation to practice a profession where he could be "of use." (Edmund Wilson, more of a Calvinist than he liked to admit, once told me in conversation that all he hoped for with his writing was to be "of use.") Out of this sense of public responsibility and out of the same sense of inner necessity that had led Justice Oliver Wendell Holmes to choose the law, Acheson as a young man chose diplomacy, believing it to be a significant public enterprise in which he would not only be able to attain intellectual control over a *corpus diplomaticum*, but over the crass stupidity of low-level politics. He would also be able to confirm – as a puritan soul – his own personal salvation.

Once he was in Washington, Acheson serviced and maintained the mechanism of active American power abroad. Though he was a born patrician and though, as the President's man, he was able to stand somewhat apart from the Senatorial and Congressional bottom feeders of the McCarthy years, he was – after all was said and done – in service to a State that belonged to the bottom feeders as much as it belonged to Boston's Brahmins and therefore he was in service to many craven McCarthy-like men. And so, by his own admission, he often seems – in his career – to have been an ambitious marionette tied to both the ideals *and* the stupid vulgarities of the State. Such is the sullying fate of those among the elect who hope to justify themselves before God, or History, or the State, by a rigorous faith alone, but who end up having to operate at the bidding of the many vacant minds who hold elected office.

Acheson began his career as Acting Secretary of the Treasury under FDR. He became Secretary of State in 1949. Within a year and a half, there had been internal spy scandals in the U.S. (the Hiss and Rosenberg trials), the Soviet Union had unexpectedly exploded its first atomic bomb, Mao Tse-tung had driven Chiang

Kai-shek out of China and on to the island of Formosa, and the Chinese Communists had crossed the Yalu River and had attacked General MacArthur's troops in Korea. Both the mealy-mouthed *and* the mindful in Congress went for Acheson's throat, saying he was Secretary to a State that had become militarily and politically soft in the underbelly. Guileless men and gullible children had waking dreams of mushroom clouds. Strong men spoke openly of being afraid. Because they couldn't throttle those they feared, the enemy without – the Red menace – they looked for enemies within. Betrayal was in the air, it was on television – at the McCarthy hearings, where intimidated and terrified men and women, neighbours and fellow workers, squealed on each other. The adroit Acheson did not falter in these times. He showed astuteness and resolve as he advised Truman on how and why to fire General Douglas MacArthur; he showed only scorn for the Washington Commie-hunting demagogues (he refused to rat on his friend Alger Hiss though Hiss, charged with being a spy, had been found guilty of perjury) and he showed an even deeper contempt for that favourite among anti-Communist patriots – the old pirate, Chiang Kai-shek. He complained that Chiang had been gifted with "a great chance in China and he'd thrown it away" because – once the United States had defeated the Japanese – they had not only rearmed and re-equipped Chiang's Chinese Nationalist troops but they had stationed those troops in centres of control in China so that Chiang could successfully confront and contain Mao Tse-tung. But Chiang's "political and military folly had lost him the position to which he had been returned . . . ." As a result, Chiang had ended up as a gangster-refugee on the island of Formosa, a peacocking stooge propped up by the Formosa lobby in the United States, while China, the incomparable prize, "had been unified (under Mao) and was started on the road to power, but not by us or in our interest."

Acheson's regret is not that Chiang was corrupt, or even that he was malignant – it is that Chiang was a fool – and in his utter foolishness he had cost the United States – always intent on coordinating its conditions of containment – a base of influence and power. Acheson's urbane cynicism is chilling but instructive, because the fastidious Secretary of State suggests in no uncertain terms (the supporting evidence is in full supply in his memoirs) that the United States will enter into political and military deals in the name of democracy with any rat-brain in a uniform who will at first guarantee and then efficaciously provide local stability and support for American policy, that policy always being foreplay for an American economic incursion.

Which leads to Acheson's assessment of Harry Truman.

He says the former haberdasher with his bird-quick eyes had "the priceless gift of vitality . . . and no need for papers predigested into one-page pellets of pablum." But better than that, Truman could act decisively: "No one can decide and act who is beset by second thoughts, self-doubt, and that most enfeebling of emotions, regret. With the President, a decision made was done with and he went on to another . . . ." But, Acheson notes, "the capacity for decision does not produce, of itself, wise decisions." Truman had rightly supported the Marshall Plan and the creation of NATO, he had been steadfast and thoughtful in his pursuit of the war in Korea and in his firing of General MacArthur, but – Acheson says – he did make one mistake of real consequence . . . when, at a crucial moment, he acted out of emotion and compassion. In Acheson's view, Truman seriously jeopardized "the totality of the American interest" by endorsing the establishment of the state of Israel.

Acheson writes:

> I did not share the President's views on the Palestine solution to the pressing and desperate plight of great numbers of displaced Jews in Eastern Europe . . . . The number that could be absorbed by Arab Palestine without creating a grave political problem would be inadequate, and to transform the country into a Jewish state capable of receiving a million or more immigrants would vastly

exacerbate the political problem and imperil not only
American but all Western interests in the Near East . . . .
I had learned to understand, but not to share, the mystical
emotions of the Jews who wished to return to Palestine
and end the Diaspora. In urging the cause of Zionism,
not just because of Jewish pressure (as the English
insisted, and most still believe) but because he had been
persuaded to Zionism by his former partner in the hab-
erdashery business, Eddie Jacobson,

Truman misled the Arabs and abandoned the British to an unten-
able position.

What nettles Acheson is that Truman, by not sizing up the tacti-
cal and strategic consequences of his act, paved the way for the
Russians to enter into the Mediterranean and the Middle East.
After all, since the time of Napoleon, the Russians had been try-
ing to establish a Mediterranean port that would allow their fleet
access to the south of Europe. Not only do the Russians now have
such a port, but they are in Egypt. Because Acheson is interested
in any dislocations that might undermine "the very continuance
of great states and empires," he sees the establishment of Israel as
folly, an act that undermines and will continue to undermine
an international American order and, ironically, the policy of
containment – that policy fundamental to the Truman Doctrine.
Acheson, refusing to justify a Jewish state on "compassionate"
grounds, confesses to a certain guilt for having, as a "useful" man-
darin, supported Truman's commitment by temperament to such
a state.

He believes that the consequence of his failure to make Tru-
man act in the strict service of American power is the present
chaos in which – he suggests – the combatants cannot be saved
from themselves. As Acheson said in a recent interview: "It's

perfectly clear that nobody can coerce them (the Arabs and Israelis) into doing something they don't want to do .... I think the struggle has to go several rounds before they'll begin to see that this is a self-punishing operation." He implied that once that lesson is learned, diplomats who have his sense of anointed ruthlessness and his essential dismay with the human condition, will be able to move in and establish order: power will then coerce, it will penalize. Until that time, lawless combatants, too far out of control, will have to punish each other until they exhaust themselves.

The Telegram, 1970

OSIP MANDELSTAM
MOVES HIS LIPS

Now I'm dead in the grave, teeth
singing in the zero:
Stalin stabbed the air
and his seraphim in sharkskin suits
dressed me in amulets of electrical

impulse, shredded my nerves
and sat listening to my heart beat,
not the beating
but the silence in between,
eternity atrophied into an ellipse

fondled by the Phrenologist's fat slug fingers,
content in his Kremlin nest
as they took me naked to the final
genuflection and fed my legs
through the scaffold's door of sprung light,

a footloose gaiety just
like Godiva's dance of ankle bells
up the stairs in Leningrad,
O Godiva, goodbye, I'd forgotten,
even when I can't breathe I want to live...

Hogg, the Seven Last Words, 2001

NATHANAEL
WEST: *MISS*
LONELYHEARTS

Nathan Wallenstein Weinstein was born in 1903. His father, a
Russian, and his mother, a Lithuanian, had come to New York as
migrating Jews in the 1880s. Max, the father, had become a suc-
cessful building contractor and he and his family had lived in a
fine home on the Upper East Side of Manhattan. When Max
died, his family gave him a half-Hebrew, half-English service at
a funeral church. His son, Nathan, told Edmund Wilson that
the undertakers had changed Max; he was "horrified when he
found that they had rouged the old man's cheeks and cut off his
shaggy eyebrows and put a great big white tie on him." Nathan
changed his name to Nathanael West. When Wilson asked him
how Weinstein had become West, he smiled: "Horace Greeley
said, 'Go west, young man, go west.' So I did."

◯◯◯

> *May I, composed like them*
> *Of Eros and of dust . . .*
> *Show an affirming flame.*
> —W.H. Auden

Nathanael West wrote four novels. Two of them – *Day of the
Locust* and *Miss Lonelyhearts* – are masterful. They are unlike any-
thing else in American writing. The laughter in these stories –

256

if one can call wizened poignancy laughter – is certainly not in the Mark Twain vein of American corn-pone satire; it is closer to the mirthless laughter of a black comedienne like Moms Mabley, where pain is a prickle-board upon which a grin has been stuck.

Miss Lonelyhearts, the son of a preacher man, a back East puritan, is a young hard-drinking newspaperman who writes the Miss Lonelyhearts column. His job is to answer letters written to the newspaper by miserable people who are ostensibly seeking some sort of solace, some kind of explanation for their sorrows, their physical and emotional deformities. These letters at the beginning of the novel – "stamped from the dough of suffering with a heart-shaped cookie knife" – at first startle and amuse him, but then Miss Lonelyhearts becomes obsessed by these plain-spoken, seemingly guileless confessions of pain – it's as if he is being told in letter after letter the grimmest of children's stories, it's as if Tom Thumb, doomed to be no bigger than a thumb, had written to him, asking *Why me, why am I a thumb*, except this is no children's story, this is – for example – the story of a girl who was actually born with no nose:

Dear Miss Lonelyhearts –

I am sixteen years old now and I don't know what to do and would appreciate it if you could tell me what to do. When I was a little girl it was not so bad because I got used to the kids on the block making fun of me, but now I would like to have boy friends like the other girls and go out on Saturday nites, but no boy will take me because I was born without a nose – although I am a good dancer and have a nice shape and my father buys me pretty clothes.

I sit and look at myself all day and cry. I have a big hole in the middle of my face that scares people even myself so I can't blame the boys for not wanting to take me out. My mother loves me, but she cries, terrible when she looks at me.

What did I do to deserve such a terrible bad fate? Even if I did do some bad things I didn't do any before I was a year old and I was born this way. I asked Papa and he says he doesn't know, but that maybe I did something in the other world before I was born or that maybe I was being punished for his sins. I don't believe that because he is a very nice man. Ought I commit suicide?

Sincerely yours,
Desperate

Another letter:

Dear Miss Lonelyhearts,
I am writing to you for my little sister Gracie because something awfull hapened to her . . . . Gracie is deaf and dumb and biger than me but not very smart on account of being deaf and dumb . . . . Mother makes her play on the roof because we don't want her to get run over as she aint very smart. Last week a man came on the roof and did something dirty to her . . . . I am afraid to tell mother on account of her being lible to beat Gracie up. I am afraid that Gracie is going to have a baby . . . . If I tell mother she will beat Gracie up awfull . . . when she tore her dress they locked her in the closet for 2 days . . . . So please what would you do if the same happened in your family?

Alone in his room, haunted by these letters, these succinct sob stories, Miss Lonelyhearts turns away from the ache and attraction of tabloid clichés to Christ. He stretches out under an image of the *corpus* nailed to the cross that he has nailed to his wall with long spikes. He is doing this because as a boy in his father's Baptist church Miss Lonelyhearts had discovered that something always stirred in him when he shouted the name of Christ, something secret and enormously powerful. Now, tormented by disfigured faces and the woes of frustrated women, he needs to feel that power, to trust that power, and in his need, in his yearning, the secret reveals itself unto him: he is filled with the earnest self-effacing yet hysterical enthusiasm of the true believer, he becomes a happiness flasher filled with love. And this is not the Sunday-come-to-meeting love felt by a country hick, by a tent Baptist. This is sophisticated love, this is Dostoievskian love. Reading *The Brothers Karamazov*, he finds confirmation of what he believes he truly believes: "Love a man even in his sin, for that is the semblance of Divine Love and is the highest love on earth. Love all God's creation, the whole and every grain of sand in it. Love the animals, love the plants, love everything. You will perceive the divine mystery in things. Once you perceive it, you will begin to comprehend it better every day. And you will come at last to love the whole world with an all-embracing love."

Miss Lonelyhearts believes that he can give his letter writers not just advice but a release, a freedom from their particular pains, by leading them, lovelorn and forlorn, out of a self-indulgent self-pity into the embrace of an all-loving Christ. Guileless and ambitious, overbearing and – like all such American idealists – optimistic, he is therefore dangerous. With an eye on success, certain that his column will be syndicated, he believes the whole world will learn to love as he has learned to love: "The Kingdom of Heaven will arrive. He will sit on the right hand of the Lamb." Miss Lonelyhearts rides his bed, chanting like a high-school cheerleader: "Christ, Christ, Jesus Christ, Christ, Christ, Jesus Christ."

No longer seeing himself as a hack reporter receiving letters from the hapless, he is on the prowl for lost souls. He encounters an aging homosexual. When the man refuses to pour out his pain, when he becomes a person insisting on some privacy, some shred of dignity, Miss Lonelyhearts – like a lamprey eel for the Lord – fastens on him and twists the old man's arm. "He was twisting the arm of all the sick and miserable, broken and betrayed, the inarticulate and impotent." Miss Lonelyhearts "felt as he had years before, when he had accidentally stepped on a small frog. Its spilled guts had filled him with pity, but when its suffering had become real to his senses, his pity had turned to rage and he had beaten it frantically until it was dead."

Miss Lonelyhearts, in his loving heart, harbours the same rage bordering on hatred that drove Kapos in the concentration camps to beat the weakest of their weak fellow prisoners, precisely because they were the weakest.

The other voice in this wilderness of sorrows belongs to a man called Shrike, a features editor at Miss Lonelyhearts' newspaper. He is a cynical blowhard who declaims nightly at Delehanty's speakeasy, the watering hole where newsmen gather. His face clenched in a smile, Shrike – as if he were the Devil's dissembler – tells Miss Lonelyhearts: "My friend, I advise you to give your readers stones. When they ask for bread don't give them crackers as does the Church, and don't, like the State, tell them to eat cake. Explain that man cannot live by bread alone and give them stones. Teach them to pray each morning: 'Give us this day our daily stone.'"

Shrike ridicules any search for a release from pain, for freedom, whether it is in the Soil, in Art, in the South Seas, or in Christ. He concludes, "My friend, I know of course that neither the Soil, nor the South Seas, nor Hedonism, nor Art, nor Drugs, can mean anything to us. We are not men who swallow camels only to strain at stool. God alone is our escape. The Church is our only hope, the First Church of Christ Dentist, where he is worshipped as Preventor of Decay."

Shrike declares: "I am a great saint. I can walk on my own water. Haven't you heard of Shrike's passion in the Luncheonette, or the Agony in the Soda Fountain? Then I compared the wounds in Christ's body to the mouths of a miraculous purse in which we deposit the small change of our sins. It is an excellent conceit. But now let us consider the holes in our own bodies and into what these congenital wounds open. Under the skin of a man is a wondrous jungle where veins like lush tropical growths hang along overripe organs and weed-like entrails writhe in squirming tangles of red and yellow. In this jungle, flitting from rock-grey lungs to golden intestines, from liver to lights and back to liver again, lives a bird called the soul."

Shrike is maddening because he is the master of a particular kind of clever shallowness. He is clever as advertising copy is clever. What he says is vivid phrase by phrase in its sadistic frivolity – each phrase alluding to a truth, each phrase attesting to nothing.

Miss Lonelyhearts, falling more and more under the spell of his own saintliness, is beginning to come apart at the seams. He is getting into fights, he tries to seduce Shrike's wife (he is sexually inept), and then he agrees to meet a Mrs. Doyle, a constant sufferer who is sexually incontinent in her heat. Coarse, repulsive, just plain horny, she wrestles Miss Lonelyhearts to the floor, pulling at his clothes. Outraged, sullied by such blatant sexual need, Miss Lonelyhearts beats her about the face, and "he kept hitting her until she stopped trying to hold him."

Miss Lonelyhearts flees to his bed. Under the eye of Christ, his hysteria leaves him. He grows calm. He "turns to stone." He feels nothing. He steps outside his skin. "The room was full of grace. A sweet, clean grace, not washed clean, but clean as the inner sides of the inner petals of a newly forced rosebud . . . . He was conscious of two rhythms that were slowly becoming one. When they became one, his identification with God was complete. His heart was the one heart, the heart of God. And his brain was likewise God."[1]

Miss Lonelyhearts, crazed by delusions of grace, is crazy as a loon.

The doorbell rings. He goes to the stairs. Mrs. Doyle's crippled husband, a meterman for the gas company, is at the door.

He, too, has written Miss Lonelyhearts a letter, a letter unmailed, and in the letter he has asked a big question: he wants to know what the point of his life is – dragging the pain in his bad

---

[1] It would be interesting to read Flannery O'Connor's stories in light of *Miss Lonelyhearts*. O'Connor has her own cast of club-foots and girls with blue faces and tattooed men and one-armed men; they are as tormented and prone to violence as Miss Lonelyhearts and his lovelorn, but O'Connor and West – even as they created strikingly similar clashes between the normal and the grotesque, the real and the surreal – intimate two incompatible truths: O'Connor, that God and His grace exist – West, that God and His grace do not exist.

leg up and down stairs for $2.50 an hour. *It aint the job that I'm complaining about but what I want to no is what is the whole stinking business for.*

Miss Lonelyhearts knows what to do: "He would embrace the cripple and the cripple would be made whole again."

Doyle, terrified by this man rushing at him – "running to succour him with love" – pulls out a gun and shoots Miss Lonelyhearts. Miss Lonelyhearts is dying, but he believes that he is now able to give the greatest gift of all to the cripple – his suffering, for "it is only through suffering that you can know Him. Cherish this gift for . . . ."

Miss Lonelyhearts, dying, does not know how to finish the sentence.

But his work on this earth is done.

In calling for compassion, Miss Lonelyhearts had been pitiless; in urging unselfish love, he had been totally self-absorbed; in offering consolation, he had left people inconsolable; in attempting to assuage suffering, he had only increased the bitterness of everyone he had touched.

As the loneliest of men himself, Miss Lonelyhearts had been blind, he had made a terrible mistake. He had not seen, he had not understood that those letters sent to him were stories, boldly told by people who weren't looking for freedom from their pain, their humiliation. They *were* their stories, their pain, their humiliation. The letter was their story and they were clinging to it. He had never entertained the possibility that people love their pain. Live by it. Miss Lonelyhearts, in the name of a greater Love, had tried to take their stories from them, tried to take away their suffering by offering them a vision of a pure Christ, as mad a venture as removing the crucifixion from Christ's own story, as if there could have been an Easter Sunday without a Good Friday.

Fittingly, Miss Lonelyhearts died insane, a crooked heart murdered by a cripple.

The Telegram, 1966-1981

AUSTIN CLARKE
RIDING THE TRANE

I walked up to the Big Man's house and I call him Big Man not because he is burly but because he has presence, he knows who he is, an island man who's ended up inland, a sunshine man who has ended up in snow country. He's got an air of stillness about him, a quiet easefulness, the public stance, I suspect, of a man who has learned how to control private terrors. For thirty-five years I have watched how self-contained he is, how relentlessly calm. I contemplate his calm as he contemplates me. In silence. We have the gift of silence. Neither of us has the need to impinge or impose. Not on each other. We don't need to talk, though we can both talk your ear off at the drop of a hat. Neither of us wears a hat. Hatless, we feel free to say anything we want to say but because we are free, we are free to have nothing to say.

He is a decorous man, a donnish man who likes to take a pew at high mass on Sunday at the Anglican cathedral, he likes to take a chair at high table at Trinity College, but he has always lived downtown, close to low life, to pimps, moochers, and drug peddlers, elbow to elbow with the street action, where he can watch how the police *do* behave and misbehave. But, for all that, low life has never laid a glove on him, not on his style. If this were 1920 he would be wearing spats and puttees. A touch Edwardian. He certainly would be sporting a Homburg hat. But it's the 1990s. Linen jackets and penny loafers are stylish. Wig hats and po'-boy cotton picker cover-alls are hip. He is too cool to be stylish or hip.

Sometimes he dresses like a cricketer, a white sweater with a maroon band at the V-neck. But he doesn't play cricket and no one he knows in his town plays cricket. Often, he shows up in a tweed jacket of an Oxford Street cut, but Oxford Street is not his alley, and for chandelier-lit suppers, he will appear in black tie – though black tie has not been called for. At one such supper, while in a tuxedo, he also wore a tiny headset. He was listening on the radio to a Blue Jays baseball game. As an elegant woman from Rome at his elbow talked on, he relaxed his paunch and fell asleep. He remembers dozing: "Dozing off is my habit, while reading, while drinking, while eating. And once, when I was a much younger man, a woman accused me to my face of dozing off while making love when she was on the brink of orgasm. I left her with no satisfaction. I do not remember her name." He does not remember the woman from Rome but he remembers sitting straight up at the supper table. As if attentive. A trick he learned at Combermere School for Boys on that bump of land in the sea called Barbados. It is his home that isn't his home: the place where he was expected to grow up stupid under the Union Jack but instead he grew up smart. Maybe that is why he dresses like he's from somewhere else. He's always been from somewhere else, even in his own family, where he was the illegitimate child, cherished, but illegitimate, in a country house.

When he laughs he laughs best when he talks country. He talks country when he gets ready to cook country – oxtails and breadfruit cou cou. "Get a fair-size breadfruit, with the stem still in; and wash-she-off; and cut-she-up in eight pieces; peel-off the skin. The skin gotta be turning almost yellow. Put she in a skillet o'cold water, enough to cover-over the breadfruit; and before you cover-she down, sprinkle a lil salt over she."

Before you cover-he down you'll soon discover that the Big Man also loves *café noir* style – Bop till you drop carrying on – Malpeque oysters and dry martinis in a long-stemmed glass (two olives), and rib-eye steak at Bigliardi's Off-Track Champions Betting Bar where, after making a modest wager on a pony, he will put on his intellectual spats and try to explain how Derek Walcott – being a black poet talking to black writers like himself – has "faced the insistent question of our schizophrenia . . . faced the question, and recognized that it is our schizophrenia, in fact, that has given us (as blacks) our most positive definition." It is true: though, of course, he is not clinically schizophrenic, Clarke does answer – 'pon the call – to two names, Austin & Tom, and he easily gets lost, caught – betwixt & between.[1]

On this day, Austin tells me that Tom is cooking – and he is stern about it – Tom *is* cooking and he *is* cooking island "food that'll bring on the bess spiritual unctuousness and grace," and he expects me to be at his house because, among others, his old friend the Chief Justice of the Supreme Court is going to amble on through the side-street downtown hookers and druggies and the Mister Chief Justice – in Clarke's house – is going to partake of pig feet and punkin, squash and chrisophenes.

"The feed bag is on."

When he say the feed bag is on is not a time to *foop* with the man in his house.

It is a writer's house behind a wrought-iron gate, except for the big flag over the door (a red maple leaf FLAG: I can't ever get used to writers anywhere who FLAG their patriotism). The small rooms, made cozy by a certain clutter, smell of pipe tobacco: Amphora, Mixture 79. There are books on the chairs, books on the floor, papers on the sofa and books on the papers. Where did he sit Malcolm X when the X-man came to see him? And all the visitin' Wessindian diplomats and the local Conservative Party honchos (Big Man, the *foop* man, is a Tory!), and Salome Bey the singer and Harry Somers the composer, and what about Norman Mailer? Did he walk Mailer through the house?

There are books, tread on tread, up the narrow stairs.

On the second floor, there is his writing room, and his bedroom, too, with a large black-and-white portrait of Billie Holliday

---

[1] He also answers to the call of being the author of nine novels and six short-story collections, most notably *The Polished Hoe*, winner of the 2002 Giller Prize, the 2003 Commonwealth Writers Prize, and the 16th annual Trillium Prize.

overseeing the bed, a wrought-iron and seemingly fragile bed on tall legs, a princely barque, afloat, "high-high, 'pon which a man or woman would have to jump up and then jump down." Most of the time when I ask him what's happening and how he is doing he says – looking grey under the eyes – that he hasn't slept for three days, being hunkered over his keyboard, writing, trying to find "the right word 'pon the page," and in trying to do so, he says he also hasn't eaten for three days. He grows curiouser and curiouser – he dozes off in public but doesn't seem to sleep at home, and though he loves to cook, he often goes without food, and though he is a man of prose he quotes poetry about being betwixt & between:

> . . . how choose
> Between this African and the English tongue I love?
> Betray them both, or give back what they give?
> How can I face this slaughter and be cool?

In his kitchen, he is wild in his airs of decorum: immaculate white shirt, a striped tie of a darker sensible hue, and his good old tweed jacket of the Oxford Street cut. Bending over a burning stove, stirring pots with a long wooden spoon, talking to me about the food he "does make," he is hassled in his head because he does not have the exact "ingreasements" so that his beans and rice will taste "good-good 'pon a fork, if you are fussy."

He is dressed as uptown Austin but he is talking down home Tom, his Bajan voice, for it is Tom Clarke that they call him in Barbados, Tom – who writes a column in the newspaper and tells his readers, "Don't lissen to no foolishness, particular the kinds and the res and talk emanating from the mouths of neither preachers nor prieses; neither vicar nor dean; canon nor bishop; neither lord-bishop nor archbishop; nor none-so. Lissen to the gamblers, first. And then, nod-off."

Mind you, when he was Tom, the barefoot boy in Barbados, he did no nodding, he *was* a *blur*. As Tom, the teenager, he ran the 100 yards in 10-flat, an island record that Austin says still stands. But now, be it Tom or Austin, he's an over-the-hill athlete with a slight paunch. We share that: old jocks, and I assure Austin that as a basketball player I was sneaky-fast, change-of-pace fast, but Tom smiles, knowing he would have left me in his dust, 10-flat. My only consolation is that Tom might have been fast then but Austin is now the slowest man I know, as slow moving as his stirring of the foods in his pots, ponderously slow so that they won't get bun bun (burnt!), and he tells me to drink up my long-stemmed martini and get myself ready to get full-up, but also *mos important* – to expect no dessert – no dessert because dessert is not eaten by Wessindians unless the meal is so light in its offerings that you need "to full-up everybody's belly."

There are no light offerings in Austin's house. He's got deep pockets, even when he's broke, and his generosity is often profligate in direct relation to his debts – and so, smiling upon self-indulgence, he fires up another martini for me, the Big Man – cooking cou cou as he dreams up new fictions to tell old hard truths, as he waits for his Tory pal, the affable Supreme Court judge, to come for a meal of pork and lima beans – he stirs his pot and turns *up* the silver knobs to his sound system, the sound of which is John Coltrane, the Trane's tenor horn, and it occurs to me that this is where Tom & Austin meet, over a pot of cou cou, smack-dab in Coltrane.

Like a Coltrane chorus, Clarke's paragraphs – as he sits writing bare-assed in the midnight hours before his computer – don't really begin, they just start, they don't end, they stop. He does not surrender the paragraph form (just as Coltrane did not surrender the 12-bar blues grid): but both perform as if form were a jail cell and a chorus is a jailbreak[1]: within the form there are dissonances, counter notes, divided metres (a study could be done of Clarke's discordant placing of semi-colons) and the extended

---

[1] Clarke's friend, the painter Harold Towne, used to speak of form as "the tyranny of the corner." He painted against the corner as Clarke writes against the paragraph.

lyric runs that sometimes invert and always imply the melody
– the storyline – while seeming to wreck it – a lyrical vexation
if not outright anger – modulated to a sweetness:

> . . . and in that time, it was he who understood that a lit-
> tle mistake, a word said under the breath but loud enough
> for Mas'r to hear; the misappropriation of one of those
> freed hens in the yards; the miscalculation in the pour-
> ing of molasses for the horse and jackass, leaving too
> deep a bottom in the bottom of the pail; and his igno-
> rance of mathematics and addition, but his proficiency
> with subtraction: twenty hams was put in the smoke-
> filled shed with the hickory leaves and the smoke broke
> out as if the whole goddamn place was on fire, Mas'r;
> and he said, under his breath, but too loud, Amma wish
> this goddamn place were going up in flame with these
> hams; but when he checked their smoking and their
> curing, one was gone. One gone! These two words became
> like a bell in the night, like a boot at the door, like a tap
> on the shoulder in a crowd, like the leather in the boot
> of the Gestapo, all over that land across the body of water.
> 'One gone!' And dogs barked. Lights came on. Lanterns
> were carried. Dogs yelped, tasting the sweetness of blood.
> Whips were cracked for suppleness. And for length. And
> for deadliness. And men jumped on the backs of horses.
> Rifles and pistols were taken from their shelves, already
> oiled and ready for use. Bullets and shots were fired for
> practice in the air. And the small children, who knew
> those two words, laughed in their sleep, and wished, and
> wished.

The prose line has been sprung for suppleness.
The ingreasements are semi-coloned.
The doorbell rang.
I'm sure the FLAG stood to attention.

I stepped out of the kitchen – out of (I thought) the music – into his tiny fenced-in downtown backyard. The air circuits were wired. Speakers were stationed at the foot of the back walls of the house: ghetto-blasting speakers: indifferent to decorum, the don was not only putting on a feed, he was pumping out Coltrane – he was *churching* the neighbourhood ... searing jolts of sweet tenor sax and bass clarinet, so loud it could not be ignored by anyone in the near distance, certainly not by the neighbours, and not even by a nocturnal racoon, an old night prowler who had come down out of its sugar maple tree to sit – with minstrel-show eyes – on the fence, betwixt and between yards. It stared at me. I stared at it. Absolutely calm. A silence. Except for Trane's horn spiralling around McCoy Tyner's triplets; they were playing "Soul Eyes." The Big Man had wilfully changed the feel in the air of the whole downtown block, in a 10-flat *blur*. Coltrane was in B-flat. And Clarke was standing in the back door of the house, the big heavy-set judge on his arm, the judge flushed from his display of goodwill, the two of them beamish, two high Anglican dignitaries, and their legitimacy – like their friendship – was beyond question. I realized there could be no recipe for knowing who Austin is, but only a consideration of his ingreasements.

The National Post, 1999

ON A LEAP YEAR NIGHT IN HAVANA: A MAN IN A WHITE SUIT WHO SAID HE WAS LEON ROOKE

At the centre of the dark stage in the courtyard there was a pin-hole of light. It widened into a white circle wherein a man with white hair who was wearing a white suit stood in the hole in the dark. He was lanky and tall, gangly, what they call in tall tale country "a long drink of water," which is what he was, a teller of tall tales rocking on the balls of his feet in the white light, warming up.

He flung his arms apart and yelled, "EEEEEAAAAAAAAAAA-AAHHHHHHHHHH."

Pause.[1] Then again, "AAAAAAAAAAAHHHHHHHHHHH." Pause. "I'm summoning the muse," he explained. "Okay, I think I've got her now. CHRISTIANS WELCOME! WIPE YOUR FEET!"

He shuffled his feet furiously. He reached into the dark as if he were scuffling with shadows.

Then he said: "There have been nights when I have trod through the city without a bell around my neck, with no gun, and

---

[1] Leon Rooke, legendary for his readings, is the author of seven novels and 16 collections of short stories. *Shakespeare's Dog* won the Governor General's Award, and he has received the W.O. Mitchell Prize, the CBC Fiction Prize, and the Canada-Australia Literary Prize.

I have spoken with the tongue of sauciness, all as a prelude to my telling you a tale that was told to me in a dream."

He paused, cried WIPE YOUR FEET, and went on: "This tale is about a man with long hair, deep eyes, and a sweet glance, an old man who was a master of the difficult art of pottery, the art of blowing life into clay so that we might hold life in our hands and eat and drink from the crucible of life. In my dream about this man there were three dream catchers who came forward and spoke to me, and the first said that he had decided not to employ the eighth letter of the alphabet, *h*, in telling me the tale."

"And why?" I asked.

And wy not? e said. You can see ow muc fun the story will be, a story wic I am now telling you, wic goes like tis:

Te pottery man's name was Noel.

E dressed simply. E gave people e met corn meal and leaves of coca, but e tried to avoid te sadow of uman company.

One day e made a serpent of clay tat wistled.

Anoter day e made te Dance of Deat.

And all te time it was said cries of pain came from is cabin.

Ten, one afternoon, aving gone to te river to wet is clay, e eard a flute and saw a man playing in solitude.

Wo are you, e asked, playing alone out ere were no one can ear you?

Wo are you, you look like my memory of myself?

I am Ekoor Noel, te potter.

I am Yrrab, te flute player.

Were did you come from?

I stepped from between te legs of a woman. And you?

I come up from te clay country, all wet.

It was the tall man in the white suit who, at that point in the story, rose up on his toes and leapt out of the light into the darkness and for a moment he seemed to be lost, darting around wildly, doing a dance, as if his bones were coming apart at the joints, but then he leapt back into the light, crying "CHRISTIANS ARE WELCOME," and "Be forewarned, the second dream catcher in my dream said he was no longer going to use the sixteenth letter of the alphabet, *p*."

The man in the white suit hunched forward to report that the flute player had asked,

Wy do you insist on staying ere alone? Solitary? You could recreate te dreams of all te men in te town.

– No. You can suffer and sing your grief on te flute I can never create wat my eyes see, I can never do wat te river does, mirror te trees as tey actually are. I do not ave colours tat reflect te ideas in my soul. My work is always inert and lifeless. So ow could I reresent a man ondering life's mysteries? My efforts are insignificant, my broter.

E led him into is wretched cabin were is aint colours were rubbed into te wall. It was a ainting of te valley around im. It was clear tat one colour was lacking, te colour of te sky at te our wen te sun, in robes of clouds, sinks from mortal sight beind te mountain ranges leaving a suffused flow of rose-coloured ligt. Te red of te ainter was too glaring.

– Tat's te colour only te Sun can roduce, te flute layer said. Wy trouble yourself by attemting the imossible?

I wis to do wat te Sun does, wat te day does tat follows te nigt, transforming te darkness, as te rainbow follows te blackness of te storm.

With arms outstretched toward the darkness, the man in the white suit uttered a sound like the nasal cry of a dying cattle beast as he became more ecstatic, suddenly whirling on the spot inside the circle of white light, chanting AAAAAAAAHHHHHHHHHH, WIPE YOUR FEET: "And the third dream catcher said the *h* was a comet whirling in the skies and the *p* was a stone angel fallen into the riverbed, but to end the story he would not employ the sixth letter of the alphabet, and so, he would go forward without the *f,*

Were is te artist, asked the lautist?

E ad a rare seed, a rare ticture to give im.

Te artist, taking te seed, decided to try one last time to colour is wall. E began to rub te new colours into te wall wit intensity, trying to bring to ass wat e ad so long desired: to aint as it really was te landscae seen troug is narrow window. E lacked someting, one ting only, a tone, a olour wic e did not ave.

Quickly, e drew is blade and slit te skin of is and. As te blood surted, warm and red, e mixed it wit water rom a jar and beold, te color. Overjoyed, e continued to aint, til e elt a surge of te oneness of everyting til e ran out of blood and e sank dead on his bed.

Te lautist saw te ainting on te wall. Wat te artist ad seen was te way it was done. Kissing the cold ace of is riend, e layed is lute at te eet of te artist.

Te last rays of te sun tinctured te artist, is otter's tools, is aints, and ten dissolved into grey, te grey of te dead artist's lesh. And e continue to lay is lute til nigt ell, one great lieless sadow covering a silent world.

Into which, the man in the white suit whispered the last words of his tall tale. He had ceased to wag his arms, ceased to shuffle, and the light he stood in slowly shrank. The darkness inexorably closed around him until there was only a pinhole of light, and then there was nothing, a complete silence, a complete darkness. He was never seen again.

Over the months, after that fateful evening, there was much speculation: was the man in the white suit actually Leon Rooke himself, appearing not only to mimic himself but, by telling the tale of the potter, to mimic his own story, or – as some said – was he an apparition of the Russian novelist, Mikhail Bulgakov, author of *The Master and Margarita*, or – are we to believe the amiably alcoholic First Secretary of the Embassy who insisted that he was not only present in the Havana courtyard for the execution of the tall tale but immediately knew by the character of the broken diction who the man in the white suit was: the former Prime Minister, Jean Chrétien? Lending credence to this possibility is the fact that guests at the Embassy are daily confronted at the front door by a hand-lettered sign, a gift of *habitant* folk art from the Prime Minister, that must obviously have suffered weather damage: WI E YOUR EET.

There is, however, a further, and more persuasive, explanation as to who the apparition in the white suit in Havana was, or more accurately, is (as great writers never die).

It is my contention that, alive and writing in Toronto, Leon Rooke is the reincarnation of another theatrical presence, a man known to be tall who often confused his friends by appearing to mimic himself by dressing in white as a ghost.

To go to the scholarly point: the particular and idiosyncratic prose in which the man in the white suit told the tale of the potter is the exact language of *The Irish Masque at Court*, first printed in the Folio of 1616 on signatures Pppp 2 verso to 4 verso. This masque, also dealing with an ambassador who is present in the audience, was performed in London in a courtyard similar to that in Havana. Beyond all doubt, Leon Rooke is the reincarnation of the Elizabethan playwright, Ben Jonson. I provide not only the authentic Jonson text as testimony but note that this *masque* marks the first appearance on the London stage of that character who will come to be known as the Paddy, that rendering of the Irishman talking as heard by the English ear:

(The ambassador being set in expectation, out ran fellows attired like citizens:)

Characters: Dennis, Donnell, Dermock, Patrick.

Dennis: For Chreesh's sake, phair ish te king? Phich is he, an't be? Show me te shweet faish, quickly. By Got, o' my conshence, tish is he! An tou be king Yamish, me name is Dennish . . . .

Donnell: Ish it te fashion to beat te imbashators here, ant knock 'em o' te heads phit te phoit stick?

Dermock: Ant make ter meshage run out a ter mouthsh before tey shpeak vit te king?

Dennis: Peash, Dermock, here ish te king.

Dermock: Phair ish te king?

Donnell: Phich ish te king?

Dennis: Tat ish te king.

Dermock: Ish tat te king? Got blesh him!

Dennis: Peash, ant take heet vat tou shay'sht, man.

Dermock: Chreesh blesh him, I shay. Phat reason I take heet for tat?

Donnell: Chreesh blesh ty shweet faish, king Yamish, and my mistresh' faish too: pre tee hear me now. I am come a great vay of miles to shee tee now, by my fait and trote, and graish o' Got . . . .

Patrick: By Chreesh shave me, tou liesht. I have te vorsht tongue in te company at they shervish. Vill shome-body shpeak?

Donnell: By my fait, I vill not.

Patrick: Speak Dennish, ten.

Dennis: If I speak, te divel take me! I vill give tee leave to cram my mout phit shamrocks and butter and vayter-creshes instead of pearsh and peepsh.

Patrick: If nobody vill shpeak, I vill shpeak . . . .

CHREESHENS VILLCOME!

White Gloves of the Doorman, 2004

JOHN O'HARA

O'Hara is O'Hara.

The accuracy of his ear is admirable. He hears thugs, psychopaths, or supper club patrons and when he tells them what he hears they believe they are hearing themselves. That is quite a feat, to apparently ring so true to your time. Yet, no matter his virtuosity, a flatness seeps in between his spoken lines, his music diminishes to a note or two, the stories pall, and, despite their immediate appeal, they fall flat.

This is because O'Hara's characters are *his*, they belong to him, they never become larger than his skill. He is in absolute control of a style that is all in his ear, but he is never more than that style, never more than the talk he hears his characters talk. Though his people are eager and ambitious for themselves, they are never allowed to be larger than what he has them say, and because what they say is often – unwittingly – at their own expense, they end up as his fools. To hear this, you have to hear him at work, and hear him at work at length:

> "Now the big question is, the all-important question – is," said Julie.
> "What is the big question, Julie dear?" said Nancy.
> "Ah, you like me, don't you? I like you, too," said Julie. "I like Charley, too."
> "And I used to like Jim, didn't I, Jim?"
> "Used to, but not any more."
> "Correct. Jim is a rat. Aren't you, Jim?"
> "Of course he's a rat," said Nancy. "He's a Franklin D. Roosevelt rat."

"I'm a Franklin D. Roosevelt rat. You be careful what you say," said Julie.

"The hell with that. What was the big question?" said Charley.

"My big question?" said Julie.

"Yes," said Charley.

"I didn't know I had one. Oh, yes. The big question is. Do we go to Harlem so I can't go on tomorrow night and I give my understudy a break? Or. Or. Do I go home to my trundle bed – and you stay out of it, Jim. You're a rat. I mean stay out of my trundle. Nevermore, quoth the raven. Well, what did my understudy ever do for me? So I guess we better go home. Right?"

"Yeah. I haven't got an understudy," said Charley. He signalled for the check.

"Jim, why are you such a rat? If you weren't such a rat. But that's what you are, a rat," said Julie.

"Pretend I'm not a rat."

"How can I pretend a thing like that? I'm the most promising thirty-year-old ingénue there is, but I can't pretend you're not a rat. Because that's what you are. Your ex-wife is my best friend, so what else are you but a rat? Isn't that logical, Jim? Do you remember Bank Street? That was before you were a rat. No, No, you weren't. If you were a rat then, you wouldn't be one now. That's logical."

"But he's not a bad rat," said Nancy.

"Oh, there you're wrong. If he was a good little rat I'd take him home with me. But I don't want a rat in my house."

"Then you come to my house," Jim said.

"All right," said Julie. "That solves everything. I don't know why I didn't think of that before. Remember Bank Street, Jim?"

"Sure."

She stood up. "Goodnight, Nancy. Goodnight, Charley." On her feet she became dignified, the star. She held her mink so that it showed her to best advantage and to the captains who said, "Goodnight, Miss Moore," she nodded and smiled. In the taxi she was ready to be kissed. "Ah, Jim, what a Christ-awful life, isn't it? You won't tell Ken, will you?"

"No. I won't tell anybody."

"Just don't tell Ken. I don't want him to think I care that much. He's giving me a bad time. Kiss me, Jim. Tell me I'm nicer than Nancy."

"You're much nicer than Nancy. Or anybody else."

She smiled. "You're a rat, Jim, but you're a nice old rat. It's all right if I call you a rat, isn't it? Who the hell is she to say you aren't a bad rat? She's not in our game, is she?"

"No."

"We don't have to let her in our game . . . ."

And on it goes, the game, the arch repetitions, the quips . . . . O'Hara says what is said and is done, but great writers have the power to say the unsayable. So he will be remembered as a writer of his time who got hold of certain inflections, and therefore, of certain attitudes, as did Erskine Caldwell who was all ears on the other side of the tracks, or, among poets – as did John Masefield in a poem famous in O'Hara's time, "Cargoes":

> *Dirty British coaster with a salt-caked smoke stack,*
> *Butting through the Channel in the mad March days,*
> *With a cargo of Tyne coal,*
> *Road-rails, pig-lead,*
> *Firewood, ironware, and cheap tin trays.*

A poetry – like O'Hara's prose – that says exactly what it says, and no more.

1981

THE SIMIAN IRISH

At the opening of the novel *Jane Eyre*, a certain Mrs. Reed is described as a woman of "somewhat large face, the under-jaw being much developed and very solid; her brow was low, her chin large and prominent, mouth and nose sufficiently regular; under her light eyebrows glimmered an eye devoid of ruth; her skin was dark and opaque, her hair nearly flaxen . . . ."

This is not all that we will need to know about the character of Mrs. Reed but it is a lot; we are being told who Mrs. Reed is – her bloodlines and the cast of her behavioural character – if you know how to read the *code* to her face.

What could that code be?

Knowing that her face, as Charlotte Brontë conjured it, is a kind of contour map we can say – given her much developed under-jaw, her large prominent chin, her low brow and opaque skin, and given the refinements of her regular mouth and nose, light eyebrows and flaxen hair, and an eye devoid of ruth – that she is not only a woman of contradictions, but she is by blood part Celt and part Anglo-Saxon, and therefore, part ape and part angel.

We know this because Charlotte Brontë believed, as did other novelists of the nineteenth century – Walter Scott, Charles Dickens, Disraeli, Trollope, Kipling and Charles Kingsley – that not only were the eyes a window to the soul, but the whole face – the bumps and lumps, the overbite or under-jaw, the simous or snub-nose, the eye of ruth in its hollow, the heavy eyebrows and low-hanging brow – were all indicators to the character of the inner self. To the schooled eye, you were your face. Who you were was an open secret.[1]

This study of the face, of course, is Physiognomy, a branch of physiology that is embedded in folklore – a belief in the evil eye, for example – that goes all the way back to the Greeks, to the Hippocratic school. By the 1800s, the idea that "the face never lies" had become conventional wisdom, and the most ardent exponents of physionomical theory were not wack-heads and quacks but medical doctors, clergymen, novelists, ethnologists, and anthropologists. The systematic study of the face as a skeleton key to human motivation and behaviour led inevitably to physionomical theories about higher and lower forms of vertebrate life – to superior and inferior forms of intelligence. Intellectuals who liked to think that certain ethnic groups were inclined to crime, began to associate facial characteristics with criminal tendencies among "the lower orders." A taxonomy of human types was proposed – a family tree of those most likely to commit a criminal act. In other words, craniologists, phrenologists, ethnologists and anthropologists decided that specific groups of men and women were born to be criminals – were "born for the rope," were "born" to be physicians – "born" to the manse, "born" to the silk, "born" to be inherently inferior or superior. Again, it was in the bloodlines and the bloodlines were in the face.

Not surprisingly, the ranking of ethnic groups on branches of a Family Tree reflected the political and religious convictions and prejudices of English society. At the very top of the tree were Aryans – the Saxon, Germanic, or Teutonic races – just above Semites and the Japanese – while "white Negroes," the simian Celt, stood at the bottom, below the Bushmen and Hottentots.

---

[1] In fact, we learn that Jane Eyre had spent her childhood in Gateshead Hall, the home of the Reeds. Though the systematic study of the face was not his concern, the critic, Robert Bernard Martin, observed: "The dominant tone of the Gateshead section is that of passion, sensuality, emotion, superstition, and the other manifestations of the non-rational aspects of man's nature. Mrs. Reed, whose capricious spoiling of her children parallels her cold dislike of Jane, rules the house, setting the tone." In other words, in Mrs. Reed, the ape had prevailed.

Specific facial features were associated with life at the bottom of the tree, life among those who were brutal and bestial, if not sub-human. These features – a low brow, a prognathic under-jaw, a snub nose, a cratered socket containing a bulging eye – these were believed to be the defining features of the Celt – the face of the irascible, unruly, discontented ape-like peasant who was given to false religion (Papism), brawling and the drink, the ape-like Paddy, the Irishman.

Through the nineteenth century, as the English were increasingly forced to confront chronic political and agrarian protest in Ireland, particularly after the famine years of the 1840s, the famine years of the "coffin boats" crammed with starving Irish, Paddy became a mythic figure in journals, in novels, and on the stage – a monstrous Caliban – a figure to be feared, abhorred and ridiculed, easily recognizable in caricature as the offspring of a gorilla father and a prognathous Irish mother. This Paddy appeared regularly in the *Fleet Street* and *Strand* journals – *The Illustrated London News*, *Cassells Illustrated Family Paper*, *The Illustrated Times*, *The Penny Illustrated Paper*, and *Punch* – whenever there were Irish protests against absentee landlords, against tithes, against the Act of Union or for Catholic emancipation – at such times of crisis, Paddy, with his pig-snout nose and fanged teeth would appear.

THE ANARCHIST
Punch, 29 October, 1881
(detail: *"Two Forces"*)

WILD IRISH CELT
Puck, Vol 8, No. 191, 3 November, 1880
(detail: *"The Simian Irish Celt"*)

IRISH FRANKENSTEIN   *The Weekly Freeman and National Press*, 6 May, 1893
(detail: *"The Frankenstein of Hatfield and His Handiwork"*)

PADDY AND HIS WIFE IN THEIR HABITAT / A KING OF A-SHANTEE
Puck, Vol 10, No. 258, 15 February, 1882 (*"Prognathism in Ireland"*)

Such a belittling and demeaning view of the Irish – as Ashanti tribal kings – Africans in the bush – certainly made it easier for educators among the English occupiers of Ireland to snuff out Irish culture by snuffing out the Irish language. In the latter half of the nineteenth century, Old Irish, the language spoken by Paddy, by peasants and the literate alike throughout the country, was proscribed in the schools, to be replaced by English, the language of the empire, which was taught forcefully – until – as we have it today all across the counties, the language of the angels is now the language of the ape.[1]

---

[1] Two comparable historical situations come to mind: in the final years of the Soviet tyranny, a "Russification program" was well underway in the schools of Lithuania, Latvia, and Estonia – a program designed to "kill off" those languages among children by making Russian the only language of late primary, and all secondary and advanced education; in Canada, all through the

John Montague, poet, of an Ulster Catholic family, has written – in English, of course – of his grandfather who, as a boy, was taught the new language in the new dispensation of the late nineteenth century. It is a poem called *A Grafted Tongue*:

An Irish
child weeps at school
repeating its English.
After each mistake

The master
gouges another mark
on the tally stick
hung about its neck

Like a bell
on a cow, a hobble
on a straying goat.
To slur and stumble

In shame
the altered syllables
of your own name:
to stray sadly home

and find
the turf cured width
of your parents' hearth
growing slowly alien:

---

twentieth century, the "education" of Inuit children in so-called "residential schools" was conducted by Anglican or Catholic priests who forbade even the social use of Inuit languages among the children, and, did so as part of a policy – abetted by government – to obliterate the culture of the Inuit. Outrage over this attack on a culture arose among the public at large only when it was discovered that the priests were assaulting and raping the children.

In cabin
and field, they still
speak the old tongue.
You may greet no one.

To grow
a second tongue, as
harsh a humiliation
as twice to be born.

Decades later
that child's grandchild's
speech stumbles over lost
syllables of an old order.

There is no stutter in Montague's poetry but as he talks he in fact stumbles over his syllables. It is an inheritance, he has a stutter. But when I first met him in Paris years ago, I was struck not by his stutter but by his high brow, his reddish-flaxen hair, his clear blue eyes, his long nose, his good regular chin, his pale skin – very Irish, he seemed to me, as he said, "You know, poetry written by the English is stagnant, dying. But it is not really a genuine kind of death. It is just moribund. The English unfortunately are no longer able to speak English. They are dying the death of the adverb, *really* this and *truly* that, all about something involving teacups and a dull day of rain, life as a faded flower in the pot, none of the tension between sex and death as Yeats would have it. And there's the great irony, it's our vengeance, you know having been forced to speak and write in their language, the Irish writers of our time – Yeats, Synge, Joyce, Behan – we've saved the English language from the English themselves."

He smiled.

It was a smile of courtly mischievous whimsicality.

Superior, with a light touch.

So it came to pass: the ape, saying the Word upon the page,
came to the aid of the angel.

1986

CECIL BEATON

Cecil Beaton, with razor-cut puffs of white hair over his ears, his lips pursed, is a figure of a certain elegance, a man of *refeened* urbanity who has cast his eye upon the old rich, the industrious rich, and those whom Scott Fitzgerald described as the coastal spew of Europe – the *nouveaux riches*. His portraits of these people are usually admiring and seldom cut beneath the well-turned ankle to the bracelet of bright hair about the bone.

There is, for example, a telling study – a set piece – of a Lady Loughborough from 1927; he has placed the head of this woman with her mournful eyes inside a bell jar and he has placed the jar on a table. She has, needless to say, an aloof elegance, since she is decapitated; a woman cut off from her body, a woman of no substance kept in a jar, a parlour-room decoration.

In his high life and high-fashion photography, where the essence of his technique is to achieve style *without* substance, gesture *without* meaning, sexuality *without* sensuality, Beaton – according to the demands of his trade – has achieved a certain excellence. His models are not dead but lifeless in their flawless beauty.

They are in Beaton's bell jar.

However, when Beaton photographs the haggard, the ugly, the aged, especially if it is a woman, something unintended happens, something compelling. His portraits come to life. Princess Marie Louise, at first glance, seems to have a kindly old face, except Beaton, catching her with her fingers raised imperiously and trying hard to haul herself out of her chair, suggests the wilfulness of an old crone who is alive like a wide-eyed plotting child, bristling on the edge of death.

Beaton, imposing a contrived urbanity on men and women who have lived out their lives, treats them in the way he knows how – as if they were young fashion models or actors. It is ironic, but these decrepit people achieve a living presence if not a dignity. As light seeds the dark, unintentionally, Beaton has seeded their individual darknesses with light.

The Telegram, 1968

KARSH AND
MACLENNAN:
POWER LIFTING

Yousuf Karsh, the photographer, is drawn to men of power and presence – generals, presidents, industrialists. He says he has tried to capture the mystery such men reveal in "an unconscious gesture, a gleam of the eye," in all such glimpses of the "innermost self behind the human face." Perhaps, but I find little or none of this mystery of the innermost self in his portraits of men of power.

I find the scenes in which he sets such men, modelled around masses of blacks and whites, too deliberate, too heavy-handed, too stylishly "composed" for the occasion. Also, he too often retouches his work extensively, tipping the glint of greatness to an eyelid, to a cheekbone. Often, the skin and the hair in these portraits are inhuman, having a white vinyl quality. Thus, in his portrait of Georges Braque, the painter's left hand is beautifully formed, but it is a beautifully formed glove made of skin. The same is true of the portrait of Jean Cocteau, whose well-shaped hands glisten in their stillness. Unfortunately, Cocteau's hands have the enamelled presence of hands I once saw in Spain, the embalmed hands of a saint in a glass case.

This enamelling of skin tones is part of Karsh's rhetoric – those revelatory gestures he has deemed appropriate to the idea of greatness: a stern unflinching eye, a dreadful odour of backlit piety, a studied repose that suggests prayer. When Karsh photographs a man of power, he does not capture the quirks of the man, the innermost self, but the solidity and stolidity of the man's Office.

The portrait of Lyndon Johnson is a case in point. Johnson, with one hand pointing to the solid earth, is leaning forward as he peers resolutely into the future, that distance beyond the photograph's edge wherein lies destiny. But I want to know where and why Karsh has hidden the toughness of Johnson, a man who bullied the Senate, who wheeled with a hand full of gimme and wheedled with a mouth full of much obliged, who groped at his belly and crotch during press conferences, who humiliated aides and scorned reporters by conducting Presidential briefings while seated on the toilet.

As for others: John F. Kennedy, a man left breathless in real life by real physical pain, a man who procured elections and low-life broads with equal ease, also has his eye on the future as if – full of amiable well-being – he is watching the movie of his own good life, hands clasped in an attitude of prayer; Queen Elizabeth and her consort, with their heads wrenched to a 90-degree angle, stand staring down peerage's hallway, looking like public works officials who have been forced to listen to a reading of Leviticus; Martin Luther King, eyes uplifted to preacher-heaven, is not the man who faced down snarling dogs and cracker sheriffs while consorting, as some easy talking preachers do, with easy women; and Nikita Khrushchev, wrapped in furs, is no more than a hokum-beaming buffoon exuding good-natured peasant cunning with no hint of what a cold-blooded killer of thousands he was and how intelligent he must have been to outwit and outlive Beria, let alone Stalin.

Film noir's parade, shot still by still.

But then . . . we have that absolutely convincing portrait of Winston Churchill – there he is, bullheaded, self-reliant, glowering – "a man of controlled and frightening violence, a man of superhuman will and energy, an uncanny kind of intelligence which has marched far beyond the limits of cynicism, a man of so many parts that inevitably some portions of his nature are at war with others, yet withal a man whose face haunted Hitler before the war and drove him to despair during it."

That reading of Churchill's character from the face of his photograph – accurate, and even astute (I'll let the haunting of Hitler pass) – is from a surprisingly long essay on Yousuf Karsh's portraits by the novelist Hugh MacLennan. The essay is called "The Face of Power," and it was written for *Maclean's* magazine, May 1, 1947. In this essay – uncollected, and, so far as I know, the longest MacLennan ever wrote (more than 5,000 words) – he made an extraordinary if peculiar claim for Karsh: "Of all contemporary artists the world over the most likely candidate for immortality is the photographer Yousuf Karsh . . . . Quite apart from his capacity as an artist, which is great, the future fame of Yousuf Karsh will be fortified by the unique nature of his subjects. He has photographed, and revealed through the filter of his powerful brain, most of the men who guided the western nations to victory in the Second World War. When history reaches out for an understanding of these men it will use Karsh's portraits."

The unique nature of his subjects . . . .

Those subjects, those men, and not Karsh, are really MacLennan's subject, and what he has to say is extraordinarily revealing, not about the men but about himself. We have come to know MacLennan from his novels and his other essays, and we have come to know him as a man of stern puritan temperament whose characters suffer from a certain constriction of the heart. But after reading his essay on Karsh it seems to me that we are dealing with a MacLennan we have never known, a MacLennan whose innermost voice – an innermost enthusiasm opens up in the essay like a black flower – an enthusiasm, not alien to a puritan temperament, for power. You can feel the force in his prose, even a thrill, as he says, "somebody must assume the burden of power . . . . Power issues its own rules. It is a separate world. It creates its own climate. To wield power with integrity, a man must accept a sort of poison within his veins."

I quote him at length:

For many years European thinkers have been telling us that the age we live in is decadent. For them, as Europeans, this may be true. But we in the British Commonwealth and the United States are no longer dominated by Europe, not even in the realm of ideas. The supreme attribute of decadence is weakness in the will. In a decadent society leaders are almost always capricious, unreliable and devoid of inner confidence. At their best they see too many sides of any public question to commit themselves to a single bold plan of action. They become like Hamlet, dissipating their force by too much speculation. At their worst they are cynical tyrants, irresponsibly and hysterically cruel and they retain power because they surround themselves with men as vicious as themselves. Karsh shows us that whatever else our society may be, it is not decadent. Not yet.

The single quality which unites all of Karsh's men of action amid their many differences is the obvious fact that they have wills like steel. In nearly every one of his faces willpower and logic completely dominate imagination. One looks – as Karsh makes us look – at Eisenhower, Admiral King, Cunningham, Churchill, Alanbrooke, Roosevelt, Marshall, Portal and Arnold. Then one thinks of the creatures they vanquished. Suddenly the Axis leaders seem amateurs of power compared to these men. Compared to Churchill and Roosevelt, Hitler was a screaming hysteric. Compared to Admirals Cunningham and King, Doenitz and Raeder were a pair of sour-minded, shifty little bureaucrats. Beside Portal, Milch looks like a circus showman. These men Karsh photographed lack many qualities. Not very many of them invite affection. But few of them lack the supreme quality necessary for a great leader. They have character. They have immense moral force.

Moral force, let us note, has nothing to do with whether a man is morally good or bad. It depends on a man's absolute inner conviction that he can carry through the job in hand without breaking under the strain, without losing his judgment, without becoming theatrical. It is quite as much a weapon as it is an attribute . . . . A close study of most of these men of power leads one to believe that their strength comes, not from reliance on a present deity, but from a sure belief in their own integrity. By integrity I mean nothing more than the inner strength which prevents a man from betraying himself. The faith of most of Karsh's subjects seems to derive from their sureness that they have the know-how to win and the willpower to get the results they want.

These men are strained, isolated, specialized. They are products of an age of exact science and massive technical power. Many of them have been disillusioned. They have learned, to their bitterness or satisfaction, that such variables as human courage, faith, loyalty and resolution are helpless against the blind and exact power of machines . . . . We see Lord Alanbrooke, who – we are told – more than any other soldier, created the British Army after Dunkirk . . . and looking at Alanbrooke's face one knows that . . . once decided, nothing – absolutely nothing – would deflect him. One reads with initial surprise in Karsh's comment, which accompanies the picture, that Lord Alanbrooke likes birds. Then one is no longer surprised. Birds are high and lonely too . . . .

Of all these faces, the one which seems to me to reflect the distilled essence of the spirit of our time is that of J. Edgar Hoover, the leader of the G-Men. Here is a terrific concentration of relentless, nervous, lonely ability harnessed to a single purpose by a will so strong one wonders how his tense body manages to contain it. Here is a man who knows that to enforce the law in the modern industrialized United States one must be as precise, efficient, merciless and unreflective as a machine. Surely Hoover is a man for whom nothing counts but results. His stubby fingers lock into each other like the jaws of a bear trap. God help the criminal who crosses him. He will think further, act faster, and strike harder than any of them would dream of doing . . . .

Henry Adams said: 'Power is poison.' Accepted superficially, as it usually is, this is the statement of a man disgusted by what he has seen of public life. But if we think about it more carefully, we realize that the statement is essentially tragic, whether Adams intended it to be so or not.

Somebody must assume the burden of power if organized society is to exist. Power issues its own rules. It is a separate world. It creates its own climate. To wield power with integrity, a man must accept a sort of poison within his veins. He can afford few friends among his equals lest it become his public duty to betray them. He can afford few luxuries lest he soften his purpose. He must starve his spirit lest his imagination revolt against the narrowness of the life he leads. In fighting against villains he must often use the methods of a villain, and be prepared to take advantage of fear, shame, hatred, vanity and ambition in the men with whom he inevitably must deal. In guarding civilization he must on occasion act like a savage.

With a few exceptions the subjects of Yousuf Karsh come under this latter definition of power. However much they may differ in capacities and aims, they have this one thing in common. They are tense, lonely men, controlling the destinies of a tense, lonely age.

Whether I find MacLennan's reading of Karsh's faces to be ludicrous is not the point. The point is power. Power and how it should be wielded, power and who is prepared to take the poison, power and who is prepared to act like a savage to save civilization.

I do not know of anyone who has commented on how close MacLennan is by temperament to Heidegger – to his belief that there are men who, by the nature of their being, are driven to exercise power as the *will to will* – or how urgently MacLennan has been drawn, without saying so, to the idea of the Nietzschean *übermensch*, the superior man who – like J. Edgar Hoover! – thinks further, acts faster, and strikes harder. In recent years in the public world of politics, MacLennan has all too often assumed the role of the tense lonely man who has been left no alternative but to castigate the self-indulgent, faithless, decadent young, and those elders who encourage the young. He has grown more lonely, and more openly sorrowful in his isolation, because the Québécois, and not just the young, have refused to do what he has told them to do. He has stamped his foot in the dust. But, in his own imaginative world, in his novels – it has been another story. His characters, as he has created them, have had to do what they are told. As a novelist, MacLennan has yielded almost entirely to his temperament, to his preparedness to take the poison, a tendency that points to the great weakness in all his work.

Too often, he is the hectoring, instructive power behind the story, telling his characters what to think, telling his readers what to think. When his characters do talk, when they do speak up (and *Return of the Sphinx* – his response to the ambiguities and confusion of the Quiet Revolution – is the worst), they have little life of their own – they are his mouthpieces or the butts of his scorn, and their conversations add up to little more than engineered explication of his point of view. He never lets his characters be themselves, he has never turned them loose. That would be a risk: they might not only turn out to be "decadent" – self-indulgent and self-pitying – they might become their own men and women and even worse – their own worst enemies. They might turn out to be Madame Bovary or Jay Gatsby, characters too reckless for MacLennan and, as it happens, too commonplace for Yousuf Karsh.

The Telegram, 1967-1973

ABOUT FACE:
JOHN REEVES

John Reeves, the photographer, is like a man who has turned
inland so that he can then push to the edge, attack all boundaries
from within. Men like that know how to stand their ground. His
ground is the face. Most photographs of the face are not seri-
ous. They are a matter of courtesy, not truth. A truth is always
a little embarrassing. There are many ways to come at truth. You
can come at it from outside, dolling up space or cropping space
as you close in on the face. That is how some sculptors try to put
a good face on stone. But there are other sculptors, and photog-
raphers, who take what they are given, not what they can get.
They take the face that's already in the stone, in the camera eye.
They take it with humility, and then like Reeves, they attack from
inland.

Many photographers bring to a face what they think it lacks,
the lighting of greatness, the dimmers of taste, the claptrap of
cultural gestures from someplace else, gestures from the outside.
Not Reeves. He is parochial, not provincial. He goes to ground.
The person, the face, can be from anywhere, but – where a Karsh
goes for the pose – the face is where Reeves is. It is his place, his
locale.

There is a deep trust at work here, and a faith. While the
colossal, the glamorously neon, the minimalist, and the makeshift
are collapsing, Reeves is at the centre, believing not only that
the centre can hold, but that the centre – the face he's attacking –
will hold, no matter how hard he pushes to the edge, to the ear,
the jawline, the brow. He trusts not tricks but the strength of

character inherent in each face – and it is remarkable how often he gets the face to bespeak the being of the person – the impenetrable Stalinist gloom of Guillevic, the schizophrenic terror of Margaret Gibson, the beneficent melancholy of Amichai, the "weight" of Mavis Gallant, or Timothy Findley, defiant in his bewildered anguish – and by trusting that inherent character, Reeves is always moving from sentiment to the edge because he knows that on the edge is best.

Exile, 1992

A PERFORMANCE OF
THE EXILE AT CAFÉ
TRISTAN BERNARD

The curtain rose on the interior of a frontier dacha. The frontiers-man sat in front of his fireplace. There was a knock on the door. The exile entered.

EXILE: Whoever you are, have pity on a hunted man. There is a price on my head.

FRONTIERSMAN: How much?

The exile hurried out as the curtain fell.

Hogg, the Seven Last Words, 2001

SALT AND TOYS

Germany is not a social enterprise.
It is a poetical and demoniacal conspiracy.
—Jean Giraudoux

"The evening – clear after rain. In the west, far away, the pale yellow light, the sky swept clean and looking as cold as jade" on the road south into the mountain chain toward Bad Tölz, a town of healing spring waters, hot baths.

Mountains are alien to me but not to Gertrud Fussenegger, not to Gertrud Fussenegger as I find her behind the wheel.[1]

"Crossroads, bend. Steep hill."

I'm at ease alone on gunmetal water and in among stone islands covered by thin soil and dwarf pines, or in desert heat watching rubble and grit turn mauve at dusk.

"Always the signposts call out: Danger! Danger!"

In these foothill valleys, the Alpine earth is opal black, there's the tang of ice in the air. It is not the landscape that unsettles me: *I recalled a man who had lost his arms during the war. He claimed that despite his loss he had not ceased to feel his hands and finger tips; he said it was as if his absent limbs had become organs sensing through echoes.* Echoes and images inhabit me: black milk at daybreak, baby shoes, scuffed by barbed wire, falling in silence like confetti made from torn family photographs, the torn face of Eva Braun, showing a turn of leg and her new red shoes . . . .

"Everything coming towards us goes swishing past like a ghostly apparition. Everything ahead of us is caught up, over-

---

[1] Gertrud Fussenegger is a German author. Her story, *Woman Driver*, quoted in parts here, has been translated by Patrick Bridgwater.

taken, obliterated . . . woods and rocks like backdrops, come reeling towards us and past, bridges, walls, railings – out of some ghastly chasm a trail of water is blown . . . . All things dissolve into spray . . . there is no love in us, only a yearning for the void."

Bad Tölz is a small trading town of pearl-grey and jade-green houses. They are pocketed in the valley on both sides of the Isar River. On the front walls of the houses, under the eaves, there are old frescoes of stalwart saints, their eyes alive in old plaster, eyes wideopen to confront evil (during the Hitler War, Bad Tölz – like so many other towns – had its own satellite slave labour camp: *We worked at draining swamps, twelve hours a day, on a liquid diet and one ounce of bread, wearing only a striped shirt and striped trousers, nothing underneath, nothing against the cold, and the rawness, the rawness between your bottom cheeks because there was no paper, this was the worst, and the rawness, the bleeding right to the bone of your heels because your shoes in the morning, that were sopping wet at night, were frozen like wood, but you had to walk like you were happy to go to work otherwise they would select you out for deportation to the death camps*) an evil that seems not to have sullied or scarred the scrubbed men and women on the street – who walk and talk with a sense of unswerving firmness, the no-nonsense goodwill of those who live day to day by forgetting. They have the cast of their houses: big-boned, squarely set, pink from the crisp air, at ease with their own fleshiness on the bone, they look cleansed.

> *To be watered we went there, Lord.*
>
> *It was blood, it was*
> *what you shed, Lord.*
>
> *It gleamed.*[1]

---

[1] Poems quoted are by Paul Celan, translated by Michael Hamburger.

At the bottom of a blue cobbled street, feeling a chill on the back of my neck, I step into an onion-domed church, Mühlfeld-kirche.

Above the main altar, a fresco of a plague procession, skeletal bodies twisted in pain, buboes, flagellants whipping themselves raw, a death grimace, the death lurch. At a side altar, there's a life-size carved Christ caught in mid-stride; he has big bony feet and a haggard peasant's face – a short man, one of the locals, a valley man wearing a brushed, off-the-shoulder carmine velvet cape, floor length and belted across the breast, naked except for a gleaming gold-leaf loin cloth.

Christ in a drag queen's dream . . . .

The next morning: reading D.H. Lawrence – *as you go among the Bavarian uplands, you realize here is another land, a strange religion. It is a strange country, remote, out of contact . . . . The beauty of the people is this, they are convivial, they are almost the only race with the souls of artists. Still they act the mystery plays . . . they sing strangely in the mountain fields, they love make-belief and mummery, their processions and religious festivals are profoundly impressive, solemn, and rapt . . . the crucifixes seem to create a new atmosphere over the whole countryside, a darkness, a weight in the air that is so unnaturally bright . . . . So full of strange radiance . . . the eternal, negative radiance of the snows . . . there is no flux nor hope nor becoming, all is, now and forever.*

On the crest of a hill behind the town I come across a large mound and a cave and a carved man of my height sleeping inside the cave, and nearby, another carved man sleeping on his side; then, on the top of the mound, half-hidden by bushes, a bronze Christ, the colour of charred wood, kneels in an agony of prayer. The final moments, life-sized, in a garden of Gethsemane (far below, where the roofs of the town slant at coral angles, the wide Isar snakes through the hills, and in the distance, the pearl-white snow caps of the Benediktenwand, Zottenjoch, the Juifen). Built into a further mound, there is a cave-house of cut stone, dismal and damp, and inside, life-size stone statues of the apostles keep watch . . . ever alert, penitential, over an enormous Christ, larger than myself, bloodied, torn, His flesh gouged and hammered, and He is not only within my reach, but there in the light of votive candles, a man could lie down in the arms of his Lord and whisper the names of the dead . . . .

the names, all their
names
burnt with the rest. So much
ash to be blessed.

. . . The body of the Bavarian *Christus is locked in one knowledge, beautiful, complete. It is one with the nails. Not that it is languishing or dead. It is stubborn, knowing its own undeniable being, sure of the absolute reality of the sensuous experience . . . . Christ dreaming, brooding, enduring, persisting. There is a wistfulness about him, as if he knew that the whole of things was too much for him. There was no solution either, in death. Death did not give the answer to the soul's anxiety. That which is, is. It does not cease to be when it is cut. Death cannot create nor destroy. What is, is.*

Berchtesgaden: film clips in the memory: it is always unnerving watching him, it *is* him, there, Hitler in a double-breasted, greenish-blue suit, and not only is he sitting in an easy chair, the chair covered by an ivory print with pale blue flowers, but, looking small, even huddled, he is holding his head in his hand, and then he lets his hand hang down, limp-wristed . . . he is relaxed, drained of distemper, at ease, at home in his stone mountain chalet overlooking Berchtesgaden . . . and Eva Braun has a home-movie camera (the two of them are preserved in Agfa-colour) . . . and she is picking field flowers in a red-checked peasant girl's dress (this means he played at photographing her . . .) or in another peasant dress, blue with white polka dots, she is dancing around an apple tree, swinging from a branch thick with white blossoms . . . and then, as Hitler makes notations on his "Strength Through Joy" program, she is wearing a dark-striped dress suit with a jaunty red hat; she is playing with a red squirrel, a gay child-like woman who had once tried to kill herself . . . not here but in Munich, not here, high in this chalet overlooking the world where she does no harm to herself, where she hides in the back stairs when company comes.

Images that explain nothing.

But then, why should there be an explanation, as if an explanation could be a palliative?

The Königssee is a swollen finger lake between enormous mountains close to Berchtesgaden . . . .

O one, o none, o no one, o you:
Where did the way lead when it led nowhere?

On a boat ride down the Königssee, a man on board cupped his hands and hollered across the water and waited . . . a gap of silence, a voice thrown into the emptiness, the abyss, and then it came back, clear, the mirror-voice of himself; a man alone in this eternal mountain light, dwarfed by snow and stone, hoping to confirm his uniqueness, his voice, by hurling it out into the abyss. And always, as confirmation, it came back.

Staring up at the huge concave valleys, the uppermost snow like inlaid ivory, I understood why a man would want to ski up there alone in the emptiness of eternity, drenched in radiant light, crouched forward, leaving the assertive sweep of his skis in the snow, the downward speed reverberating into his bones, because – no matter the dogged struggle to the top, the meaning, the exhilaration, the risk taken toward excellence is always in the movement down, in the necessary yielding return to earth-bound humanity, a leap back into the penitential world through the tree-line.

Berchtesgaden is a town settled and built around an ancient abbey. That abbey had been dependent upon salt mines worked by bondsmen and serfs; in the fields, serfs, when they weren't work-ing the mines, had decorated their cows with headdresses of flowers and had made beautifully intricate carved toys.

Toys and salt.

Always, it seems, there is this kind of dichotomy in these val-leys. Ships loaded with salt and toys, sent out into the world, to Antwerp, Cádiz, Genoa.

I went down into the earth, into darkness, into the salt mines.

There was earth inside them, and
they dug

They dug and they dug, so their day
went by for them, their night. And they did not praise God.
Who, so they heard, wanted all this,
Who, so they heard, knew all this.

Narrow-gauge railroad tracks had been laid along the tunnels – herringbone salt patterns in the walls having the dull lustre of tin, a greasy feel to the stone and a brackish salt taste on the fingers – tracks, trunk lines, transport spokes converging on a gouged central "hall" for the salt carts – a huge circular hub, an under-ground wheel lying flat on an axle to hell, thousands of dark-faced day-blind men carrying pine torches, men in black aprons and black caps, serfs, slaves, moles hollowing deeper and deeper into salt.

I dig, you dig, and the worm digs, too,
and that singing out there says: They dig.

◯◯◯

Coming up for air, driving toward the Obersalzberg and Hitler's mountain retreat high atop the salt mines. "The town is falling away now behind the slope . . . the road is climbing, curve after curve . . . getting narrow here, damn! . . . these narrow roads, chock-full with cyclists, pedestrians, children, and dogs . . . . There it is now at last – clearway. Houses and people are being left behind, the road is tearing towards us and the wind, the sweet singing sound sweeping its leaves against the windows. Faster! Faster! The white line is running ahead of us, the red cat's-eyes on the kerb-stones, faster and faster the signs flash past," driving toward the Eagle's Nest, Hitler's chalet, his dream, his toy, five miles of winding road up to the houses Bormann, Göring and Himmler had holidayed in, until it was impossible for them to go further, impossible for all but Hitler who had bored a hollow straight up through 400 feet of solid rock, mining his way toward eternity, rising, with little Eva Braun beside him in the lift, upward with a woman who often wearied him.

Still, sometimes of an afternoon, he would stand beside her in her polka-dot dress as he threw his voice toward the treeline, as he blew his death kiss over the world, and no echo came back – his voice fell to the earth, a squeal, the rat-like squeal of steel boxcar wheels on steel – the mole man in his bunker in the clouds, limp hand hanging in the air, listening to his astrologers, while humming along to Wagner, to *Parisfal* from Bayreuth on the radio, posing for home movies, letting his piano player – Ernst Franz "Putzi" Hanfstaengl – teach him how to eat an artichoke, and then, singing a little folk song, *duh duh te duh,* bent over his war maps, the maps of his mind, and for a moment he looked up waiting for his voice to come back.

Standing where Hitler had stood, up in the ethereal, radiant light, I asked myself – for one of the few times in my adult life – whether some little song might be heard from the other side of mankind, whether God is not an impossibility?

Standing where Hitler stood, I asked . . . .

Is it only the refusal to turn towards Him that makes Him impossible?

Is it a matter of the *will* to believe?

Is it a matter, as Pascal put it in his *Wager*, of accepting that God either exists or He does not exist, understanding that once you've asked the question you must take sides, you must make the bet, because once you've asked the question you have no choice.

The Pascalian wager would be this: taking into account the rules of probability, if you bet that God exists and it turns out that He does not, what do you lose? Only your finite life, a life you may have lived through with some ease of heart, even dignity, but it was a life you were going to lose no matter what. However, if you bet against God, if you wager that He does not exist and it turns out that He does, you lose everything, you lose "an infinity of life."

Obviously, the no-lose or win-win position is to decide for God. Since you cannot bet both sides against the middle, what is required – and the language is appropriate to a land drawn between salt and toys – is your unconditional surrender to the bet, and therefore an unconditional surrender to God.

Standing where Hitler stood I wondered if I should make the bet, if I should throw my voice out over the world.

Would it come back?

Would I hear the voice of God instead?

> *Our eyes and our mouths are so open and empty, Lord.*
> *We have drunk, Lord.*
> *The blood and the image that was in the blood, Lord.*

Pray Lord.
We are near.

◉◉

I came down from the mountain and set out for Herrenchiem-
see, set out for the dream, the toy, the palace of Ludwig II, King
of Bavaria, that melancholy patron and protector of Wagner,
that lover of peacocks, and lover of the echo within an echo of
himself in mirrors.

Born in 1845, at Schloss Nymphenburg in Munich, he grew
up to dance with villagers under the lime trees, jumped through
hoops of fire, yodelled and, late at night in the moonlight, he
went out in a small boat alone, a slender young man with blue
eyes and milk-white skin, to slowly row in circles while reciting
Schiller:

> *With this kiss let me embrace*
> *The many millions of the world.*

Often, of an afternoon, he would sit silently on a piano bench
beside Wagner and one day he said to him, "You don't care for
women either, do you? They are so boring."

Wagner asked him what he thought a woman should be and
Ludwig said, "A beautiful soul in a beautiful dress with a voice
like music and perfumed with lilies."

"Ah! But that's the impossible," said Wagner.

"Well, who wants it! It's only a dream."

Only a toy!

These people, who are the salt of the earth, you can feel a weight
in them, in their haunches, their hands, the thickness of their
necks, and yet there is some deep yearning in them, as if they
wanted to escape their own flesh, an almost mystical need to dis-
appear into the light, to be weightless in eternity, which makes

*them dangerous, given to extremes, given to a pursuit of beauty
through a love of pain, God-fearing while afraid of no one, cau-
tious but in love with speed . . . .*

A toy within a dream.

Ludwig offered his hand in marriage to a cousin. He staged
fireworks.

And then he turned away and retired into a dayblind world
of swans, falcons and peacocks, and a pond in an indoor grot-
to. He rowed in circles within circles on the pond, and then, draw-
ing deeper into his own darkness, he built Herrenchiemsee, a cas-
tle on an island in Lake Chiemsee. It was an incarnate vision of a
formal French garden, and a long white gravel walk to a three-
storey façade of a faux Versailles . . . an echo of an echo . . . a huge,
blue-enamelled peacock in the white vestibule, an *escalier des am-
bassadeurs,* a glass roof, an enormous gold bed in which Ludwig
never slept, a Sun King who shunned the sun so that he could
stroll at night into his Gallery of Mirrors under 52 candelabras
with three rows each of 11 hanging chandeliers, 2,300 candles
– with 27 arched windows facing 27 corresponding mirrors . . . .

"Eternity and infinity," Ludwig said, "I am in eternity and
infinity," walking alone, listening to his own footsteps in the
middle of the night . . . walking into mirror reflections in mir-
ror reflections as if he were trying to lose himself down a long
shining tunnel.

Pronounced mad, he was confined to his quarters at Schloss
Berg on Starnbergersee, but one evening, wearing blue and white
swan's feathers, he went walking with his doctor. He apparently
strangled the man, and then walked out into the water, and,
though a strong swimmer, he sat down in the muck, called out,
listened, heard nothing, and mouth open, drowned himself.

*Silence, cooked like gold, in
Charred, charred
Hands.*

"How did it come about – driving like this" she asked, "or did we dream it? . . . this drive up into the mountains; and, as dreams always are, everything was larger than life and fantastic, giant scenery, giant like the night, and the road, ever upwards, upwards, endless, spiralling, giddy viaducts towering one over the other. In front, a blue car. From some foreign country, a foreigner on the road, keeping in front all the time, faster and faster still, going too fast to be overtaken. Is he going to get away? No, catch him. Afraid that he may elude us, afraid because the road is getting so narrow, sweeping in tighter and tighter circles round ever narrower bends, and the stranger – not a car at all – opens his silvery wings, smiles from behind his blue visor . . . .

"And now the road has vanished into thin air – bottomless space is swallowing us up."

Fingers, insubstantial as smoke.

Toronto Life, 1979-82

THE G SPOT

Gambling, the French novelist François Mauriac once said, is continuous suicide. There is no past, no significant future, only an eternal and always optimistic present tense.

Continuous suicide!

It is a peculiar view, if I can put it that way, and I should, because Mauriac was peculiar: he was a fierce Jansenist and, as such, in his great metaphysical scheme of things, there had to be many losers and very few winners and those winners had long since been chosen, predetermined in the eye of God. They were either among the outcast or one of the elect, among the damned or one of the saved.

It is a severe view of existence.

Many a Jansenist has spent many an hour seeking a sign, any sign, no matter how small, of his or her salvation, some sign of the gift of grace – because in such a predetermined world grace is a gift, a gift all too frustratingly given, so it seems, to the unwitting, the undeserving, the unworthy.

I was standing one blustery September afternoon among men in grey toppers at one of the Ascot oyster bars, contemplating the race course – a right-handed triangular circuit of a mile and three-quarters that favours the galloping runner – and as the horses came around the final turn, a bell was tolled, tolling for those hearts about to be broken as the jockeys whipped their horses into the long uphill stretch, 14 horses about to cross the wire. I had bet on the race with optimism, with confidence. A couple in front of me at the oyster bar were talking:

"I suppose I'm 36, or is it 37?" he said. "What're you, dear?"

"I should think I'm 37," she said.

"Really?"

"Or very nearly 38. It's a question of the months in the middle of the year. Middles nearly always muddle me. It's like halves and quarters. Fractions virtually ruined me in school."

"Quite."

"Actually, now that I think about it, I'm 38."

At that point, the horses crossed the wire.

"Oh dear," she said, "I think I've actually won."

"You don't say."

"I do. One . . . seven."

"Yes, it really seems so."

"At 40-1, my dear."

"How ever did you pick that?"

"My youngest sister. She's 17 today. So I bet 1 and 7."

"Well done, I say."

I had bet 4 and 2. A little gift of grace had been given to the unknowing, the uncaring. Metaphysics? Grace? I sauntered off in a small sulk to one of the outlying bars to contemplate suicide.

Not really, of course.

Still, Mauriac had a point. I had to face the fact that in all great beliefs, there is always a grain of truth.

After all, a gambler, having bet on ten races of an afternoon, has risked continuous death, ten little deaths – and, despite his optimism, and because he has lost, he may blame his loss on God, saying, "I got killed," but he knows he has done the deed to himself.

An afternoon of continuous suicide.

Except – like everything else in life – how you look at those deaths is a matter of temperament.

Ten little deaths, *dix petites morts*.

That's more to my liking.

Ten little sexual orgasms.

And why shouldn't one, from time to time, hit the G spot: Grace.

Grace, the big win.

Since I am not a Jansenist (nor a Calvinist, Protestant cousin to the Catholic Jansen), I see no reason why I should not expect to win. To die a little, yes, to die a lot, maybe, but always to come back from the dead, resurrected, to not only win, but to win big, big enough to make the corrupt and fallen world my oyster.

The Prix de l'Arc de Triomphe is run on the first Sunday of October at Longchamp, a 12-furlong course set in the greenery of the Paris Bois du Boulogne, and since 1857, when the Emperor Napoleon came to the afternoon races by boat (the fashionable way of reaching the Bois at that time), racing at Longchamp has been a highlight of the Paris social calendar.

The carriage procession to the course was described in detail by Zola in his novel *Nana*:

> Carriages still continued to arrive. They now comprised five rows along the barrier bordering the course, and formed quite a dense mass streaked here and there by the light hue of the white horses. Then beyond, there were numerous other isolated vehicles, looking as though they had stuck in the grass, a medley of wheels and of teams in every possible position, side by side, slantwise, crosswise, and head to head; and horsemen trotted across the plots of grass that were still comparatively free, whilst foot-passengers appeared in black groups continually on the move. Overtopping this kind of fair-ground, amidst the strangely mixed crowd, rose the grey refreshment tent, to which the sunshine imparted a white appearance. But

the greatest crush, an ever-moving sea of hats, was around
the bookmakers, who were standing up in open vehicles,
gesticulating like quack dentists, with their betting lists
stuck up on boards beside them.

"All the same, it's awfully stupid not to know what horse
one's backing," Nana was saying. "I must venture a few
louis myself."

Little has changed. "All of Paris" still goes to see those horses
that have already proven they are champions: among them, the
winners of the Derby, the Jockey Club, the King George, the
Grand Prix, the Grand Criterium, the Gran Premio di Milano,
the Irish Oaks, the Irish St. Leger . . . .

A man of about 35, freckle-faced, with the front brim of his grey
fedora pushed up (like a gamin from the movies: he was a coin
dealer from Lyon), smoking a big cigar, said with an infectious
boyish smile – though I had not said a word to him: "A man who
doesn't care about money is a dangerous man."

We stood side-by-side watching the rippling changes of odds
figures on the electronic board.

"That's not an easy view to take of a man," I said.

"There are those," he said, "who think life is all a massage,
with ice cream and free jewellery. Do you fancy Nuit d'Or, if he
goes to 6-1?"

"Would you?"

"I would."

Nuit d'Or went down to 6-1 and lost.

During the early afternoon, my coin dealer friend lost money,
certainly several thousand francs, but he kept smiling, his big
cigar still unlit.

"We're having a hard start," I said, admiring his affable air.
"You've suffered a blow."

"But I don't care, I don't really care about money," he said, jabbing his dead cigar at me, beaming. "It's why I'm a dangerous man to deal with, you see," as he turned at the sound of the starter bell to watch a new run of horses break from the gate, and for the first three furlongs, in a loping stride, they maintained their pace, the pace setters (who are never expected to win) leading the field up a half-mile hill . . . with the lesser horses then beginning to tire, to fall back . . . and at the halfway point as they galloped into the big turn – the winner – from somewhere back in the pack – began to improve, so that with little more than two furlongs to go, he charged with an elegance that could not be denied through the flagging frontrunners (equine elegance, as with women, comes from turning a flaw to an advantage . . . in horse racing this is called pace: knowing how to discover the strength that is in a horse's weakness, how to put the flash of speed together with the severe demands of endurance) until, at about 2:28.5 – having taken some 345 strides and having pumped 650 litres of blood through his body – the winning horse crossed the line.

I had begun to find my own pace at the betting windows. A loss, but then a win. And another win. Not big, but a bulge of 500-franc notes.

After much military bugling and after a formal single-file parade in front of the grandstand and a trot out to the distant Start on the edge of the woods, 20 horses eased into a lineup for the Prix de l'Arc. Having made a bet, I found that my coin dealer from Lyon had disappeared. I was now standing behind the Italian owners of one of the favourites, a soft choice, but a favourite nonetheless, named Carroll House, Irish-trained and Irish-ridden. The horses broke, the crowd strained. The horses sorted themselves into position, becoming a pear-shaped cluster that seemed, from so far a distance, to move as one on the backstretch.

With three furlongs to go, Carroll House shouldered through the front-running pack, his barrel chest banging and bumping, his jockey switching to the left-hand whip. He was nosing ahead, taking the race, seizing the day. This was no gift. This was a take. The wire was his by a long neck. The owners of the horse and their wives yelped like schoolchildren, throwing their hands into the air. They kissed and kissed again, and then – with exuberant recklessness – skidaddled down three flights of stairs to the paddock.

I thought Carroll House should have been taken down, disqualified for severe bumping, for interference – and there was an Inquiry posted, a jockey's complaint, the sign suddenly flashing – but after a three-minute delay the stewards let the win stay. The Official prices went up on the board. In the walking ring, the crowd crushed around the horse and the jockey still mounted in his canary yellow silks . . . the crowd shoving and hugging . . . so dangerous if the horse were to panic and kick. But he did not. As if to the manor born, ears pricked, he pranced under the plane trees and the owners preened.

I had not bet on Carroll House. Though I'd had a fair day, it was not good enough, not for my purposes. Too many little deaths. Paris is an expensive city. The ponies were supposed to pay not just for my hotel and my suppers but for the grace notes of living, the concupiscence.

I walked out at my own shuffling pace, amidst the milling crowd, thousands suddenly swelling onto the road and into the trees, with no nearby metro, no lineups of taxis. Just reserved limos and dozens of dun-and-yellow chartered buses. I felt, in the oncoming dusk, an increasing desolation, an exhaustion after too many *petites morts*, all optimism of the moment deflated – now hurrying forward as if I were evacuating a ruined city (it is a feeling of bleakness after losses at the track that has to be beaten back otherwise you end up susceptible to the tenets of M. Mauriac). When some loutish Englishmen called a bus driver who looked like he might be Somali a *nigger*, I felt sullied and knew

I had to quickly shed the after-air of the Arc. I found a lone taxi driver surrounded by gesticulating, frustrated, jabbering men all wanting to hire his car. He explained that he was waiting for a gentleman who had hired him to go to Chartres. "He's late, he's a liar," someone yelled. *"Peut-être,"* the driver said wanly. *"Peut-être."*

There is a reason for all wins big and small. Here was a reason. Sensing that he wanted an excuse to get out of the woods, too, I folded 1,200 francs into his hand and suggested he take me into town. With a darting eye, he acquiesced, angering the crowd, some of whom pounded the trunk of his car. By the time we reached my hotel on rue de Lille he was showing me family baby pictures. He was a grandfather. From Algiers. Did I like *cous-cous*? His brother had a small restaurant near the Bon Marché . . . .

It had been a day of limited clarity at the track ending in an occluded light in my room. Though I had shaved in the morning I decided to shave again. Hot towels, and then at last refreshed, feeling worthy of Paris, I dressed to go to supper at the Closerie des lilas, eager to be with my old friend from La Rochelle, the poet Robert Marteau, and his woman, Neige. He, after all, had been given his own gift, he had seen

In sable mirrors,
Caballeros, ebony on black,
Rise over reefs of surf . . .

Sadly on that day, the horses had not risen for me.

I had come home feeling I was still half in the grave at Bois du Boulogne. A friend told me: "Half out of the grave, not half in, and you're lucky for that. Nobody beats the nags, not all the time, not even part of the time. That's the way life is, the House – The Eye in the Sky – He always wins." I shrugged.

I was sure that Paris and her horses had more to give me. I had to wait, however, for a month, for the Breeder's Cup, the series of million-dollar races that are run on one Saturday in America in early November, races brought in on closed circuit television to Champions, the bar at Woodbine.

I was reading the *Form*. I studied the changing odds on a bank of TV screens mounted over the bar. I had lost five races in a row. The last, however, had been won by a 30-1 shot and I was not glum about that. You cannot expect to easily pick 30-1 shots. There is a reason why they are 30-1. And if they win, God knows why. So I take them as shooting stars, omens out of the east, a sign of what's to come, not of what has been lost. For the upcoming race, I felt a rush of confidence, curiously light on my feet.

A man who worked at the track, a man with a bounce to his walk – always on his toes – who liked to say, "I'm in hospitality," stopped by the bar.

"What's new?"

"I'm down ten bucks," the hospitality man said.

"I thought you didn't bet."

"I don't but I do."

"What're you talking?"

"Look, I start each day with 40 bucks in my left-hand pocket and I bet ten bucks on who I like by moving the ten to my right pocket so I just put ten to the right so I'm down ten."

"Jesus . . . ."

The hospitality man moved on, but after the million-dollar race for *Juvenile Fillies* he came back.

"How'd you do?"

"I'm down 20," he said morosely.

After the *Distaff*, he said, "I can't make a win."

"So, I can't make a face."

We laughed.

After the next race, the hospitality man stood with his arms folded. "I'm broke," he said. "What the hell am I going to do the rest of the day?"

"You've got money, you've got 40 bucks, so bet."

"I never touch the righthand pocket. It's like my bank."

"So make some money. Be a businessman."

"I'm in hospitality, thanks."

"It's your bank, make yourself a loan, short-term, 10 per-cent. Be easy on yourself."

"No way."

"Move the 40 to your left pocket. At 10 percent, already you're up four bucks."

"Are you kidding?"

"If you're the bank it's like being the House."

"Right."

"You've got it both ways. You're in hospitality, you're a suc-cessful banker . . . ."

I opened my *Form* to the *Turf* race. "Give me a winner," I said without looking up, but the hospitality man, now a respectable banker, had hurried off to the buffet table, both hands in his pockets.

I studied the *Form*.

And had the feeling of emerging clarity. A horse called Sierra Roberta had run at the Arc. He'd come fifth behind Carroll House, and running behind Behera, he had been bumped badly by Car-roll House . . . and now Behera was at 2-1 while Sierra Roberta was at 29-1. In the Prix de la Nonette at Longchamp in September, Sierra Roberta had beaten Behera by a length-and-a-half.

This was it.

Without hesitation, I wheeled Sierra Roberta in an exactor, betting him top and bottom (first and second) with six other horses, especially Prized who had won the Molson Million in Toronto and was going off at an incredible 6-1 simply because he was running on the turf for the first time.

The horses broke from the gate.

I stood taut, intent, yet strangely calm, certain that – bidden or unbidden in the eye of God – I had actually seen into the future, I had actually seen the end in the beginning, a sighting to be confirmed at the finish line: the horses 6 and 11. And that's exactly how it happened. Prized won, and Sierra Roberta – though boxed in and rough-handled on the turn into the stretch – came up the inside on the rail to be second. He should have won. Never mind. The exactor paid 1,600 dollars for a 2-dollar bet. I had made the bet for 10 dollars, total outlay, 120 dollars: payoff 8,000 dollars. It had been a day of continuous suicide but now grace abounded. The circle was closed, hotel and travel bills from Paris would be paid. The future was bright. I'd learned to live with all the little deaths; even a big death or two. And so why not move on to Santa Anita in December, Gulfstream in Florida at New Years and St. Moritz in February . . . ? Yes, racing on the ice. Think of that: sitting on a balcony of the Palace Hotel in St. Moritz, eating eggs benedict, watching horses race on a frozen lake, and drinking a champagne toast to Jansen right in the heart of Calvin's home country.

City & Country Homes, 1990-2003

EDMUND WILSON

1

I went to stay with Edmund Wilson in upstate New York. I had my three-year-old son with me. It was early in the morning and going to rain. After a good sleep I stood barefoot on the stair-case landing of Wilson's stone house in Talcottville, stood by the window with panes of glass that had been put in place by the Talcotts, the old panes marbled, and through them the trees were bent and twisted. Poems had been etched with a diamond point in some of the panes:

> *What is peculiar is never to forget*
> *The essential delight of the blood*
> *Drawn from the ageless springs*
> *Breaking through rocks*
> *In worlds before our earth*[1]

How peculiar it was to look through the windows of Wilson's house and see the world fade and come clear and fade through words as clouds mottled the early morning light.

The solid, wide centre-hall door was decorated by a brass knocker and stood ajar. Flanking the door were leaded circles and diamonds of glass. A white porch and balcony ran the length of the stone house, and at the rim of the porch were ferns and high

---

[1] The poems throughout, and the drawings, are by Edmund Wilson – with the exception of this etching that is in the window pane, done, I believe, by Stephen Spender while he was visiting in the house.

raspberry bushes and stone hitching posts cut from the nearby Sugar River quarry. The lawn, scorched from the August sun, dropped down to a broad-shouldered two-lane highway from Boonville, and across the road, a large farm stretched to the Sugar River.

Edmund had come into the hall from his study. He was in white pyjamas, a ragged black-paisley dressing gown and slippers, and he held a broad-brimmed grey felt fedora in his right hand. "G-G-Good morning," he called out as he saw me on the stairs. He put on the fedora and wrapped the dressing gown around his stout stomach. "Did you sleep well? Come outside," and with a short rolling stride, staring straight ahead, arms hanging like a stubby-legged club fighter, he elbowed the screen door open, announcing, "I was just thinking of your dear old family . . . you know, your father is . . . quite different from mine, who was kind of . . . a tyrant."

There was something mildly wacky about the way Edmund often blurted out what he was thinking (a habit I think he inherited from his mother on whom he doted – a woman who had bawled out whatever it was that crossed her mind). So formidable in photographs, in his senatorial stance, and in his stentorian stutter, he could suddenly be guilelessly foolish. (I had found him late one night with my father – I'd gone to fetch Morley from Edmund's suite in the Park Plaza hotel in Toronto – and he had come out into the corridor of the high-toned hotel in his old pyjamas, his fly open, in order to say goodbye to us at the elevator, as if the corridor were his hallway. He'd been so enjoying what he had to say that he got into the elevator – ignoring the couple already there – continuing to explain his point, his pink pecker readily there, too, and it wasn't until the doors opened onto the lobby that he sensed the light of another world than his own and people standing in it, so he said goodnight heartily, his hand in the air as the doors closed.) He shuffled in his slippers along the planks of the porch and sat in a weathered rocking chair. The mail truck, he assured me, would be by in a moment and I could set my watch by the truck. I said I didn't wear a watch. He shrugged. The truck, he said, passed every morning at nine o'clock. "Nine o'clock. Would you like a drink? A vermouth?"

☙❧

Edmund Wilson was born in Red Bank, New Jersey, May 8, 1895, the son of parents who had connections with the puritan Mathers, and with the Talcotts, a Tory family who were among the first to go West after the American Revolution. A treaty with the Oneida Indians had opened up what is now northern New York State, and the Talcotts, having claimed land at the Sugar River north of Utica, had built this solid, expansive house out of the local limestone, a house that became hostelry, town hall, post office and social centre.

The Talcotts were land speculators who expected that a railroad would run through here, but the railroad passed Talcottville by . . .

Or else to imagine
History as a crystalline sea-anemone

and so the village green is an unused field and the village itself has remained a small settlement strung along a relatively unfrequented road. Some who stayed in the area drank far too much and some kept on selling pieces of their immense estates. Yet, Edmund says, the house perfectly pleased his father.

His father had been a hard man to please. Unstable, he'd come to a dark finish, a finish that not only troubled Edmund but sometimes made him feel that he was walking in his father's shadow. Edmund has always returned to the stillness of this stone house, returned to this link with his past, his family history, under threat from that shadow.

Edmund Senior had been brought up in the wake of the Civil War. It was a period "both banal in a bourgeois way and fantastic with gigantic fortunes," a difficult, and even a terrifying time for men like Edmund Senior, educated in the old traditions. He had aimed at public life, but the political career he had hoped for had been conceived of in the old republican terms of each man responsible for his own property and responsible also for the institutions designed to protect that property. It was a time, however, when his "kind of education and the kind of ideals it served no longer really counted for much," a time when institutions had become weapons of exploitation, when men no longer worked the soil, but were enthralled by money. Edmund Senior, a successful lawyer who had been the Attorney General of New Jersey – a lawyer who had lost only one case in his life – a man burdened by the overpowering pressures and the insidious diversions of post-Civil War capitalism – had first retreated to his house at Red Bank,

> *The ugly stained glass window on the stair,*
> *Dark-panelled dining room, the guinea fowl's fierce clack,*
> *The great grey cat that on the oven slept –*
> *My father's study with its books and birds,*

His scornful tone, his eighteenth century words,
His green door sealed with baize . . .

and then to Talcottville, where he had buried himself in a "hypo-chondriacal gloom . . . which blanketed the future with darkness: no real desire to live, no hope of doing anything further." Stranded and hamstrung by neurotic depressions, he had spent much of his later life in sanatoriums or shut up behind a felt-covered door. His moments of relief were few; "his eclipses, by the time he was fifty, were lasting for months and years," and these bouts with darkness wore Edmund's mother down. It did not help that she was deaf and used an ear trumpet, it did not help that she and her husband had very different tastes, different temperaments. She was extro-verted and loved long Cadillacs. He had no particular urge to ac-quire money and was reclusive. She tried to be interesting to him, she played bridge and read a book a day, but he disdained cards and "no longer paid any attention to her." Still, "she refused to leave him," Edmund told me, "and instead, she had herself a collapse."

After Edmund the barrister died in 1923, Mrs. Wilson told her son, "Your father . . . would go into court when he knew that the judge and the jury were prejudiced and public sentiment was all against him, and try his case and win it." She added, with a hint of bitterness *and* forewarning – as if visiting the disease of the father on the son – "these brilliant men always have something wrong with them."

in a modesty of death I join my father
who dared so long agone leave me

Edmund, at his desk at Talcottville, sitting in his father's room, wrote:

"*To have got through with honour that period from 1880 to 1920! – even at the expense of the felt muted door, the lack of first-class companionship, the retreats into sanatoriums. I have never been obliged to do anything so difficult. Yet my own generation in America has not had so gay a journey as we expected when we first started out.*

"*In repudiating the materialism and the priggishness of the period in which we were born, we thought we should have a free hand to refashion American life as well as to have more fun than our fathers. But we, too, have had our causalities . . . we admired the heroes, the affirmers, the 'lords of life,' but later on, when we had some experience of the difficulty of practising an art, of surviving to grow old in its practice, when we had seen how many entrants had dropped out, we must honour any entrant who finishes . . . . Too many of my friends are insane or dead or Roman Catholic converts – and some of these among the most gifted; two have committed suicide.*

"*I myself had an unexpected breakdown when I was in my middle thirties [just after he separated from his wife, the actress Mary Blair]. It was pointed out to me then that I had reached exactly the age at which my father had passed into the shadow. I must have inherited from him some strain of his neurotic distemper, and it may be that I was influenced by unconscious fear lest I might be doomed to a similar fate.*"

He wrote:

> *Back home – dark now –*
> *High eaves – hard light –*
> *Dogs bark far*
> *On dark farms –*
> *Hard now – blank tonight!*

"I did not recover wholly for years," he said, "and there were times when I was glad to reflect that I had covered more than half of my three score and ten – 'on the home stretch,' I used to phrase it in reassuring myself. But now that I am farther along, I find I want to keep on living."

⚬⚬⚬

The air was heavy, humid. The sky, in layers of pewter, glistened, and in an eastern corner, there was a sour smear of sunlight. A Buick convertible with night-lights on sped by, and after the roar of dual exhausts, the silence marked the isolation of the stone house, fortress-like off to the side of the road, this curious relic, this memorial to the failed ambitions of his ancestors: walls a foot-and-a-half thick, foundation beams secured by enormous handmade nails.

Edmund hunched forward, his elbows on his knees, his hands soft and fleshy, and he let them hang between his spread legs, the tips of his fingers pressed together in an upside-down steeple. A general store with a gas pump had been built some years ago on the lot along the highway to the south, a store run by a bulky woman with a long curling black hair growing from her chin, and Edmund searched past the store and on down the road for the mail truck. Though he had recently been in Israel for several weeks and then at his summer home on Cape Cod, his face was white, almost pasty. There were blotches of pink in his cheeks; he was suffering from attacks of angina and the lines at the corners of his mouth were deep. He settled back in the rocking chair and said, "The truck is orange and has a flashing light on the top which gives it the appearance of an insect. It is an orange bug" (more and more, Edmund has tended to describe contemporary life in terms of insects, bugs, vermin), and with his feet set squarely before him, his hat on his head, he faced the fields that were supposed to have been the town of Talcottville.

"You've got two beauties up in Canada in Marshall McLuhan and Northop Frye," he said, chortling. "That fellow Frye is very powerful in the universities, and McLuhan, as far as I can determine, is a fake. Thank goodness I avoided meeting them when I was up there." He spoke in short declarative sentences or in paragraphs, the flow broken only by stuttering. With him, even gossip was a deliberate exchange of information. He prodded anyone he met for opinions and facts and listened and then, if necessary, straightened them out ("No, no, Thorton Wilder's *The Eighth Day* is much the best thing he has done. I have reservations, but it is much the best thing he has done . . . . No, no, Podhoretz, his book, it's ridiculous . . . .). He eased forward in the chair, amused by himself, looking for the mail truck.

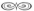

Edmund is a force. It is the first thing you feel about him. And he is so forcefully who he is not just because he is intelligent (T.S. Eliot said "there is no method to criticism but to be very intelligent") but because he seems from the beginning to have believed in the authority of his intelligence, in the singular authority of his voice. He had once complained that Eliot had taken on the tone of "the agèd eagle," but Edmund seems to have been born an agèd eagle. He has put the matter boldly: "The implied position of the people who know about literature . . . is simply that they know what they know, and that they are determined to impose their opinions by main force of eloquence or assertion on the people who do not know."

How he came to know what he knows has been – as the police might say – a matter of due diligence. In 1921, writing from France, he tried to explain himself to F. Scott Fitzgerald: "In America I feel so superior and culturally sophisticated in comparison to the rest of the intellectual and artistic life of the country that I am in danger of regarding my present attainments as an absolute standard and am obliged to save my soul by emigrating into a country which humiliates me intellectually and artistically by surrounding me with a solid perfection of standard arrived at by way of Racine, Molière, La Bruyère, Pascal, Voltaire, Vigny, Renan, Taine, Flaubert, Maupassant and Anatole France. I don't mean to say, of course, that I can actually do better work than anybody else in America; I simply mean that I feel as if I had higher critical standards and that, since in America all standards are let down, I am afraid mine will drop too."

He has brought to this pursuit of critical standards, though he would insist on saying that he is an atheist, a religious sensibility. The fervour of his commitment has been readily apparent in the fervour of his language. He has, for example, been intent on *justifying* the lives of men like his father's ancestors, who were betrayed by their own *failures of faith*. They were betrayed even more, however, by a catastrophic, if not *apocalyptic*, breakdown in the *ideals* of the republic itself. Given such a breakdown – the triumph of the spirit of loansharking and corporate capitalism, political whoring and guttersniping, and mere careerism – he has gone about the *saving of his soul* by pursuing *a solid perfection of standards*. He has made a solid *commitment* to his literary *salvation* though such salvation has had to entail a penitential passage through mortification, a passage that has enabled him to *proclaim* the superiority of his intent while disclaiming the superiority of his talent, to proclaim his submission to a higher purpose while affirming his own individual power.[1]

This has been true of Edmund, as it was true of the Puritan Divines.

"Don't talk to me about God," he said.

"I won't," I said.

---

[1] This last thought, a nice turn of phrase, was first applied to Edmund by the critic, Larzer Ziff.

While he waited for his mail, growing more anxious as a mantel clock chimed nine, I idled back into the house and poked about the front rooms. Creaks and noises and voices carried along the walls, and where they came from I was not quite sure; for a couple of days, I'd had the eerie sense of being in touch with empty chambers, with hollows under the eaves, wondering which was the door that Edmund's father had covered with green felt so as to cut himself off from his family, those eyes of his, the fixed startlement in photographs, the eyes of a morose man suddenly aroused from deep gloom.

On the walls are pictures from Edmund Senior's world: John Bull and the Baltimorians and John Bull and the Alexandrians; The First Reformers, and over the carved mantelpiece, primitive china-like figures of early Americans partying on The Day We Celebrate. The flags these tiny pioneers hold have different numbers of stars; fifteen, twenty-two, nine, ten – the growth of the republic? Are these the emblems of the house, these remnants from the past, some stirring, some quaint, some ugly – like the bust of a young girl which stands on a pedestal in the upper hall; her hair-ribbon and ruffles glisten white in the light and the carefully engraved pupils of her eyes are empty? Decades ago the girl who had posed for the bust bribed a man with a truck to take the bust away and sink it in a pond, but the bust was dredged up and – though Edmund thinks it is horrible – it is in his hall, close to an engraving of Corday, feather pen at her forehead, a verse attached:

> . . . *adieu Citoyen*
> *je me recommand au souvenir*
> *des vrai amis de la paix*

I stepped back on to the porch. He was standing shoulder to the wall, staring down the road, looking a little forlorn, or maybe he was just lost in thought, even lost in a little dream about morning sex. He liked thinking about sex, he liked writing about his sexual affairs in his notebooks.[1] The porch overhang cast shadows on his face; one side was soft and femininely round and the other lined and harsh. Essentially, he has his mother's features, square-jawed and plump in the jowls, and eyes with crescent lids. But his eyes are curiously at odds with each other. The layers of lid on the right eye are delicate and there is a slightly bemused look in that eye. From that side, the rigid line of his lips seems almost prissy. But the lid of the left eye lies heavier and the look is determined, even sinister. From that side, his mouth is grim and turned at the corners in contempt. His face is a blend of genuine warmth and genuine toughness, a toughness also felt in the slope of his shoulders, for, despite his age, there is a thrust about the way he holds himself, planted in position, the stance of a man ready to endure mortification, ready to endure those eruptions in his own life and the life of his republic that he accepts as inescapable.

He has written that even before the Crash of 1929 he had felt in his body a nervous apprehension of the national collapse, and when the crash came "like a rending of the earth" – like a judgment visited upon Big Business – he was so "exhilarated by the sudden collapse of that stupid gigantic fraud" that he went out on the American road – as reporter and sometime *feuilletoniste*, writing for *Vanity Fair* and the *New Republic* – to see what he could catalogue of the carnage, travelling week after week across the country, mixing – despite his doughty stuttering patrician manner – with communists and cops, judicial lynchers, vaudevillians,

---

[1] Reader after reader of his fiction, and those who have looked into his notebooks, have commented on his "cold clinical eye" – his detailing of a woman's body as if it were a "still life" and some have found the lack of sentiment attached to the detailing repellant. Myself, considering the reportorial positions he has had to have assumed amidst the heat of lovemaking to "see" the precise colouration of the layering of folds of flesh around a clitoris, highly comic.

bootleggers with suitcases full of scotch, coal diggers and Indian corn dancers, nabobs of the tennis clubs, the stokers at the open hearth furnaces of Detroit, the guano gatherers of Carlsbad, and of course, for New York relief, with Mr. Ziegfeld's "Glorified American Girls" – "girls who have not only the Anglo-Saxon straightness – straight backs, straight brows and straight noses – but also the peculiar frigidity and purity, the frank high-school-girlishness which Americans like. He does not aim to make them, from the moment they appear, as sexually attractive as possible, as the Folies Bergères, for example, does. He appeals to American idealism, and then, when the male is intent on his chaste and dewy-eyed vision, he gratifies him on this plane by discreetly dis-robing his goddess. He tries, furthermore, to represent, in the manoeuvres of his well-trained choruses, not the movement and abandon of emotion, but what the American male really regards as beautiful; the efficiency of mechanical movement."

Having hit the American road, he assessed the situation and concluded that American politicians had become "unique among governing classes in having managed to be corrupt, uncultivated and incompetent all at once." Too much of American life had become like a dance marathon, the exhausted dancers asleep on their feet.

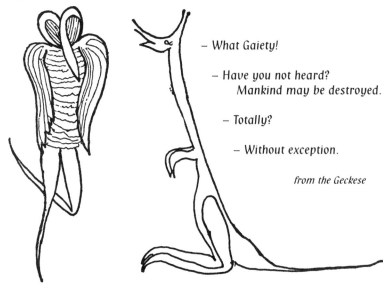

– What Gaiety!

– Have you not heard?
   Mankind may be destroyed.

– Totally?

– Without exception.

from the Geckese

The "mechanics of middle-class society," he wrote, the manu-
facturers, businessmen and bankers "who live on or deal in invest-
ments, so far from being redeemed by culture, have ended by
cheapening and invalidating all the departments of culture,
political, scientific, artistic and religious, as well as weakening
ordinary human relations: love, friendship and loyalty to cause
– till the whole civilization seems to have dwindled."

Having converted reportage and anecdotal storytelling and
portraiture into a grave, gracefully stern moral act, having man-
aged to maintain his admiration for certain "lords of life ... young
poets, ridiculous and rare," he quit writing so incessantly about
the American political and industrial grain. In 1935, he travelled
to the Soviet Union and stayed for five months. Though none
knew it as such at the time, the Terror had begun. Every day he
absorbed as much as he could, filling his notebooks with what he
had seen: plays, ballets, the cinema, conversations, his dreams, the
Peter-Paul Prison where a revolutionist had set her hair on fire in
her cell, the general hatred of the clergy, and lonely avant-garde
couples dancing to jazz. He stood in line in Moscow's Red Square
to look upon the embalmed face of Lenin, which he thought
"extraordinarily fine, intellectual, distinguished." He met with the
old and respected aristocrat and scholar, Prince Mirsky, and he
met Dos Passos' translator in Leningrad. He went to a collective
farm and sailed on the Volga to Odessa, was quarantined for more
than a month with scarlatina, and then "woke up repressing hys-
terical laughter and tears," thinking – a little bewildered by the
Soviet Union – *I mustn't let Russia get to me.*

He came home to the stillness of his stone house and went
to work:

Between the study and the bed,
Liquor stand me in good stead.

Fascinated by the Marxist-Leninist urge to "establish a soci-
ety in which the superior development of some is not paid for

by the exploitation . . . the deliberate degradation of others," he set about, for seven years, to the completion of his book, *To the Finland Station.* It turned out to be an extraordinary unravelling of the roots of socialism in Europe, a brilliant evocation of various "actors" in history, revolutionaries like Lassalle, Bakunin, Engels, Trotsky. He seemed to put on their skin so that he could dance in their bones – men engaged in a battle, the forces of integrity pitted against the forces of brutality and bestiality, men like the historian, Michelet ("a man of an unsettled and passionate generation . . . [who] forged his own personality, and established his own place") and that singular misanthropic mystic – Karl Marx – who had "built a stronghold for the mind" in the eye of the materialist storm ("When I was writing about him," Edmund told me, "I developed horrible boils. Marx suffered pain from boils all his life"), – and the solitary Lenin, a man "of unusual intellect and formidable tenacity of character, of historical imagination combined with powerful will."

Concluding his book with Lenin's arrival at Finland Station in Leningrad in 1917, Edmund put aside his boxes of notes and foolscap manuscripts and settled on to his front porch, feeling at some ease among "the frank accents and friendly eyes" of his family. He sat back with his bottles of scotch and amused himself by recollecting fragments of his father's language: "Weltering around in a Dead Sea of mediocrity . . . . Making some sort of a fist of it . . . . It rains. It snows. It makes no matter. Cataclysm." And then he counted up the decade's casualties, those companions of his, who, either insane or drunk, had died or switched horses in the stretch. However, rather than subside into the darkness of demoralization, he now was able to be sardonic and jocular about it,

> *John Dos Passos*
> *No longer writes for the Masses*
> *And when he returns to his Virginia estate, he*
> *Is greeted by a chorus of "old Massa!"s.*

> *On account of Soviet knavery,*
> *He favours restoring slavery.*

and he was able also, in contemplating his own Talcottville land-scape, to escape, touchingly, into a recurrent dream: "It is sum-mer; I pass by a strange summer forest, in which there are mys-terious beings, though I know that, on the whole, they are shy and benign. If I am fortunate and find the way, I arrive at a won-derful river, which runs among boulders, with rapids, between alders and high weedy trees, through a countryside fresh, green and wide. We go in swimming; it is miles away from anywhere. We plunge in the smooth flowing pools. We make our way to the middle of the stream and climb up on the pale round grey stones and sit naked in the sun and the air, while the river glides away below us. And I know that it is the place for which I have always longed, the place of wildness and freedom, to find which is the height of what one may hope for – the place of unalloyed delight."

Having passed through the valley of his father's distemper and the shadow of his nation's depression – and having passed through a World War and into a time of Cold War and a place that is "charred and sterile, littered with rubbish and bones," he some-times picked up *Life* magazine and scratched his head and mused, with a touch of the mischievousness that is in his drawings, "Am I then in a pocket of the past? Am I peripheral?" He began talking out loud to himself (actually interviewing himself in the *New York Review of Books*) and he began to wonder aloud, as a further sign of dislocation, not from life but from life as he saw it in *Life* mag-azine, if he hadn't become an old fogey. He liked the sound: an old fogey. But it was a question worth asking because he had come to regard the Talcott clan and their house – the ghost of his father, his aunts and uncles – as the deeply affirming experience of life:

What is peculiar is never to forget
The essential delight of the blood
Drawn from ageless springs

He'd had, of course, his bleak moments of dread in the house – it is not surprising to me that Elena, Edmund's wife, says that she once saw a ghost in the upper hall of this house – because just the other day Edmund told me that for a long time he has been suffering auditory hallucinations in his rooms. He hears the telephone ring in the morning as he wakes up, and he says he used to get up to answer the phone – only to find it wasn't ringing – and he believes he has also heard his daughter, Rosalind, who lives in her own house at the other end of town, calling to him. But whatever voices, whatever murmurings he hears, whatever the deep sense of dread that worms away at him, his fate at least has not been his father's. Old fogeyism is not a felt door. He's out on the road, day after day, investigating his home territory. And it's no secret: he is in his grey portly years, still randy. Through contemplation of the Kimball, Mather and Wilson clans, their sins of commission and omission, and his own, he has achieved in this house a certain confessional contentment, a revival of spirit, a strengthening of discipline and a summoning of moral resources. He has, by bringing his clan back to their home ground with him, found himself to be "at the centre of things – since the centre of things can only be in one's head."

⬯

Then the mail truck rolled slowly toward the house and Edmund, tugging the lapels of his paisley gown around his throat, went to the side of the road. As he waited the breeze caught his white pyjamas at the cuffs. He was standing peculiarly at attention, eyes straight ahead, like a soldier on review. The truck pulled up and it was just an ordinary truck painted a violent orange with a twirling light on top, and an amiable local fellow sorted through stacks of mail piled in the back seat.

As I stood there waiting, trying to see Edmund for who he was, trying to understand why he – so far from me by generation and by ancestral background – meant so much to me, the truck shifted into gear and Edmund, hugging a bundle of letters and papers against his body, came up the walk and he passed into his study.

◎✕◎

"Breakfast will be ready soon," he said, "and then I've got to go to Utica. Mopping up some material for my book on Lewis county."

He moved to his writing desk and sat down, tearing open his mail. "You know," he said, "I'm not going to stay in this house. It's too tough up here in the winters . . . . Wellfleet is becoming my base of operations now." Then he laughed and pushed some papers aside. "I'm going to send your dear old father a card. Yesterday, I was in a town called Sodom, and I'm going to write and remind him of the sins of the people." He riffled through a stack of postcards and snapped one out.

From the back kitchen came a call from Mabel Hutchins, who cooks and cleans for him, and he said, "Breakfast at last." He laid letters and papers on a little table and I noticed a new magazine, *Famous Monsters of Filmland* in with his letters – a menacing two-headed beast with fanged teeth, burning coals for eyes, a cuckold's horns, and arms hanging loosely to his horned feet, glowered on the cover.

"How come you've got that?"

"Uhn," he shrugged, going quickly toward the dining room, "Give it to your boy."

We sat down to breakfast at a round table in the dining room. The room was dominated by a grandfather clock and we ate cold hard-boiled eggs, dry shredded wheat with cold cream poured over it, toast, bacon, and strong coffee. My son ate only the bacon and toast. Edmund whispered – not wanting Mabel Hutchins to hear – that he had been hoping for griddle cakes. He seemed preoccupied with plans for the day, his trip to Utica, and then he went upstairs to dress, leaving me with Mabel, a modest countrywoman who is firm about his place in her life. (He had asked her once why she had never remarried and she had told him, "Who'd look after you?") As for ghosts and Elena, his wife, saying that she'd seen one in the house, Mabel told me with a country matter-of-factness: "That might have been old senile Annie Carpenter who used to live across the road – all the doors were always open in this house – she used to wander in and out of houses – once, I found her in the morning, sitting in the kitchen, and my guess is it was her."

Thumbing through Edmund's film magazine – *Bride of Frankenstein, The Wizard of Ooze, The Walking Dead, The Man They Could Not Hang* – I recalled that he had once asked: "What is the reason then – in these days when a lonely country house is likely to be equipped with electric light, radio and telephone – for our returning to these antiquated tales? There are, I believe, two reasons: first, the longing for mystic experience which seems always to manifest itself in periods of social confusion, when political progress is blocked; as soon as we feel that our own world has failed us, we try to find evidence for another world; second, the instinct to insulate ourselves against panic at the real horrors

– Guess who!   – Tsk tsk, must you use scent?

340

loose on the earth – Gestapo and G.P.U., tank attacks and air-plane bombings, houses rigged with booby-traps – by injections of imaginary horror, which soothe us with the momentary illusion that the forces of madness and murder may be tamed and compelled to provide us with a more dramatic entertainment."

Edmund came back downstairs and hailed me from the hall. Dressed in a blue suit and a roll of white collar, he was on his way to Utica. His driver, his constant companion, the young local Hungarian woman, Mary Pcolar, was waiting at the end of the walk. We stood on the porch, my son Michael between us, and he suddenly dumped his grey fedora on the boy's head. The hat settled down around Michael's ears and for a moment Edmund stood erectly beside him like a sergeant major on parade, and then he took his hat back.

"Let that be a lesson to you," he said, enigmatically.

Going down the walk, he gave us a jabbing wave, then got into the car. While waiting for the car to pull away, I saw that some teenagers were in front of the general store, drinking from cans and flicking cigarette butts high in the air. Then a white convertible swerved off the highway. There were yells and the driver, a straight-haired kid in black swimming trunks, socks halfway up his calves and wearing heavy black boots, got out and went through a round of hearty shoulder punching. His girl, her hair high in a ridiculous beehive, beamed in the front seat. Then he jumped back into the convertible, honking, and he tore off at high speed, stopped about four hundred yards down the road and returned, and sat revving up in front of the store. His friends grinned. They had passed the previous afternoon in the same fashion; aimless, putty-faced kids with nothing to do, with no purpose, stranded out in the foothills. Edmund was sitting very stiffly in his car, looking distressed at these aimless louts and presumably was giving Mary Pcolar instructions. Then the car pulled away and passed the kids and he did not look back.

2

Edmund and his fourth wife, Elena, live by Cape Cod water in Wellfleet and in the summer his grandchildren gather there in the home that is sheltered by tall spreading trees and where I always feel ocean currents swinging on the air, not the cold menace of dark ingrown hills. I can smell bayberry and sweet tufts of long lemon-green grass, and the cleansing salt, too. The house (one of two identical houses built by two ship's captains) is back behind a rise of sand and yellow field daisies. It is three frame storeys, white with green shutters. Though the front yellow room is darkened by overhanging branches, the rest of the house is washed in light, a light different from Talcottville (the house was bought by his doting mother as a gift to him shortly after he had married Mary McCarthy). There is no silence embedded in stone in the Wellfleet rooms (if there are voices that run along the walls then they are recent voices, perhaps nettling and acrimonious – Edmund has often been cantankerous and cruel to his women – but not haunting, though there is a photograph of his ghostly mother on a bookshelf, his mother in a profile set in an oval frame with a pink matting). The light seems to pick up the soft colours, especially the pale blues. These are rooms of wood and paint, not stone and plaster. These are rooms in which laughter does not lose its timbre.

Edmund's schedule is monastic; he rises early and works until the afternoon. All intruders are intercepted at the door by Elena, who is in control of the mechanics of the household, and then at three o'clock of an afternoon, after a short drive, the Wilsons perch on a small dune beside the ocean on the bay side or swim in one of the five freshwater ponds, particularly Duck or Gull Pond (where Thoreau walked his rounds). After the plunge and the return home, Edmund pours drinks for friends, if they've been invited around, in the central sitting room, and then he goes off to bed with a glass of several fingers of scotch in hand.

He sits alone in the middle of the sofa, a quilt covering the wall behind him; checks of white and washed out Wedgwood blue. Hung in the centre of the quilt is a painting – I think it is an old *New Yorker* cover that Elena liked – and it is of a doorway opening out to the sand dunes (it is tempting to look through that door, back to his days on the Cape with Dos Passos, "Volodya" Nabokov, Mary McCarthy, e.e. cummings . . . the home-brew whiskey, the *Partisan Review* crowd of editors, the wrangling with Mary McCarthy, his isolation in the winters, his courting of Elena . . . .).

On another wall, to the right of where I sit, is a Pavel Chelish-chev painting of rich but muted colours. Edmund says proudly that Elena fished it out of a wastebasket years ago where it had been thrown by a magazine editor. The room is a little cramped by a three-quarter bed covered in dark blues, and guests loll back on it. There's a coffee table in front of Edmund and on it stand an ice bucket and bottles. Everything is in order, yet nothing formal. While carrying on conversation, he carefully lays out cards on the table, playing a complex double solitaire. Elena has come in with the grandchildren, three pretty girls, and as he stutters his affection they hug his knees.

In her black bathing suit, Elena is slender and striking for her middle years. She has quickly sent the children to the front room and sitting on the edge of the bed, she stretches her fine long bare legs, crossing her ankles. As she talks she wiggles her toes. She is from the Mumm Champagne family: she hardly drinks at all. Edmund has been telling with relish how he and Elena had visited a painter in Paris, Leonor Fini. This woman and her lover had owned a pair of exquisite antique candlesticks. They had told the playwright, Jean Genet, a convicted thief, that he was to come and visit their apartment. He had warned them that he was liable to steal anything. They'd laughed at him and told him to come for his visit anyway. He'd stolen the candlesticks. Edmund laughed heartily, saying, "I like Leonor." Elena said over and over, "She's sick, quite sick, what!" and insisted that Leonor Fini was the only person in Paris she would not allow her daughter, Helen, to visit. "Sick, quite sick, what!" She said that the Fini apartment was done entirely in black velvet and everything had been covered in black cat's hair and Fini had been wearing knee-high black leather boots. "Leather, leather, what!" Edmund, his chin jutting out, said simply, "I like her."

◎✕◎

My boy, Michael, was banging a chrome opener on Edmund's whiskey bottles. Huffing through his nose, charmed as he always seems to be by children, Edmund fetched a coin from his pocket and put it out in front of the boy, holding it between his left thumb and forefinger. He drew the coin back and forth with Michael watching suspiciously, and then he shoved the coin into his other hand and waved his closed fists in front of the boy. After deliberation, Michael punched the left hand and got his penny.

Edmund tried once more, and then again, losing each time. Defeat didn't bother him. He wasn't interested in winning. He was busy teaching the boy. In slow motion, he went through the coin manoeuvres, showing him how to hide the penny. Rocking back on the sofa with laughter, Edmund was alive in the child's world, in his own love of magic, fairy tales, sleight of hand, puppets and fantasy. But, as Michael – now holding the coin – jabbed at Edmund's stomach, saying, "Guess again, guess again," Edmund, pointing at Michael's closed fists, began to talk about power, power in education, in politics, power at the end of a gun. I asked him why he had applauded Israel's military strikes, because, after all, he had not only deplored what he called the "death dealing characteristic of our time" – the military option – but he had said back in 1954 that "the real unconfessed preoccupation in Israel . . . is a kind of imperialistic drive to expand in a territorial way and become a power in the Middle East" – and in *Confessions of a Non-fighter* he had said that he could not imagine killing men he did not know.

"I mean," I said, "you've always been a pacifist."

He rose, colour suddenly in his cheeks, and he said loudly, "I've never been a pacifist."

"But you said yourself you'd declined to fight during the Great Wars."

He was angry: "I disagreed with what those wars were all about, what was at stake in those wars. I've always believed in fighting for what you believe in. I've always been a fighter. I've always fought for what I believed in."

Extricating himself from between the table and sofa, he snorted, and for some reason – as if he were confused – he handed me his empty glass, hunched his shoulders, and went off to the toilet.

I topped up his glass, and filled my own. My son made the coin disappear into his pocket. I reached over Edmund's cards on the table and moved a red nine on to a black ten . . . but then put the nine back, thinking that that went beyond playing the imp of provocation in his conversation, that was a real incursion into the solitariness of his world. He didn't just play solitaire every evening, it was double solitaire, the game of an embattled man . . . a man who has always been determined to try to beat the game, beat it on behalf of the solid perfection of standards, on behalf of new writers, new causes, old writers who should be newly seen . . . an embattled old patrician seemingly locked in the past – beating the bushes on behalf of the renewal of his republic, "a society, a political system, which is still in a somewhat experimental state . . . ."

He was right. He has always fought for what he believes in. He has, despite the sometimes air of being an out-of-work bishop – soft-skinned, looking lettuce-fed and aloof – Alfred Kazin once chided him for wearing a rolled collar and tie to the beach: and he'd replied huffily that he had only one way of dressing – he has been a battler all his life. In consequence, power has been an obsession: force *majeur*, the wielding of power, the flaunting of power, the collapse of power, and even the magic of power – making coins disappear and appear, making puppets dance and speak – the power of the imagination informed by rational critical powers, by the authority of intelligence, in fact, the authority of his intelligence as it has been put to work wherever his interests and instincts as a reporter have taken him. It has been an act of freelancing out on the razor's edge, an act that could only have driven a man to become difficult and to drink (he'd told me, "I do not drink to turn on, I drink to turn off"). He had fought and is still fighting to impose his standards, his opinions on people by the force of eloquence, by force of rhetoric – so that he might, in a modesty of arrogance ingrained in his secular Calvinism, say of his role in society, "I have been of use." That is what he had told me one day with disarming unaffectedness. "I want to be of use."

Sitting on his sofa, he took a new drink and swept up the cards and shuffled them and began again to lay them out in rows, huffing with quiet laughter, recalling a "mopping up party" at which the waif-like Québécois writer Marie-Claire Blais had appeared with the wealthy artist Mary Meigs and the peace activist Barbara Deming – and how some folks at Wellfleet had not wanted to believe that there could be a *ménage à trois* of lesbians in their midst. Pleased with the little story, he was nonetheless hard at work moving the cards – numbers against numbers – suit against suit – moving them within the inexorable logic of solitaire. It occurred to me as he hunkered forward, head down that his writing has always been heavy with images of "mopping up operations," of battle and beasts and invading insects, red-eyed horrors coming down the road. Even his conversation has a drill sergeant's flavour: his house is his "base of operations," a visit to a friend is "an expedition" to meet a "pilot-mind" where he is "briefed," after which he hopes – in a phrase I still find hard to believe he ever uttered – he hopes to prove himself as "a soldier in the Liberation War of humanity." But then, as his good friend, the Haitian poet-in-exile, Phito Thoby-Marcelin, cautioned me – "He is a battler, yes, of course, but he is also romantic, timid and romantic. He is absolutely loyal, or absolutely indifferent, and this is the mark of a certain innocence, which is very American and lends to his terrible sense of betrayals, combat, horrors, catastrophes . . . and so, as a pessimist with his innocence wounded, he presents himself as a naked historical force pitted against other forces."

SUPERAT

Edmund will always be a force because he will always be read and he will always be read because his style is based on observation – he is always trying to see the object for what it is

– and because he sees the object so clearly, we get an instant feeling not just for the tone and the intent of the work at hand, but we get a feeling, too, "for the literary image that will convey social crisis, for the scene that will instantly evoke a historical moment." It is this that makes his book, *Patriotic Gore*, so astonishing, for in it he has seen and heard the history of the American Civil War through the country's writers; he has heard that history as if those writers were a grand choir of voices, great soloists, all under Edmund's direction.

The War, of course, and its fields of almost unimaginable gore, are his subject. He recreates that carnage by recreating, through journals, letters, diaries, and novels, the personalities – in a "theatre of glove puppets – not the kind on wires but the kind you put your hands in" – of Ambrose Bierce, DeForest, Oliver Wendell Holmes, Ulysses S. Grant (his terse prose, as the style of a participant, carried "the accent of decisiveness"), Stonewall Jackson, Alexander Stephens, Henry James (his prolix prose, as the style of a non-participant, "was ambiguous and ironic"), Abraham Lincoln and Harriet Beecher Stowe. North and South, these "actors" were impassioned by a vision, a sense of high purpose . . . none more so than Lincoln, who'd "sought to attain for his nation that it should have, under God, a new birth of freedom and prove to the sneering old world that such a government as the Revolution had tried to establish could survive internal dissension." So, too, Mrs. Stowe had "believed that the republic was consecrated by some special dealing of God's providence" and it was therefore to be saved from itself, it was to be saved over and over again, and insofar as Edmund was concerned, they and others had saved it. Not only that, it had been renewed in the wake of the war, lifted out of its gore by men like Justice Oliver Wendell Holmes, a non-believer who had brought a believer's intensity to his defence of the republic, a man who had so "*identified* his own interests with those of the American Republic" that at his death, he had willed his entire estate, his fortune, to that republic.

Recurring redemption amidst recurring carnage, the commitment of the rational critical moralist to the repeated rescue of the republic from its collapses – these are Edmund's great themes.

Edmund, however, also wrote a Preface to *Patriotic Gore*. In that preface, he says: "Having myself lived through a couple of world wars, and having read a certain amount of history, I am no longer disposed to take very seriously the professions of 'war aims' that nations make . . . . We Americans have not yet had to suffer from the worst of the calamities that have followed on the dictatorships in Germany and Russia, but we have been going for a long time now quite steadily in the same direction," pursuing with "panicky pugnacity . . . a blind collision with the Soviet Union." In the Civil War, "The North's determination to preserve the Union was simply the form that the power drive took . . . . The institution of slavery, which the Northern states had by this time got rid of, thus supplied the militant Union North with the rabble-rousing moral issue which is necessary in every modern war to make the conflict appear as melodrama. In a recent Walt Disney film, showing life at the bottom of the sea, a primitive organism called a sea slug is seen gobbling up smaller organisms through a large orifice at one end of its body; confronted with another sea slug of an only slightly lesser size, it ingurgitates that, too. Now the wars fought by human beings are stimulated as a rule primarily by the same instinct as the voracity of the sea slug."

He went further, arguing that murderous acts committed in the name of "virtue" and "civilization" only make a mockery of "morality" by turning struggle and conflict, ambiguity and upheaval into mere melodrama. Songs about glory and God – like the "Battle Hymn of the Republic" – and speeches about the national ideal of democracy are only "a kind of window-dressing to cover up the gore."

The editors of *Life* magazine and several men of sluggish wit called him anti-American.

They refused to accept that their nation was a sea slug of the deep, or that they, as intellectuals and patriots, were mouth-pieces busy providing just cause for mindless biological mayhem. They certainly did not want to be told that Abraham Lincoln, as he struggled to preserve the Union, was instinctually voracious as Lenin and Bismarck had been instinctually voracious. But there was Edmund saying that each of these men, through the pressure of the power he found himself exercising, had become an uncompromising dictator, and each had been succeeded by agencies – even into our time – which continued to "exercise this power and to manipulate the peoples he had been unifying in a stupid, despotic and unscrupulous fashion." Then, as if to rub salt in patriotic Virtue's wound, he quoted the Great Emanci-pator's statement – not often cited in American textbooks – made during the Douglas debates: "I have no purpose to intro-duce political and social equality between the white and its black races. There is a physical difference between the two, which in my judgement, will probably forever forbid their living together on the footing of perfect equality."

It seemed as if Edmund, sometimes sardonic by implication yet always firmly rooted in a straightforward reading of the texts, was moving a coin, the readily acceptable and received stan-dard of belief and good opinion that people wanted to main-tain in themselves and in their republic, from closed fist to closed fist, from outright cynicism to absolute idealism. And each time he opened a fist, it was found to be empty – but in between, in his reading of the ambiguities, the righteousness and the contradictions, in all the attesting and detesting, the persua-sion and evasion and "the impotence of well-meaning people, and the outbreaks of violence and its sudden bereavements," through all the gore and its aftermath, the coin, the *res publica*, was glimpsed.

It had a living presence that was real if elusive.

It was in the silences between the words as his great choir sang.

Patriotic Gore concludes with a portrait of Justice Oliver Wendell Holmes. In him, Edmund says – and his abiding attachment to Holmes is felt – "Calvinism has faded, but its habits of mind persist." Moreover, at a time when "the law has broken down in America; the Constitution has gone to pieces," he "achieved isolation, remaining unperturbed and lucid," and "was never corrupted, never discouraged or broken . . . he was a tough character, disciplined, and not a little hard." Continuing to function through a corruption of standards and the contagion of values, he defended the republic by adhering to a solid reading of the law. As a non-religious man seeking clarity, he brought a religious fervour to that law as if the law could be made sacred, while admitting that the law was no more than a "complex accretion, a varied assortment of rules." He believed that "force, mitigated so far as may be by good manners, is the *ultima ratio,*" and such force in any given society was to be used to enforce general propositions, like established laws, while at the same time he unashamedly confessed "that no general proposition is worth a damn." And finally, operating as he did with the egotistical sternness of an idealist while deploring idealism, if ever he'd been asked in which fist he held the true coin of the republic, he might well have answered, "Guess." So much of Holmes sounds so tonally like Edmund that many thought that the way to understand Edmund was to understand Holmes.

It is true that they seem to share a good deal – including a certain bleakness – and Edmund's admiration for Holmes is palpable in his prose, but Edmund could never be so removed from his own flesh and kin as to leave his estate to the republic. And more importantly, he could never have written the words Holmes uttered over the nation's war dead in Washington:

"There is one thing that I do not doubt, no man who lives in the world with most of us can doubt, and that is that the faith is true and adorable which leads a soldier to throw away his life in obedience to a blindly accepted duty, in a cause which he little understands, in a plan of campaign of which he has no notion, under tactics of which he does not see the use."

To throw away life in blind duty, ignorant of why, or how, or to what effect!

That gainsaid everything Edmund has stood for. In fact:

Holmes was misanthropic and sorrowless.

Edmund is misanthropic and sorrowful.

Holmes said man was of no consequence in the cosmos.

Edmund has said a man constitutes his own cosmos.

Holmes was a man of moral precision, moral detachment and disdain.

Edmund is a man of moral precision, moral engagement and outrage.

As an outraged moralist, he is given to satire (if he had been a graphic artist he'd have been George Grosz), by temperament closer to Swift and Karel Čapek[1] than to Holmes, let alone Hal Holbrook.[2]

In a poem about power from 1951, "Reversals, or Plus ça change,"[3] he wrote of a stranger on the road who, because he has the *slink* and *shift* of the felon about him, is turned away by a seemingly upright barkeep:

---

[1] Karel Čapek, Czech playwright 1890-1938: *R.U.R.* (Rossum's Universal Robots – the first use of the word *robot*), *The Insect Play*, and the satirical novel, *War with the Newts*. He died on Christmas Day, just before the Nazi invasion of Czechoslovakia.

[2] Hal Holbrook, American actor who made a career of a one-man stage show playing Abraham Lincoln.

[3] Along with taking his shot at J. Edgar Hoover, Edmund explained in a note that this poem, "Reversals, Or Plus ça change," is in "backward-rhyming meter, known as amphisbaenics, which is often found in late twentieth century poetry, and is a characteristic product of that baffled and ambiguous period." That amphisbaenics is often found is, of course, a joke. The amphisbaena is "a fabled serpent with a head at each end, and able to move in either direction," or a "complicated monster capable of walking equally in opposite directions." (Oxford Universal Dictionary)

Said the stranger:
I have ridden for days without stirrups,
Misled by invisible spirits,
Not daring to stop at a town
In dread of the noose or the knout.

As it turns out, several reversing couplets later (town/knout), the barkeep recognizes the stranger as:

That monster whose mere nod annihilates
Millions. "Good God, you are Stalin, a
Fugitive! What a mean face
Without whiskers! Must I keep you safe?"

The barkeep is Hitler, who says:

"Come in: such occasions are rare if
One dwells in the wilds. I was Führer!"

Suffering a shared reversal of fortune, a shared loss of power, they drink a bottle of kirsch, and agree that they know who their successor is, a man who is wearing Stalin's shaved-off moustaches for a wreath, none other than J. Edgar Hoover:

Be at ease: we shall gossip, shall review.
Who is this new tsar, say? One Hoover –
An old pro-consul of theirs.
My moustaches make bays for his wreath.

At the time, Hoover had become the G-Man, the Crime Fighter, the face of public virtue, the public defender of the nation's morality.

We drove along one of the curving roads across the Cape to a beach on the bay side. Elena led us between small hump-like dunes, past wild plum trees and grey pine roots with the sand blown out from under the roots, the pine cones of last fall lying like charred knuckles in the sand. The sun was hot and we sat down quickly near clumps of grass. Edmund, in an old Panama hat, a long white shirt and brown shorts and white beach shoes, slowly traced figures in the sand with a gold-topped walking stick that he'd inherited, I believe, from his priest Kimball grandfather. The June '67 war in Israel had come to an end; Wilson had been in Jerusalem until twelve days before the outbreak of hostilities.

He raised his stick, levelled it at the water, and said again that, Yes, for the first time he had taken sides in a war. Yes, the Israelis were a new race who had bred the old national squabbles out of their blood. Yes, they were producing a people who were scholars and men of action, handsome and beautiful, "a new breed."

He had written about his trip and the young lawyer and wife with whom he had stayed. Their prime aim in life, he'd said, apart from their family, "was patriotic, it was not just to work but to demonstrate virtue" – as if they had been reborn into his *res publica* – on behalf of the new State. They were accomplished but modest people. The wife wore a waistless gown, the lawyer drank little, and both considered card playing somewhat decadent. They were certainly not like the Jewish bourgeois from America whom Edmund saw tromping into the King David Hotel for a couple of days. Those Jews were another breed, they were right out of *Life* magazine: "Pale and fat and amorphous – all bulges and bay windows and thick ankles and necks – and, though evidently prosperous, dowdily dressed."

The sun was on the nape of our necks, there were biting flies, and there was no breeze, so Edmund took a short stroll along the beach, poking at seashells with his priestly stick, staring out over the water. I wondered what would happen if he looked back. Would he turn to a pillar of salt (we'd been talking earlier about Pasternak – "the courage of *his* genius" – and how Pasternak had explained that Lot's wife was the only one who had shown any compassion for the dying because she had looked back)? But he wasn't in a mood for looking back, he was looking stern, so when he sat down again I said, "Did you meet any Yemenite Jews in Jerusalem?"

"No, no . . . ."

"I've a friend, one of your new breed . . . ."

"Yes."

"He calls them niggers."

Edmund looked at me coldly and whacked the small rise of sand with his walking stick but said nothing.

"Those niggers probably look," I said, "more like Abraham did then anybody else over there now . . . they look like Arabs, and they don't care who Agnon is . . . ."

We drove home. He told me, quite abruptly, to come around a little earlier than usual the next day. I said quietly that I would. I wondered if I'd carried my prodding impishness into abrasive impertinence.

The next afternoon, he was alone. He wasn't working, he was waiting. He seemed unfocussed, shuffling forward and then back. He said, "Come up to where my books are, I want to give you something, something of mine." We went upstairs to a stifling library. He was out of breath, white-faced. "I've never given you anything," and he fumbled through his books. "How about this? This is my marked-up edition of *To the Finland Station,* all my corrections." I said I didn't think it was something I should take. "Well, what would you like?"

"How about a little something from the Geckese?"

He burst into laughter and found one of his privately printed pamphlets. It contained a drawing and a Geckese verse I'd never seen before.

A dizzy old duchess named Sarah
Designed a delightful tiara.
It was made of live shrimps,

Alternating with imps,
Who sometimes tormented the wearer.

He told me to come with him into his bathroom.
It is a big clean well-lighted room at the back of the house.
He sat on the closed toilet, I sat in a small chair. "Now," he said,
"should we call your dear old father?"
"Why not? Tell him we're talking to him from the toilet."

"You think so?"

"On your throne."

"Perhaps not. I spoke to him yesterday, you know. Called him up."

"No."

"He asked me if I knew Balzac's story, *The Masterpiece*, about a painter who paints one picture all his life . . . turns out to be nothing but a big blob . . . your father always cheers me up!"

He chortled happily, sitting on his closed toilet in a room full of light, everything sharp and clear, and I couldn't help smiling myself – not only because I was sitting in the bathroom with Wilson, but because I was remembering something he'd written when he was closing in on sixty, something about cathedrals and bathrooms: "I have had a good many, more uplifting thoughts, creative and expansive visions – while soaking in comfortable baths or drying myself after bracing showers – in well-equipped American bathrooms than I have ever had in any cathedral. Here the body purges itself, and along with the body, the spirit. Here the mind becomes free to ruminate, to plan ambitious projects. The cathedrals, with their distant domes, their long aisle and their high groinings, do add stature to human strivings; their chapels do give privacy for prayer. But the bathroom, too, shelters the spirit, it tranquilizes and reassures, in surroundings of a celestial whiteness, where the pipes and the faucets gleam and the mirror makes another liquid surface, which will render you, shaved, rubbed and brushed, a nobler and more winning appearance. Here, too, you may sing, recite, refresh yourself with brief readings, just as you do in church; and the fact that you do it without a priest and not as a member of a congregation is, from my point of view, an advantage. It encourages self-dependence and prepares one to face the world, fortified, firm on one's feet, serene and with a mind like a diamond."

We were in the sitting room and he was laying out cards methodically for his game of double solitaire, playing each hand until he had no chance of winning, until there were too many kings blocking his way, and then he scooped up the cards and began again as we talked about Timothy Leary, Ken Kesey and LSD, and Edmund explained that he had no interest in the drug, "Because I do not want to turn on, I want to turn off. I've been turned on all day. I drink to turn off." With that he rose, shot out his hand and said, "Goodbye, we'll see you soon." And so, turned off, he went to his study and then to bed.

Edmund's goodbyes are disconcerting. Suddenly his hand is before you; you clutch it, you leave, smiling, but left at loose ends by the abruptness of it all. It is not brusque, just abrupt, as abrupt as his first arrival at our house in Toronto had been, when he'd come looking for breathing space, feeling betrayed by his country.

He'd come around early one morning, almost without warning, taking us a little off stride, especially my father who seldom got up early and wasn't sure what to make of this man he knew so slightly. He had come to my father disheartened, looking for a friend, and they had settled down together on the back porch, the blossoms from the crabapple tree that shelters the flagstone stairs falling into the garden, the morning sun filtering through the lattice-work wall leaving little dabs of light on Edmund's worried face. He'd come, he said, because he felt a closeness to my father, somehow felt he could confide in him. My father, unsettled by this openness, uncertain of what was expected of him, and shocked at how mortified Edmund felt and how certain Edmund was that he was going to be financially crippled by the U.S. taxmen,[1] had wondered whether he should offer to lend him money, and if so, how much and how could an offer be grace-

---

[1] "The Cold War and the Income Tax: A Protest." His pamphlet. Having failed to pay income tax for several years he was being hounded by the IRS. They seemed determined, as a branch of *big government*, to crush him until they were ordered to arrange a settlement by President John F. Kennedy.

fully made between men who hardly knew each other, yet felt a bond by temperament. But Edmund had not needed money. "I need to confide in someone," he'd said, looking a little spooked. During the afternoon, they discovered that they shared a wry sense of the serious things that mattered. "This has been wonderful for me," he'd said as he left. He'd come and he'd gone. And that is how it is with Edmund. You have hardly said goodbye before he's gone and you've hardly said hello and let go of his hand before he is picking up a conversation where you left off several months before. As Elena saw me out to the door, and as the screen door snapped shut behind me she called out, "Edmund's going back to Talcottville in a few days. Stop off and see him, what. Edmund always gets lonely up there by himself."

3

Through those years I saw Edmund almost every summer, but the last time was brief. As usual, he was seated on the small sofa and he served me a big glass of scotch. The cards for double solitaire were laid out but he was not playing. He was not feeling strong. I had been in Jerusalem. I told him about a swearing-in ceremony that I'd seen, a ceremony for the élite paratroopers in front of the Western Wall, at night, with huge burning letters . . . words on fire in the dark sky. He said he'd seen something of the same kind in a stadium, that it was all very frightening in a way, but he'd also found it exhilarating. We talked about the writers there, about Agnon, whom I'd also met, but he didn't really know anything about the younger writers, and I don't know why – perhaps because he talked about wanting to find his puppets, perhaps because he was always so friendly despite his senatorial head and paunch – perhaps because I'd come to love his need to correct me, saying, "I'll give you a little talk on that," stuttering or huffing – but I could never resist at least one moment's impudence with him, and so I said, "I think maybe you met all the wrong writers, they kept you away from all the good poets, the ones who have a worry on their minds . . . ."

"Like who?" he said.

"A guy named Amichai, he's a lovely guy, and good, and I heard about another guy, Yehoshua . . . ."

"Well," he said with a sudden, almost limp weariness that I'd never seen before, "you can get around, I can't get around anymore. I see who I can manage to see," and I felt ashamed for having pricked him, for having forgotten how old and ill he was – though, in a way it was a compliment to him, because I could not think of him being out of touch, could not think of him being anywhere but at the heart of his own interests, at the centre of his own cosmos. But the cards were still on the table, he was pasty-faced. I kept silent. Then, he reached out into the silence and signed his name on a paper in a book of blank pages for me. It was quick, it was deft. He might not have met all the new boys in Jerusalem, but he'd signed his name in Hebrew, the language of the place ...

I didn't know any Hebrew to save my life. Then he started to play double solitaire. It was the last time I saw him.

He died in the house at Talcottville. Two days before he died a chipmunk came into the house and up on to his bed and sat beside him. Mabel Hutchins, who came every morning, afraid that she would find him dead, now can't believe he is gone. I can't believe he is gone either, but as I look back, I remember how he was and he certainly could be gruff, and direct, and he had his unalterable prejudices, but he had always been amiable to me. His affection for his friends was genuine; you could see it as his eyes sparkled as he got right down to his best talk and scandal and laughter. He could be brutal when he was blunt, but it was plain that he preferred jokes and magic to the role of magistrate. I'd seen him drunk only once and he'd spoken in a nasty voice I did not know, inflicting pain. I'd seen him perform his puppets only once and they'd spoken in a voice I did not know, inflicting pain. He was entirely open to children, and twice I found him bewildered by his need to make some kind of gesture to me, sentimental and open, but he did not know what to say or give, and so he stuttered and laughed at his own loss for words. Those were the only times that I saw him at a loss.

In his last years, he had been sick, and as it always is when a man is old, one pain brought on another. He had constant attacks of angina; he caught malaria in Jamaica; there were colds and the gout. He worked with the same determination, never letting up his pace, full of ideas and curiosity, but more and more he seemed to be putting his life and work in final order. The last time I saw him, on that August afternoon, he looked terrible – white-faced and haggard and thinner; on a trip to New York he had fallen and hurt his back and I was told later that he couldn't get up from his chair, not even to find his puppets. Talking tired him. But his wry sense of humour was there: we'd spoken about Jerusalem and he had said that he had been given the Jerusalem Prize, but when he'd made it clear that he was not well enough to travel to the ceremony in the Holy City, they'd taken it back and given it to Borges. Edmund, who knew about the politics of prizes, was nonetheless a little wounded, and he laughed and said, "I don't know what the devil Borges ever did for the Jews." Anyway, there was another prize: he had just been given the Golden Eagle of Nice, which neither of us had ever heard of before, but that didn't matter; it had a tag of a little more than five-thousand dollars and the eagle came in a gimmicky red box with little doors and brass hinges – like a gimmick from a bowling tournament.

– *Gimme the gimmick, Gustave!*
– *Ah, that, my dear fellow, you will have to find out for yourself.*

We laughed. He liked showing that red box. But he was in bad shape, he was finishing his lovely but melancholy memoir, *Upstate*, about his world passing away in Talcottville.

So, it was a shock, but no surprise when he died in June. He died and was cremated and brought to the Cape. On a bright afternoon, the young local priest had a scotch-on-the-rocks in the family kitchen, and then several of us went in a small group to the Wellfleet Cemetery. The grave, a hole for the urn, was off and away from the other graves, alone under tall old pines.

It was strange that Edmund, so great a man, should have had so small a funeral. But then, he'd always been private. Anyway, there were some literary people there – Arthur Schlesinger, Renata Adler, my father and myself, Lillian Hellman, Jason Epstein and his wife. We stood in a loose circle on the soft sand and grass and pine needles. Rosalind, his eldest daughter, had planted his favourite flowers: a clump of ladyslippers. We waited. Then, one-by-one, couple-by-couple, the neighbours began to arrive: men with shocks of white hair drifting through the pine trees, and the priest waited, and when he was about to begin, another couple appeared, and slowly they made an outer circle.

At last there were about thirty of us. The priest adjusted his glasses and began to read passages picked from the Knox translation of Ecclesiastes and the Psalms.

A man who had been a friend for years read a short tribute to Edmund, saying that Edmund was a religious man, that if religion meant anything, it meant his kind of spirit, his kind of devotion to the study of what was excellent in Christian and Jewish thought. Then, with the sudden startling gesture of a medieval courtier, this elder Ivy League gentleman drew away from the grave with a low bow and a sweep of the arms, saying, "Shalom, Edmund." The priest went to his knees, taking the urn, and disappeared arms-first into the hole, like a bird diving for fish, his surplice falling around his shoulders, putting Edmund down into the earth. Most of us watched with that passivity that is a defence against awful melancholy.

The family, Elena, the son and two daughters, took turns at the shovel, slowly filling in the hole. There was some confusion, with no one sure of what to do, and from the children, the embarrassed little laughter you use in public to protect your private emotions.

With the sod at last set, the elder neighbours, long attuned to funerals, quickly drifted away – as unobtrusively as they had come. The family, the writers and editors, were left, and no one spoke very much. They splintered apart, yet refused to leave, as if Edmund were not a man given up easily. The priest sat by the edge of the road, staring into the long grass; I stood with my father, farther along the road; and there was Renata Adler, walking by herself, head down, going home alone; all of us alone, yet held together by Edmund's importance in our lives. What rare thing was it that we refused to give up? What beyond a man's life did we feel we were losing? We knew we were losing it.

Back at the house, there was a sea bass cooked by the neighbours and some wine. Soon, we could feel the family drawing together into that protective knot for the hardest night, when the body is down in the ground, and I wanted to flee, not from the memory of Edmund, or the pain of the family's loss, but from the loss itself, for I kept thinking of how Edmund had described himself in his memoir of Talcottville – disciplined, gracious, the very virtues of his old house, sitting watching the decay and demoralization of his countryside, the highway widened in front of his house to four lanes for no good reasons, the old elm tree cut down to do it – sitting, waiting for the mail by the highway, the local young men on their motorcycles or in their cars speeding up the road five miles and then back five miles, frenetic, making noise, showing off, frustrated and bewildered with nowhere to go, driving cars that soon would be repossessed.

I thought that's how Edmund was for me: in a world of literary and political motorcyclists – destructive and showboating, waiting to be repossessed, he was a man of complete integrity and faithfulness to himself, and that, after all, is the root of love, that kind of respect for oneself and others. Maybe that was what we all knew was going out of our lives as we stood around the grave; maybe that was what the old neighbour had in mind with his courtly bow – a rare kind of love for literature and life had gone from us and we weren't quite sure where we would find it again.

Just as we had stood alone after the burial, we would now have to find that integrity in ourselves. Edmund had found it in himself. Though we may want to weep that he is dead, his triumph makes a man just a little ashamed at how little he has done; yet, at the same time, we are encouraged by what he achieved to go on and do more, to be true to our own best talents: obstinately, with as much grace as possible, with all energy. That is how Edmund lives with me still.

After Edmund died, his daughter, Rosalind, who lived alone in her own house in Talcottville, asked me to stay in Edmund's house, to keep prowling academics and reporters away from her. For two weeks, I slept in the room (but not the bed) in which Edmund had died, met many of his relatives during the day and spent most evenings, after supper, drinking vodka with Rosalind. "How's it been for you being the child of a famous writer?" she asked me one night, answering before I could ". . . 'cause it hasn't bothered me at all. I never go into New York." She had isolated herself to the south end of the tiny town. Walking into the stone house one night, after some hours with Rosalind, I saw a ghost at the top of Edmund's stairs – a figure in a long nightshirt. I was not scared. I was rather pleased. Whether it was the ghost seen by Elena, or whether it was Edmund himself, or whether I was into the whimsy of drink, I can't be sure, though I do know that it was not Mabel Hutchins' neighbour, the old and senile Annie Carpenter.

The Telegram, Exile, 1966-2004

Notes

As I said in *Raise You Five*, the man of letters I most admired in my time was Edmund Wilson. In 1966, to announce that I was the new literary editor of the *Telegram*, my immediate editor, Tom Hedley, asked me to write about Wilson and his work. Over the years, that piece evolved into its present form. As a matter of nostalgia, I have reproduced the pencil-and-ink drawing by Dennis Burton that was commissioned to accompany that *Telegram* piece. O Canada, indeed: Wilson's work has had no discernible effect on Canadian letters.

Edmund Wilson's poems and drawings are from his book, *Night Thoughts* (Farrar, Straus and Cudahy, New York 1961).

I was made aware of François Mauriac's aside on gambling in an essay, "Blood, Neon, and Failure in the Desert," by Joyce Carol Oates.

The quotes by various sports figures in "Muhammad Ali" are from Thomas Hauser's *Muhammad Ali, His Life and Times* (Simon & Shuster, New York, 1991), an extraordinary compilation of statements, remarks, and editorial observations about and by Ali.

A complete discussion of the Irishman in Victorian caricature can be found in *Apes and Angels* (Smithsonian Institution Press, 1971) by L. Perry Curtis Jr.

Rumours of War by Ron Haggart and Aubrey B. Golden (new press, Toronto, 1971), remains the most authoritative investigative response to the War Measures crisis. Like all readers and researchers of the period, I am in their debt.

"Crime and Redemption" is predicated on Ramsey Clark's book, *Crime and America* (Simon & Schuster, New York, 1970).

The prose selections used throughout the "LeRoi Jones" text are from *The System of Dante's Hell* (Grove Press, New York, 1965), a novel by LeRoi Jones.

The prose selection from John O'Hara is from "We're Friends Again," *Sermons and Soda Water* (Random House, New York, 1960).

The verse selections from Paul Celan, used in various essays, are from *Paul Celan: Poems* (Persea Books, New York, 1980), translated by Michael Hamburger.

"Year of the Horse" first appeared in *Toronto Life*. I included it in my memoir, *Barrelhouse Kings*. Its proper place in my work, however, is here, in association with my other tale about horse racing, "The G Spot."

After "A Motiveless Malignancy" appeared in *Toronto Life*, and then in *The Ontario Review*, and the Ploughshares Prize anthology, several writers suggested that it had the narrative "feel" of short fiction. I published it as such. Adding a few post-modern gestures, I included it in my collection, *A Kiss Is Still a Kiss*. I am reprinting it here in its original non-fiction form. The facts of the story in both are the same.

B.C.

I WISH TO EXPRESS MY GRATITUDE TO:

At *The Telegram*: Tom Hedley, Ron Evans
At the CBC: John Kennedy, Richard Nielsen, Robert Patchel,
   Terrence Gibbs, Robert Weaver, Bill Casselman
At CTV: Tom Gould, David Sobelman
At *Punch*: Alan Coren
At *Toronto Life*: Tom Hedley, Marq de Villiers
At *Leisure Ways*: Jerry Tutunjian
At *The National Post*: Noah Richler
At *City & Country Homes*: Charles Oberdorf
At *White Gloves of the Doorman*: Branko Gorjup

ACKNOWLEDGEMENTS:

Most of the selections in this book first appeared in the following periodicals and books. As I explained in Raise You Five, *I am prone to revision. The end dates for each essay or encounter indicate first publication and the time over which changes and revisions were made. Grateful acknowledgement is made to:*

The Telegram, Maclean's, Leisure Ways, Punch, The National Post, Toronto Life, White Gloves of the Doorman, City & Country Homes.

BOOKS BY BARRY CALLAGHAN

Fiction

A Kiss Is Still a Kiss: Stories

When Things Get Worst: A Novel

The Way the Angel Spreads Her Wings: A Novel

The Black Queen Stories

Non-fiction

Raise You Ten: Essays and Encounters 1964-2004, Volume Two

Raise You Five: Essays and Encounters 1964-2004, Volume One

Poetry

Hogg, the Seven Last Words

Hogg, the Poems and Drawings

Stone Blind Love

As Close as We Came

The Hogg Poems and Drawings

Memoir

Barrelhouse Kings: A Memoir

Translations of Books

Wells of Light: Selected Poems of Fernand Ouellette

Flowers of Ice: Selected Poems of Imants Ziedonis

Fragile Moments – Jacques Brault

A Voice Locked in Stone – Miodrag Pavlović

Singing at the Whirlpool – Miodrag Pavlović

Eidolon – Robert Marteau

Interlude – Robert Marteau

Treatise on White and Tincture – Robert Marteau

Atlante – Robert Marteau